LATINO HEARTLAND

Latino Heartland

Of Borders and Belonging in the Midwest

Sujey Vega

NEW YORK UNIVERSITY PRESS

New York and London

NEW YORK UNIVERSITY PRESS
New York and London
www.nyupress.org

References to Internet websites (URLs) were accurate at the time of writing. Neither the author nor New York University Press is responsible for URLs that may have expired or changed since the manuscript was prepared.

ISBN: 978-1-4798-6453-9 (hardback)
ISBN: 978-1-4798-9604-2 (paperback)

For Library of Congress Cataloging-in-Publication data, please contact the Library of Congress.

New York University Press books are printed on acid-free paper, and their binding materials are chosen for strength and durability. We strive to use environmentally responsible suppliers and materials to the greatest extent possible in publishing our books.

Manufactured in the United States of America

10 9 8 7 6 5 4 3 2 1

Also available as an ebook

This book is dedicated to my parents, Miguel y Theresa Vega, and the countless other immigrant families who struggle, persevere, and make home in places that are not always welcoming. ¡Sigan luchando, sigan ganando, sigan mejorando el mundo!

CONTENTS

Pioneering Ownership of Greater Lafayette

I met Mercedes at her home on a crisp spring morning. It had been a year since she and I had first met and developed an immediate connection. We were both daughters of Mexican immigrants, both college-educated, both trying to understand the latest arrivals to Greater Lafayette.[1] Throughout 2006 and since then, my personal and professional friendship with Mercedes grew. We attended birthday parties and aqua-aerobics together. I went to her bridal shower, wedding, and baby shower and got to know several of her family members. Because both of us worked for the school district, she as an English as a New Language (ENL) teacher and I as a Hispanic Outreach Coordinator for the local high school, we often collaborated on school field trips for our Latino students and discussed how best to address student needs. By early 2007, I was starting to write and reflect about what the community had taught me over the past few years and to lay the foundations for this book. Mercedes, now married and proudly carrying her newborn baby boy, wanted some adult time and to find out how the project had developed.

As the granddaughter of one of the first Mexican workers who settled in Lafayette, Indiana, in the 1950s, Mercedes viewed work on this book with personal and pedagogical interest. Her father was raised here, she was born here, and now she sat across from me rocking the fourth generation of Sandovales who would call central Indiana home. Working toward her master's degree in literacy, culture, and language education, Mercedes was fully aware of the value of collecting Latino narratives in the Midwest. Conscious of the stories, struggles, and accomplishments laced throughout her family's history in this town, Mercedes brought that experiential knowledge to the classroom to connect with and encourage her students, the most recent Latinos to arrive in central Indiana.

With her maternity leave over and my writing just beginning, our time with each other was less frequent. We scheduled a time to meet and check in with each other, and as is often the case with two academics, casual conversation veered eventually toward the research. Mercedes asked about my writing and what I was planning to include. I responded by bringing up "belonging" as a possible direction for a chapter. We talked about moments throughout the past year when Latino residents exhibited notions of belonging that were ignored in the national debate. I pointed to the graduation sash displayed in Mercedes' living room as an example of this type of belonging that often went overlooked in strict assimilation narratives. Mexican flag colors made up the right part of the graduation sash while the left side had red, white, and blue stitched on it; Mercedes explained that she had asked a local seamstress in town to make these sashes for her and her friends to wear on their graduation from Purdue University five years earlier. We spoke of the sashes, the public displays of ethnic religiosity, the immigrant marches, and the basic yet critical ways her own family unapologetically lived out their ethnic Mexican and American lives in this midwestern landscape.

Seeking her input and curious to see if I was accurately reflecting the local feelings of Lafayette's Latino community, I asked Mercedes what she thought about belonging as an approach toward understanding the local dynamics. Mercedes confidently responded with a resounding, "Not only do I belong, but I feel a certain sense of ownership because of my family. We were the pioneers." Asserting ownership of Lafayette, Mercedes declared historical lineage and a legacy of established belonging to the area. Without missing a beat, she asserted herself as a resident and "pioneer" of the community regardless of the ethnic claims she still held on to. Notably, feelings of belonging, of claiming a right to exist and to be included in the moniker of "we" in local and national contexts, was not limited to English-speaking pioneer families. Spanish-speaking Latino residents encountered moments of tension and denied belonging; still, new and established families exhibited a resiliency to claim community in the face of exclusion. Instead of accepting the multiple obstacles that limited their incorporation, Latinos invested in their own conceptualizations of a midwestern home.

Though they may not have had the pioneering lineage of Mercedes' family, Latino families found other means of connecting to the local

La Naturaleza, the Fall foliage of Central Indiana. Photo by author.

landscape. Indeed, some Latinos even grew attached to the physical setting. Comments of "*la naturaleza*," or the natural flora that surrounded this river valley, illustrated how the physicality of greenscapes and small-town quaintness reminded some immigrants of their rural homes in Mexico. The cornfields that surrounded the town and the plant life that dotted tree-lined streets and luscious creek beds all provided familiar ties to nature missing in more urban settings. As Caridad, a Mexican female, expressed, "Nos encantó Lafayette. California es de ciudad, freeways, y carros. Aquí hay plantas y árboles como en nuestro pueblo. Se me hace increíble ver las mismas cosas, la naturaleza de allá" [We loved Lafayette. California is all city, freeways, and cars. Here, there are plants and trees like in our village. I find it incredible that one could see the same things, the nature from over there]. Comparing this setting to California's cement cities and traffic-clogged roadways, Caridad found beauty and inspiration in the farmlands of Indiana. Similarly, other families recalled California with a uniquely working-class perspective. The high cost of living and lack of disposable income in California left many limited in their West Coast experience. Far from memories of beaches, theme parks, or other amenities often associated with California, working-class immigrants recalled urban cityscapes, freeways, and traffic that defined the daily drudgery of working to survive, not working to live.[2] The high cost of living coupled with a lack of recreational time and disposable income led to a West Coast experience devoid of tourist attractions or positive feelings. As one longtime resident explained, "En México la situación es muy difícil. Puro vicio. En California gangas [*sic*]. Aquí es muy tranquilo" [The situation in Mexico is very difficult, all vice. In California [there are] gangs. Here it is very tranquil]. These families preferred the small-town atmosphere of Lafayette to what they perceived as disadvantages in more urban locales.[3] Central Indiana provided a steady income, a lower cost of living, and more time to spend with family to enjoy *la naturaleza* and tranquility so many appreciated. Opportunities to connect with one another and enjoy the midwestern landscape provided many families with their sense of belonging and ownership. Their homes, their families, their memories were here in central Indiana, and no politician or national debate could take that away from them.

Guided by an earlier research project I had conducted on the ethnic appropriation of space in the Pilsen/Little Village area of Chicago, I was drawn to Greater Lafayette as a site for comparative analysis in a "new," nontraditional destination. My introduction to this river valley came in 2001. At the time, I was dating a young man who was attending Purdue University's American Studies program. Though the campus itself existed in West Lafayette, my partner chose to live east of the Wabash River, where his graduate student income could stretch further.

Because of my own affiliation with the University of Illinois's Anthropology program, I initially lived primarily in the Champaign-Urbana, Illinois, area and visited Greater Lafyaette nearly twice a month on the weekends. During these brief visits I drove around town and began developing initial contacts in the community. Even during this early exposure, it was immediately evident to me that Greater Lafayette existed as two very distinct midwestern cities. West Lafayette was a classic college town catering to university students and faculty. Across the Wabash River, State Street transformed into South Street and almost immediately revealed a class distinction between the two towns. The town–gown divide was apparent. Grocery stores, shopping districts, and residential neighborhoods were noticeably different on the "West Side."[4] In Lafayette, multiple Spanish-surname car dealerships, *panaderías* [bakeries], and Mexican grocery stores dotted the landscape. The *panadería* was a special favorite because it had been years since I'd lived in proximity to a Mexican bakery. I'd grown up in a Mexican suburb of Los Angeles, San Fernando, that had all the amenities of a Mexican ethnic experience. Moving years later to a suburb of Dallas/Fort Worth, I found these comforts harder to come by and certainly farther away. In Greater Lafayette, the *panadería* was small but had fresh *bolillos*, *conchas*, *churros*, and my personal favorite, pumpkin *empanadas*. These ethnic businesses triggered my own memories of a sense of home. Visits to these eateries were frequent and certainly expanded my waistline during the time I spent in central Indiana.

Latino businesses dotted the scenery and physically altered the landscape with a unique ethnic familiarity not often seen outside of historically Latino metropolitan cityscapes. Symbols of a Mexican presence weaved in between other, less distinctive commercial venues and created a "multiethnic adaptive streetscape" in Greater Lafayette (Miyares 2004). Neighborhoods and streetscapes reflected the demographic changes in the area and showcased the strategies of Latino residents to appropriate space with their own unique signs of familiarity. Small ceramic statues of the Virgin of Guadalupe appeared in gardens, Spanish-surname businesses revitalized otherwise abandoned strip centers, and area parks hosted adult soccer tournaments while the aroma of *carne asada* wafted through the fields.

This ethnic entrepreneurial spirit and the location of these commercial spaces in otherwise older and abandoned areas of town solidified my interest in the region. As with the Pilsen/Little Village area in Chicago, I wanted to explore how Mexican immigrants revitalized the physical and economic environments of their "new" communities. Focused on the physical and social palimpsests of the town's ethnic inhabitants, I began archival research to explore the history of the spaces now frequented by Latino residents. In addition, I asked people to recount a history of Mexican arrival. These narratives revealed a town that was still undergoing transition and whose Spanish-speaking population was not limited to a Mexican heritage. Though a majority of Spanish speakers were of Mexican origins, Latinos from various backgrounds also coexisted in this small town. A Mexican presence outnumbered that of Puerto Rican and El Salvadoran families, but together they criss-crossed this area of central Indiana to produce a particular Latino experience. The term "Mexican" was a self-identified term used by even the second generation of U.S.-born peoples of Mexican descent. Rather than divisive, the term "Mexican" to describe the community was used by first-generation immigrants and multi-generational Mexican Americans and signaled an attempt to maintain solidarity across their experiences; similarly, Puerto Ricans and El Salvadorans also self-identified with their specific national and ethnic markers. Still, I decided to prioritize the term "Latino" to speak to the larger Latino collective that made up the Spanish-speaking community. This gesture toward a wider Latino ethnic identity was used during the 2006 national immigration debate and allows for the multi-generational co-ethnic relationships built between Spanish-speaking residents of Lafayette regardless of immigration status. Moreover, there was a prevalence of mixed-status families wherein residents who were undocumented, permanent residents, and citizens all lived in the same household. Thus, unlike labels like "immigrant," "undocumented," or "Mexican" to segregate experiences, the term "Latino" allowed for that level of ambiguity which reflected the complex lived realities present in central Indiana. With regard to other terminology used in the book, while some other researchers do not capitalize the "W" when referencing people racially categorized as White in our society, I firmly believe that in capitalizing terms like "Black" or even "Latino" as designators of community, we must contend that "White" is also a moniker of community and not just a descriptor of color. Thus, in capitalizing the "W" in "White" I seek to highlight that it too is a separate and distinct term referencing a particular experience in the United States and not just the normative or white (lowercase) way of viewing the majority population.

Initially focused on the Latino appropriation of midwestern space, this book underwent a restructuring as a result of elements at the national level that affected the local social environment for Lafayette's Spanish-speaking population. No longer having commitments in Illinois, I moved to Indiana in the summer of 2005. During this time, I spent every day archiving, interviewing, and participating in events around town. By late 2005 and early 2006, a national political climate surrounding immigration was building. In December 2005, U.S. Representative Jim Sensenbrenner, from nearby Wisconsin, introduced H.R. 4437, the Border Protection, Antiterrorism, and Illegal Immigration Control Act of 2005, which supposedly addressed a midwestern immigrant "problem."[5] In Greater Lafayette, debates in the newspapers, online commentary sections, and in casual conversation signaled that the immigration debate had reached the midwestern United States. The heightened national debate on immigration was supposedly focused on undocumented immigrants, but in practice it drew on familiar and historic tropes that marked Mexican residents as always and already worthy of suspicion. In both local and national narratives, anyone who spoke Spanish or looked phenotypically Other could be identified as possibly "illegal" and therefore a threat. In Lafayette, families whose history in central Indiana dated back decades were accosted on streets, sneered at on job sites, and bullied in the schools. For their part, resilient Latino residents contested the antagonism through various forms of protest and continued to live out their daily ethnic experiences regardless of how the majority non-Latino population perceived them.

In interviews, I asked participants to reflect on the surrounding geography and asked if certain ethnic spaces provided some level of comfort or familiarity. More often than not, responses reflected concerns and fears regarding the national political focus on immigration. Business

owners voiced concerns about undocumented clientele whose anxieties led them either to stay away or limit their spending habits to save
money should they be deported. Conversations shifted to discussions
of verbal and felt attacks at the hands of non-Latinos who increasingly
looked upon them with disdain. The analysis of space remained a critical concept for understanding where and when these encounters happened, but it was obvious that the community was dealing with larger
issues of discrimination. Aware of the changing atmosphere, I shifted
my research to include the ways in which Latino Hoosiers used alternate
measures of belonging that positioned them squarely within, and not excluded from, the Lafayette community.[6] Additionally, I felt it necessary
to include non-Latino Hoosiers in the research as a way to complicate
how the politics of immigration was influencing their views. Bringing
non-Latino, mostly White, residents in dialogue with Latino narratives
would broaden understanding of how residents in these type of communities developed ties or distanced themselves from one another. Thus, to
do justice to these participants, I would need to address the politics of
immigration in the study.

Feeling unfairly attacked and positioned as criminals, Latino residents sought refuge and comfort with one another. They created their
own sense of belonging and comfort. Latino-owned businesses coordinated and raised funds to show a united front at immigration rallies.
Religious centers provided a sanctuary for ethnic spirituality. Women, in
particular, found the religious networks particularly helpful for combating feelings of despair and denied acceptance. Female *comadrazgo*, or
religious social networks, strengthened in these circumstances wherein
women often lacked biological family networks. Women found emotional anchors in prayer groups and Sunday services where other Latinas
offered communal support. In 2006, these religious networks provided
empowerment in the form of ethnic and spiritual belonging. Taking
belonging as a point of departure, this book explores how community
membership was determined yet simultaneously remade by those struggling to widen the scope of who was imagined as legitimate resident
citizens of this midwestern space. Informed by intersectionality as an
analytical framework, it explores the intersecting power relations of gender, race, class, immigration, and citizenship in the making and marking
of community. Debates surrounding immigration obsessed on the topic

of "legality," as if that were the single axis by which belonging could be determined. In actuality, larger complicated framings of exclusion relied on phenotype, language use, gender, and class, among other indicators. These enmeshed factors of belonging determined acceptance such that actual immigration status had nothing to do with the way someone was or was not treated as a legitimate member of a community. Phenotype and language use, for instance, determined if someone was judged or presumed to be an outsider. This dependence on external perceived markers to determine insider status was all too familiar. Historically, skin tone, class, and/or gender designations marked certain individuals as not completely worthy of citizenship in the United States. Moreover, this binary of belonging erased the very real contributions of individuals with extralegal status and marked them as always and already unfit.[7]

Often a protected concept, community belonging has been used as a tool in the us-versus-them binaries of immigration politics. In separating a "them" from a seemingly unified, static, and well-defined "us," the politics of immigration used concepts like belonging and community to distinguish legitimate newcomers from "illegal" foreigners. The narratives in this book complicate the us-versus-them discourse to widen conceptualizations of "us" that dispute the need for a "them." Regrettably, the 2006 immigration debate used historically familiar attempts to target brown-bodied individuals as threats to the nation and positioned Latinos as "outside the imagined [national] community."[8] Latinos in Lafayette still held emotional, financial, and familial connections to Latin America and the Caribbean; however, these transnational identities did not negate feelings of connectedness to their homes in central Indiana.[9] In other words, transnational ties did not impede the construction of familiarity and community in Lafayette. Thus, the meaning of community and how Latino and non-Latino residents broached the topic of belonging to community took on critical importance in this book.

When I began research on this area, I started with books and documents on Lafayette's historical narrative, the small collection of Spanish-language *Journal and Courier* issues, English-language issues of the *Journal and Courier*, and printed materials on business or church histories. Conducting archival analysis provided a historical perspective on the way immigrants were depicted in the area's local media throughout various periods of its past. This historical grounding aided in my understanding the social milieu of the twenty-first century. Ethnographic interviews consisted of open-ended, semi-structured questions that varied according to the participant's role in the community. Direct referrals and snowball sampling, wherein one individual led to another and that led to another, yielded a number of community members who agreed to speak to me for this book. In total, I formally interviewed seventy-nine individuals and spoke casually to several others. The interviews consisted of fifty-four Latino interviews (mostly of people of Mexican descent) and twenty-five non-Latino interviews (twenty-four White residents and one Black male).[10] Of the fifty-four Latino interviews, I spoke to twenty-two men and thirty-two women. In the non-Latino interviews I spoke to six men and nineteen women. Interviews ranged between twenty minutes and three hours, with most averaging about one and a half hours.[11] While I never asked individuals directly about their immigration status, four participants made it clear to me during their interviews that they were undocumented. Here, my own subject-position played an important role in trying to navigate these overlapping experiences in Greater Lafayette. Latino participants asked me questions about my own family past, Mexican heritage, and immigrant history while only one non-Latino resident asked me to clarify my ethnic identity while being interviewed. Though most non-Latino interviewees did not address my ethnic background, I would be naïve to assume that it had no impact. Indeed, I noticed that some non-Latinos were very careful of the language they used to describe Latino residents while others were surprisingly vocal about their opposition.

With some individuals not sure of how to place me within the community dynamic, establishing a presence in the community was difficult to navigate at times. Participant observation and direct conversations via interviews helped established my role with some as an academic doing a study on the local Latino experience. To others I was simply a young woman who did not have family in the area or one who worked in any of the local manufacturing or service industries. In other words, I was an anomaly. Most Latino residents had some sort of social network in the area that brought them to Lafayette. Either direct family ties or fictive kinship networks (not blood-related but considered family through social networks) assisted in defining one's presence and social existence in the town. New arrivals were either family or longtime friends with *fula-*

nita de tal [so-and-so]. Placing newcomers within a network established their role in the community: Could they be trusted, are they approachable, where in Mexico did they come from, and what was their religious affiliation? This was rather important to many of the area's multiple Spanish-speaking congregations, who right away placed newcomers as Catholics or as possible Protestant converts. For Catholics, St. Boniface Church offered a large, thriving spiritual and communal resource and plenty of ethno-religious traditions from Mexico. For non-Catholics, the Baptists, Mormons, or Pentecostals also provided their own networks, albeit much smaller than that of St. Boniface. Some residents assumed that perhaps I was a student from across the river, from Purdue University. Though I clarified my affiliation with a different institution, this "Purdue student" association was not always beneficial. It seemed the town–gown divide was present in creating mistrust among the Mexican community. Guille, a longtime Latina resident who worked as an administrator in the city school district, warned, "These families are used to undergraduate students' coming in to 'research' their lives and identify their issues for some class credit and then never do anything to actually improve their lives." Moreover, across the river lived affluent Latin American students (undergraduate and graduate) and professors. Rarely did these Latin American West Side residents venture into the social spaces of blue-collar Lafayette Latinos.[12] More times than not, it was the children of working-class Mexican immigrants who attended Purdue University and attempted to bridge that divide.

Without parents or close friends in the community, I attempted to establish myself through other means. I volunteered to teach English at the Lafayette Adult Reading Academy, offered my translation skills to Purdue's Health Initiative to meet Spanish-speaking service workers, joined the Lafayette Mayor's Commission on Hispanic Affairs, interviewed and volunteered with various Latino-based organizations, worked as Hispanic Outreach Coordinator for the local high school, and attended baseball games, cultural events, public performances, and different denominational religious services to help familiarize people with my role in the community. As the secretary of the Mayor's Commission, I disseminated meeting minutes and at times offered organizational advice. In the process, I became acquainted with local activists and their roles within the community. As the Hispanic Outreach Coordinator, I interpreted for Spanish-dominant students and English-dominant staff. Additionally, I also interpreted for parents when they came in for meetings and organized Spanish parent workshops that familiarized them with high school expectations and curriculum standards. My outreach coordinator role also included informing Latino students about higher education. I answered their questions about higher education, assisted them in applying to college and finding financial aid. By way of these various activities, I developed my own activist research agenda that not only provided necessary exposure to the community but also gave me the opportunity to contribute in some way to the local dynamics of the town and not just "research" for my own benefit.

Admittedly, the affiliation with the high school brought about its own set of challenging situations, especially when I was called upon to interpret for Spanish-speaking students involved in disciplinary issues. However, I felt that my role was to advocate for the students and parents. Oftentimes, this meant interpreting information to the school officials regarding cultural differences, religious holidays, language use, working-class experiences, and fears associated with the contemporary climate against immigration. Additionally, my age assisted in my attempting to build a bridge between teenagers and their parents. I was often visited by parents who spoke to me about troubles they had with their children. Tears and frustration often accompanied interactions with Mexican fathers and mothers who were at their wits' end with a rebellious teenager. Conversely, I made myself available to students and worked with administrators and teachers to address some of their (the students') concerns. With both parents and students, I listened to and answered questions regarding cultural expectations and the streaks of independence that teens were picking up from their peers and the social climate. Though I made my research agenda and role in the community clear to everyone I came in contact with, my exposure to students and parents was strictly geared toward assisting the community in any way possible. My role in the area was more clearly defined by this involvement with the schools; however, I never directly used these contacts to elicit interviews. Personally, I felt that my role as researcher should not rely solely on this position of power in the community and I never wanted the parents or students to feel that I was mining their concerns at the school for the purpose of the book. On the other hand, events and situations at the school did inform my perspective toward the interaction and response between Greater Lafayette's non-Latino residents and the Mexican community.

Whether at the school or in interviews, my interactions with individuals often came with a particular introspection regarding my own subject-position. At the school, I calmed both parents and students by relating my own experience with teenage angst and explaining that they were not the only ones going through this culture clash in parenting U.S.-born children. In interviews, I painfully sat across from undocumented immigrants tearfully retelling their struggles and dreams of a future in this country. The personal experience of watching my parents, aunts, uncles, cousins, and friends all struggle through the U.S. immigration system was intensely present in these conversations. That a majority of my relatives, like many families in Lafayette, benefited from earlier immigration reform only made the pain and despair of contemporary undocumented immigrants even more acute and personal. Sheer happenstance resulted in the citizenship status of my parents, and as I sat across kitchen tables and admired family photographs, I could not help but wonder how it was determined that these families did not merit the same consideration that previous generations had gained. This troubling reality was present especially when I spoke to non-Latino residents who insisted on calling these neighbors "illegals" and dismissed the contributions of undocumented immigrants. I often struggled with a commitment to the research that halted my intervention during these interviews. Paralyzed from the shock of facing participants who felt compelled to tell me that undocumented immigrants were not worthy of immigration reform, I struggled to control my reaction. I knew that part of this analysis relied on my understanding this very visceral response and my attempting to get participants to open up about their feelings regarding Latino residents. On multiple occasions I felt obligated to intervene and inform interviewees of their false assumptions and damaging accusations. Usually, though, I sat and took notes. I absorbed their anger. I collected the research with the full awareness that I, as a Chicana, would have to find a way to make sense of, or at least ethnographically describe, these situations. In the end, I dealt with these feelings the only way I could—I carried the frustrations and my own visceral reactions home with me and allowed these participants the space to be honest, even if incorrect. It was a difficult decision that I still find myself struggling with even as I listened to and transcribed those painful exchanges. Methodologically speaking, this was a necessary choice aided by the need to understand how the non-Latino community was truly responding to Latino residents. Ethically, my activist subject-position is still left reeling from the filthy feeling of sitting through these conversations. As an anthropologist, as a daughter of once-undocumented immigrants, and as a confidant of contemporary undocumented families that still struggled daily, I am unsure of how best to devise a methodology that addresses opposing perspectives on such a complicated issue. Still, I feel that this kind of work is increasingly necessary to address how the politics of belonging and the immigration debate continues to divide the contemporary United States.

Conducting research on race politics and systems of inequality is necessary, but it is increasingly difficult when we include individuals who hold deeply problematic and at times racist perspectives. If, as Ruth Behar (1997) has suggested, there is a need to always do the kind of anthropology that "breaks your heart," what about doing the kind of anthropology that infuriates you? Do we intervene at the time of our exposure to these participants or do we gather their perspectives to understand them, even if we fiercely disagree with them? Can we do both? I hope this book offers a step toward building methodological strategies that somehow include multiple, if at times oppositional, perspectives on community and culture. Recognizing that Latino residents do not live in a vacuum, this book approaches the complexity of multiethnic, multiracial, and multicultural communities through an examination of how these residents interact with or isolate themselves from one another in the same space. By exploring the politics of immigration and belonging in this small midwestern city, we can better understand how other spaces across the United States confront their own notions of community when faced with an increase in racially or ethnically identifiable residents.

I would like to take this opportunity to thank the community of Lafayette for welcoming me, telling me their experiences, and trusting in me to do their stories justice. I was invited into people's homes; attended their weddings, bridal showers, and birthday parties; and all along developed incredible friendships with and admiration for the individuals whom I got to know in my years of living in Lafayette. The resiliency and beauty of shaping family, friends, and cultural solidarity in this central Indiana region was inspiring. Specifically, I would like to thank the Salazar, Del Real, Muñoz, and countless other families for assisting me in understanding their unique experience as Latino Hoosiers. The community leaders and organizers' commitment to improving the lives of Lafayette Latinos has been inspiring: Maribel Salazar Masoodi, Aída Muñoz, Cari Muñoz, Mari Muñoz Del Real, Ivan Hernandez, Tony Del Real, Hector Vargas, Angie Vargas, Karen Demerly, Monica Casanova, Fermin Recarte, Nohemi Lugo, Mida Grover, and so many others who could not be named. I thank Paul Shueller for his incredible knowledge of and assistance in researching Lafayette's history. My thanks to all those whom I worked with at Jefferson High School; the office staff, faculty, and students all shaped and influenced the book in one way or another. Specifically, my contact with the high school students was extremely beneficial. Their teenage angst and continual questions about college and life after high school contextualized the project within a different generational level. Indeed, it was one of these students whose artwork graces the cover of this book. I thank Alejandra Carillo-Muñoz for her talent and amazing artistic touch. While they are faced with incredible obstacles, there are still so many other individuals who seek out justice and community understanding across race, language, and ethnicity.

My success in this world is a testament to the struggle and resiliency of my own parents, Miguel y Theresa Vega. As once-undocumented Mexican immigrants themselves, they too encountered the multitude of fears and anxieties that accompany a move to the United States. Though it pained them to leave their mothers and siblings in Mexico, they made the best of a painful situation and survived. They successfully raised four grateful children and in the process taught them love, tenacity, and family unity. I am saddened that my father did not live to see his youngest daughter publish a book on experiences like his own, but I am comforted in knowing that his memory and legacy live within my own commitment to fight for a better life and defend those who find themselves where he was for forty years, economically exiled in the United States.

The sweat equity he built working backbreaking, tiresome jobs was what allowed me to come to academia in search of those stories and lifeways I observed every day in his home. Through her own experiences—including the loss of her husband and surviving breast cancer—*mi mamá* taught me amazing strength and gave me the will to succeed in an unfamiliar environment. My mother inspired tremendous academic perseverance. As she walked me hand-in-hand to that first day of pre-school—my *mochila roja* slung across my back—I would never have guessed the long and treacherous road my mother was leading me to. *No seas mensa hija*, don't be dumb, get an education. You don't want to rely on a man for the rest of your life. Now as an educator myself, I am fully aware of the lessons both my parents taught me and absolutely cognizant that without them this scholarly work would have never materialized.

I am also grateful to my emotional and intellectual rock, Lee Bebout. I am indebted to the support, encouragement, and collaborative suggestions he provided throughout these years. His continual scholarly advice and attentive ears have strengthened this book and will continue to influence my academic progress. Without him I would not have been introduced to Lafayette; without him I might not be who or where I am today. My heartstrings are also fully aware of the gifts my son, Jayden Michael Bebout-Vega, has provided me. His blessing in our lives and his willingness to let Mommy spend a few hours in her office have paid off. No more worries *chiquitin*—your mommy will spend countless hours playing with you to make up for it.

Additionally, I am sincerely thankful to my siblings—Sergio, Faby, and Adolph—for their willingness to always understand why I could not make it home for birthdays and holidays. Through their combined efforts, my parents were more able to understand these personal sacrifices. Additionally, having grown up in a household with all of them has provided me with the skills necessary to collaborate and work as a cohesive whole with others, and the wisdom to know when to take that last scoop of ice cream for myself.

To my scholarly family, all of you have provided amazing insight in my personal and scholarly development. To Alejandro Lugo, who introduced me to border theory and borderland studies in general, I am grateful for the intellectual support and personal encouragement he has provided all these years. Our initial interactions at the American Anthropology Association Meetings in 2001 cemented the collegial relationship that led to my choosing the University of Illinois for my doctorate. Moreover, the excitement and enthusiasm he has always given this project has been incredibly essential to its success. Alejandro has worked closely to challenge me when I needed to be challenged and to encourage me when I need encouragement. His commitment to the department and involvement with students has also shaped the ways in which I hope to interact with students in the future. Arlene Torres has provided comfort on countless office visits when my fears and frustrations concerning academia were at times debilitating. Arlene listened and observed while also directing and inspiring me in professional directions. Her example of service to the university and attentiveness to a scholarly commitment of dissecting and combating racism and poverty has certainly affected my development. Through Martin Manalansan, I have learned the art of entertaining through pedagogy. Through his scholarship, I have learned to interrogate the banality of everyday lived experience and look to those subtle yet pervasive signals of race, place, ethnicity, and gender as they operate throughout different spatial experiences. Martin's motivating message of "This is not your magnum opus; just finish the damn thing" rings daily as I continue to work on my scholarly writing. Ellen Moodie's attentive interest to this research in her hometown has been encouraging, especially at times when I worried whether anyone else would care as much about Indiana as I did. Ellen's experiential knowledge of the area and scholarly expertise in trauma and violence add valuable insight to this project. Janet Keller's attention to early drafts of some of these chapters and her willingness to navigate the worlds of memory, nostalgia, linguistics, and discourse have had a tremendous impact on the direction of this and future projects. Finally, thank you to Gilberto Rosas for walking me through the manuscript process at a time when I needed it most and his willingness always to lend a supportive ear.

In Lafayette I am particularly indebted to individuals who supported me, regardless of my ties to a Big Ten rival—at least I attended U of I and not IU. The students and faculty of Purdue University's American Studies program have all been unbelievably supportive and essential to my fieldwork in their campus town. I am truly thankful to Dr. Susan Curtis, Dr. Bill Mullen, and Dr. Charles Cutter, as well as to their students Katie Armstrong, Heidi Renée Lewis, Charles Park, Erick Wade, and Brian McCammack for their observations and suggestions on this book. The research assistance and friendship of Young-In Kim was extremely valuable to my personal and scholarly development in Lafayette. I am indebted to Drew Lopenzina and April Shemak, who not only read early versions of these chapters but also helped me survive east Texas. At Arizona State University I have been blessed with sister colleagues throughout all four campuses. The Women and Gender Studies unit in the School of Social Transformation has been a godsend in an otherwise difficult academic trajectory. I am in deep gratitude for the confidence that Mary Margaret Fonow and Georganne Scheiner Gillis had in my work and the supportive acceptance that Lisa Anderson, Cecilia Menjivar, Karen Leong, Alesha Durfee, Heather Switzer, Wendy Cheng, Karen Kuo, Michelle Tellez, Carlos Velez-Ibañez, Rosa Jimenez, Rudy Guevarra Jr., Kathy Nakagawa, and so many others have provided me. The Institution for Humanities Research (IHR), particularly the director, Dr. Sally Kitch, and the assistant director, Kathy Holladay, was instrumental in my arrival to the ASU campus and the completion of this book. Indeed, the IHR helped with the publication of this book through their subvention program for humanities faculty. Additionally, IHR fellows Leah Sarat, Yajaira Padilla, Wei Li, Francoise Marguet, and Claudia Sadowski-Smith all provided wonderful feedback. I am also thankful for the brief but meaningful visits with fellow anthropologists Ruth Behar, Leo Chavez, Arlene Davila, and Jane Hill, who were instrumental in finalizing this book. I also want to thank the University of North Texas's Ronald E. McNair program for all its staff did to prepare me for a life in higher education, especially Judy Morris and Diana Elrod, who acted as surrogate family, therapists, and career counselors to so many of us McNairites. You were the first educators to believe in me, and for that I will be forever grateful. And to that high school assistant principal who suggested I should work at a daycare center when I asked about going to college to become a teacher, thank you for solidifying a permanent drive to prove you wrong. I received strength, perseverance, and encouragement from all the individuals listed and so many more. I hope to do this book justice in their name.

Introduction

Bienvenidos a Hoosierlandia: *Asserting Ethnic Belonging at the "Crossroads of America"*

Escucha pueblo
La canción del inmigrante
Y el canto alegré
De que espera la justicia.

Ven pueblo sigue luchando,
Sigue buscando dignidad.
En que los hombres volverán
Hacer hermanos

[Listen everyone
To the song of the immigrant
And the joyous song
That awaits justice

Come everyone, keep on fighting
Keep searching for dignity
Where all men will return
To being brothers]
—Himno al Inmigrante, Indianapolis, April 2006

In April 2006 an estimated 20,000 immigration rights support-ers marched onto the streets of Indianapolis.[1] Sung to the melody of Beethoven's "Ode to Joy," the "Himno al Inmigrante" [Hymn for the Immigrant] elicited boisterous cries from thousands who traveled, some for hours, to chant, sing, and collectively voice opposition to the national debate against undocumented immigrants.[2] Calling for a return to human brotherhood, marchers pleaded for an imagined community

Father holding up daughter at Indianapolis rally. Photo by author.

that was inclusive and flexible. Demonstrators wanted to create awareness of a broken immigration system that gave many no other choice
but to enter the United States "illegally"—this action was not criminally
malicious but driven from desperation.[3] Marchers peacefully asserted
a "*dignidad*" [dignity] that went otherwise denied in popular rhetoric
against immigrants. Their voices reverberated against downtown buildings. The march ended at a public green space called the Mayor's Action

Center (MAC), where people continued chanting and rallied together even as police looked upon them from atop the Marion County jail just across the street. The marchers gave speeches directly outside the MAC offices—a space designed for citizens of Indianapolis to request city services—as a symbol of formal request to the city and the police watching from the jail across the street that immigrants should not be deemed criminals based on undocumented status.

Immigrants and non-immigrants, Latinos and non-Latinos all gathered on those Indianapolis streets and reflected a spirit of solidarity that traveled much further than those tear-laden streets in the Midwest. All over the nation, Spanish-radio personalities, church leaders, labor organizers, business owners, and individual immigrants coordinated to express their frustration. Indeed, the coordinated events of 2006 reflected a reality of mixed-status families, neighborhoods, and communities implicit in a U.S. Latino experience. These massive demonstrations, many of which shattered historical records of public protests in the United States, called attention to the tentacles of the immigration debate. Reduced to stereotypical lawless tropes, undocumented immigrants and

Youth raising a flag for justice at Indianapolis rally. Photo by author.

their supporters affirmed a different image during those spring marches, one of families, workers, and contributing members of society willing to participate and belong within the national collective imaginary. On the streets of Indianapolis, Latino Hoosiers from Mexico and El Salvador to Puerto Rico and Venezuela, all with various residential statuses, gathered to showcase their right to demonstrate and belong in *their* nation, *their* state, and *their* local communities.

(Re)imagining Indiana

Acres and acres of flat farmland used for feed corn or soybean often embody the familiar images of Indiana and the Midwest in general. Two-lane roads perpendicular to the flat horizon guide my own memories of this region. But this imagined Midwest is far from the reality. Slight river valleys notch out tiny hills and interrupt the monotony of hypnotizing uniformity. Small, barely there bumps alter the landscape and beckon drivers to take a moment and glide, coast the second-long release from gravity, and enjoy the tranquility of watching the corn grow and life take shape. In Indiana, the Wabash River wends its way through the state, carving out a rolling countryside. Beyond the flatness often associated with small midwestern communities, these hills signify a transformation worth noting. The altered landscape, the subtle yet present scenic shifts, reminds us that moments of change actually come to define space. Here, the topography may be an apt metaphor for demography, for like its slight hills and river valleys, a complicated history of settlement challenges the imagined homogeneity in the Heartland and the United States more broadly. Of course, the rural Midwest has long been a site of cultural contact and conflict. Indian communities, French traders, White settlers and African American freedmen, and the Ku Klux Klan all intermingle in the stories of this midwestern landscape. Latinos, too, look onto the rolling fields and call them home. Century-old *barrios* in Indiana's northwest and a long history of migrant labor traversing the state's rural lands established a unique, if often overlooked, Latino presence. Like many before them, these Latino Hoosiers settled, raised children, and established themselves as midwesterners. This book accounts for Latino Hoosiers in the making and marking of twenty-first-century Indiana. It argues that the concept of community has always included various entry-points and that belonging should not rely on fictitious notions of uniformity. As this book's title suggests, this volume addresses the politics of belonging and the impact of boundary maintenance on a Latino population that daily redefined what it meant to belong in the United States.

As with other areas of the Midwest, popular depictions of Indiana frame Hoosiers within a White American experience. In films and music, Indiana has been positioned as static and homogeneous. Most know Indiana through the lyrics of John Mellencamp or popular films of White male athletes, such as *Hoosiers* (1986) and *Rudy* (1993). More recently, the popularity of the NBC-TV and ABC-TV, respectively, sitcoms *Parks and Recreation* and *The Middle* have provided more fodder to the romantics of Indiana. Indeed, the state prides itself as the quintessential middle of America: the place of "traditional" American dreams where White residents just so happen to prevail. Caught in this warped nostalgia, Indiana's people of color become simultaneously erased. Thus, as the self-proclaimed core of an American national imaginary, a corrective to the romantics of the Midwest is certainly past due.[4] Privileging White Hoosiers as representative of Indiana conveniently forgets the century-old Mexican neighborhoods in the Indiana Harbor/East Chicago corridor and leaves out the state's most famous family, the Jackson 5.[5] Though northwest Indiana complicates the perceived complexion of the state's population, Hoosiers of color also lived far beyond Chicagoland.[6] Popular and cinematic representations of "Hoosiers" have typically excluded these communities of color from the normative Indiana, or middle-America, experience. But can we imagine an alternative Hoosier experience reflective of these complexities? What if, for instance, instead of famed Notre Dame player Rudy there were Rodolfo, a talented Mexican American athlete whose undocumented status barred him from traveling to the championship game? Perhaps Mellencamp's famed song of Hoosier couple Jack and Diane could include their neighbors José y Adriana "doin' the best they can" in a renewed moment of immigrant hostility. These personifications of Indiana in Rodolfo, José, and Adriana render a new, more complex sketch of this midwestern space. Instead of viewing these shifts as challenges, what if the Rodolfos and Adrianas of Indiana reflected a more accurate vision of an American experience?

This book accounts for the thorny reality of representation and belonging in a midwestern landscape mistakenly imagined as homogeneous, English-speaking, and free of political controversy. As one older resident, Ted, mentioned of his early days at Purdue University, "We never had protests on campus over the war or anything like that. It was like the '60s never happened here." Perceived as neutral, calm, and perhaps even above tensions, central Indiana typified a Hoosier composure that even Latino residents described as "*muy tranquilo*" [very calm/tranquil]. This tranquility attracted Latino families to settle in Greater Lafayette, where they were economically stable and their children less exposed to violence or drugs. The Lafayette area provided city amenities like Spanish church services, Latino-owned business, and various employment possibilities; but just as important, this exurb of Indianapolis was far from the urban cityscapes of Chicago or Los Angeles that some Latinos had fled. An hour north of Indianapolis and two hours south of Chicago, central Indiana was far enough away that it provided some rural distance and was close enough that one could drive to those cities within a day if need be. Still, Lafayette was not free of conflict. Some residents revealed kernels of discord and race-based harassment throughout their narratives of midwestern tranquility. White, Latino, and Black respondents recognized some unrest operating just beneath the surface of the midwestern-nice illusion.[7] Outright references to the KKK or subtle snubs in public all disrupted the way central Indiana residents actually interacted with one another. These tense exchanges came to a head during the 2006 national immigration debate wherein a figurative border was erected between those who could be considered contributing members of society and those who could be dismissed as criminals, terrorists, or job-taking thieves.

The border, as spatial metaphor, lends a unique perspective to the study of Lafayette during the 2006 immigration debate. The border, or what Gloria Anzaldúa (1987) so vividly termed as "*una herrida abierta* [an open wound] where the third world grates against the first and bleeds," specifically references the U.S.–Mexican border but expands to other bordering encounters where people "grate against" one another and "bleed" (3). In addition to the heightened vigilance, unsanctioned crossings, deaths, and anxieties present at that 2,000-mile long corridor, the border also encompasses a multitude of social and cultural exchanges of ideas, identities, families, and community. The physical space of what Renato Rosaldo (1988) notes as the "zone between stable places" has inspired significant scholarly attention, especially within Latino studies.[8] The attention to border theory comes out of its varied applications as a physical borderland and a metaphorical apparatus that peels away the economic, racial, gendered, and historical borders that created difference, sustained distance, and inspired unique exchanges between peoples. Whereas a border represents the territorial demarcation of one nation vis-à-vis another, border theory and borderland studies recognizes that hegemony is part and parcel of the emotion of nationalism, and the resulting identities are what indeed are being protected by such physical boundaries. As Alejandro Lugo (1997) notes, "the border region and border theory can erode the hegemony of the privileged center by denationalizing and deterritorializing the nation/state and culture theory" (45). While territorial land becomes the discourse used for border protection, "it is not territory per se that is being contested, but instead personal identities, movements of persons, and cultural and political hegemony of peoples" (Kearney 1998: 124). Migrants who traverse these borders, metaphorically and literally, can instantly become the target for this aggression.[9] Perceived as threats, those who defy and complicate the image of a homogeneous nation can be subject to the "wall in our heads" (Berdahl 1999), or that internal bordering that transplants geopolitical borders onto social interrelational obstacles.[10] Using border theory to understand the impact of the 2006 immigration debate in central Indiana "thickens the borderlands" to these nontraditional settling locations and underscores how divisive politics impinge on people's daily lives across the country (Rosas 2006).

Though defended as concerns about unauthorized entry to the United States, the immigration debate inflamed long-established disputes over Latinos as cultural threats.[11] House Resolution 4437, or The Border Protection, Antiterrorism, and Illegal Immigration Control Act of 2005 (H.R. 4437), provoked political speeches, media discourse, and local conversations that positioned Latino residents under suspicion. Notably, the interjection of U.S. Representative Jim Sensenbrenner of Wisconsin as a main sponsor of the bill marked a significant regional political leap and moved the debate away from the more familiar geographical setting of the southwest. With increases in their Latino demographics, midwesterners and southerners directly positioned themselves as victims of the "terrorists, drug smugglers, alien gangs, and violent criminals" described by Sensenbrenner in 2005.[12] Traditionally limited to state-based legislatures in California and Arizona, anxieties that marked Latinos as possibly "illegal" and therefore a threat grew exponentially across the country.[13] The actual number of undocumented immigrants in these "new" locations may have been minimal, but the racialization of all Latinos as possible "terrorists, drug smugglers, alien gangs, and violent criminals" perpetuated narratives of impending fear and takeover. Rep. Sensenbrenner and others used then-recent demographic increases of Latinos in "new" areas to promote regional angst against anyone phenotypically or linguistically identified as Other.

The word "new" dominates the scholarship of Latinos in nontraditionally recognized destinations, but neither the immigrants themselves nor the towns they inhabited were necessarily new to the migrant stream. Lafayette, for instance, had both historically established Latino families and recently arriving immigrants. Latino families who previously resided in Los Angeles, Chicago, Texas, Mexico, El Salvador, and Puerto Rico intermingled with families present for three generations. This resulted in a much more stable and vocal Latino base willing to advocate on behalf of their collective ethnic belonging. Decades of finessing their place among, or at times in spite of, White Hoosiers came under attack during the highly contentious and very vocal national immigration debate of 2006. Newspaper editorials, sneers at workplaces, and eruptions of vocal hostility on city streets positioned Latinos outside the local imaginary. Boundaries were drawn against anyone visually suspected as an undocumented immigrant. Indeed, physical distances and mental borders kept people from interacting with Latinos, who were perceived as always and already criminal. Thus, Latinos confronted a state of "exceptionality, or the status of living as a person exempt from particular rights" (Rosas 2006: 337). Regardless of citizenship status or Latin American origins, Latinos faced contentious exchanges in schools and workplaces with non-Latino residents who bought into the rhetoric of fear.

Mistakenly perceived as an overnight phenomenon, Latino Hoosiers did not just miraculously appear in Lafayette. Rather, many factors drew a variety of newcomers to this Hoosier setting. While Purdue University attracted international Latin American and Caribbean students and their families to this college town, a larger increase in Latino population resulted from other working-class employment opportunities.[14] Since the 1950s, families from the Mexican states of Jalisco and Zacatecas have worked in

Lafayette as service employees in restaurants and hotels. According to oral histories, in 1956 two Mexican workers, brothers, arrived in Lafayette after unsuccessfully searching for work in Chicago. On the advice of their parish priest, the two brothers boarded a bus to an unknown town in Indiana. In Lafayette, an old friend of the priest provided them employment in his restaurant. Soon thereafter, their families and intimate friends joined them. The arrival of these two brothers resulted in a network of families spanning four decades in this central Indiana river valley.[15] As Hilda, a Mexican resident who first arrived in Lafayette in 1963, explained, "When people know there are jobs, they tell friends and family 'Vente, acá ay trabajo. Te ayudo conseguir chamba'" [Come, there's work here. I'll help you get a job]. Once relatives and friends were told about the opportunities in central Indiana, many followed in the footsteps of earlier trailblazers.

As long as jobs were plentiful, many Mexican families in Lafayette encouraged their family members to join them in central Indiana.[16] As Hilda continued, "Ya ven que les va bien, y se traen sus familiares" [Once they see that they are doing well, they bring their families]. Partly this cooperation worked as a way to assist fellow immigrants in their fiscal needs as well as encourage some sense of familiarity in a predominately White town. By the 1990s, factory jobs enticed more Latino residents from California, Texas, and Florida as well as from Puerto Rico and different regions of Mexico. The recession and the North American Free Trade Act served to increase the profit shares of major transnational companies, but they left working-class and rural families on both sides of the border devastated. As jobs were lost and inflation rate skyrocketed in other regions of the United States, "Lafayette typically showed better employment numbers than the state or the nation" (Kriebel et al. 2000: 116). By the 1980s, three major companies invested in Lafayette and provided a dramatic increase in employment. Caterpillar, Wabash National, and Subaru of Indiana all opened facilities in Lafayette and joined the likes of Alcoa, Fairfield, Tate and Lyle, and Eli Lilly.

These trends in economic growth occurred as a result of relocation initiatives that moved manufacturing facilities from larger older cities with stronger union influences to smaller towns that offered tax and non-union labor initiatives (McConnell 2004). Historically affected by rural flight, small towns and rural areas, like those in central Indiana, welcomed the prospect of more jobs. Too often, these small areas had insufficient residents to meet the new labor demands.[17] Additionally, those workers who initially embraced the arrival of these jobs rejected the positions associated with "less-than-desirable jobs" in meatpacking and night shifts (Kandel and Parrado 2004: 257).[18] As a result, these companies recruited individuals from other regions to fill the demand. Companies like Caterpillar, Subaru, and Wabash National recruited workers from throughout the nation. Additionally, the area's service industry also expanded to meet the varied needs of the rising population. With every stage of economic expansion, Lafayette grew in physical size and population density. In the 1990s, Latino and non-Latino residents shaped the area into a very different image than it once was. My neighbor's family came from Wisconsin, and I knew other White residents who had arrived via Chicago, Michigan, and Ohio, but it was the Latino arrivals who attracted the most attention. Similar to their non-Latino counterparts, Latino workers came from other cities in the United States that lacked substantial economic stability. Some did arrive directly from Mexico or other Latin American nations, but a majority (89 percent) of those I spoke with had resided in another part of the United States prior to stumbling upon Lafayette. Additionally, other co-ethnics like Puerto Ricans and El Salvadorans also made Lafayette home. Thus, central Indiana became well known among a small circuit of Latino migrants in search of a quieter, more financially stable place to raise a family.

In 2006, the region was rife with newly built shopping centers, redeveloped condos, and housing subdivisions where once corn and soy had grown. With an overall unemployment rate far below that of the national average, Greater Lafayette reaped the benefits of economic growth. As the community expanded, established Lafayette residents worked alongside, went to school with, and lived in the same neighborhoods as newly arrived individuals. Rather than being spatially or socially segregated, Latino Hoosiers interacted daily with their non-Latino neighbors. In theory, the opportunity to meet, welcome, and relate to newly arrived residents was possible; however, in practice the public spaces, residential areas, schools, and workplaces reflected a different mode of interaction. Prior to the 1990s, exposure to Latino populations throughout the state was limited to seasonal migrant labor. The 40 percent growth from 1990 to 2000 in Lafayette's Latino population resulted in noticeable changes in entrepreneurship, places of employment, classrooms, and neighborhoods. Lafayette's already established Mexican families delighted in the growth of Latino neighbors in the 1990s. The substantial increase brought a rise in Spanish church services, grocery stores, and other ethnic businesses. This was especially appreciated by women who no longer had to make homemade *tortillas* or covertly meet in one another's homes for Spanish prayers to the Virgin Mary. However, while Mexican residents rejoiced at the arrival of other Mexicans and Latino co-ethnics, some non-Latinos noted the changes with trepidation.

The introduction of H.R. 4437 in 2005 and the resulting debates on immigration in 2006 sparked hostility and resentment toward the region's increased Latino population. More recently, state-based legislative acts in places like Arizona, Alabama, Georgia, Utah, South Carolina, and even Indiana have continued to mark undocumented immigrants, and particularly Latino residents, as *personae non grata*. The persistent politics of immigration situates undocumented immigrants, and Latinos assumed with that label, as deficient and unworthy of acceptance. This book illustrates how Latino residents positioned themselves as legitimately belonging to or "owning" the right to reside in Lafayette. Latino families of Lafayette faced daily reminders of their difference in this Hoosier space. Climate patterns, the pervasiveness of spoken and written English, and introverted cultural patterns made this midwestern space quite unlike those in Latin America or even more traditional settling locations in urban and southwestern cities. Yet, since 1956, Latinos settled in Tippecanoe County, raised families, and (re)constructed the meaning of "home" to include this Hoosier landscape. Through their bordered negotiations, Latino families claimed their own social and physical space in Lafayette.

Intersecting the "Crossroads of America"

Fittingly, the state motto of Indiana, "The Crossroads of America," provides an important entry point for exploring how Latinos and non-Latinos interacted in this American landscape. As a metaphor for coming together and departing, the crossroads presents a way to examine how people converged or diverged in a community. The crossroads can also reveal how interstitial space provided an opportunity for accord and co-existence. Indiana has certainly faced these crossroads before. The experiences embedded in this book build upon a long history of cultural contact and conflict in the region. Homes once inhabited by German immigrants now housed Mexican families. Streets traversed by horse and buggy now lead to truck dealerships where "*Se Habla Español.*" Centuries-old conflicts over settlement and encroachment became relived in the discursive battles over home, belonging, and community. This book illustrates these complex and historic intersections in the Midwest.

The crossroads metaphor also played a critical role in the lives of Mexican communities. Crossroads, or bordered experiences, can be thought of as the meeting space where multiple stimuli influence identity formation. Gloria Anzaldúa described this interstitial crossroads between national and cultural identities as a space of survival: "To survive the Borderlands / you must live *sin fronteras* / be a crossroads."[19] Thus, Anzaldúa advocated on behalf of a crossroads as bridge. Latino Hoosiers built bridges and lived metaphorically *sin fronteras* [without borders] by situating their lives both within Indiana and beyond national borders. Confronting real socioeconomic limitations and legal restrictions on their lives, Latinos in Indiana attempted to circumnavigate these "Crossroads of America" and created their own ethnic definitions of belonging in Hoosierlandia.[20] But much like the façades of Disneyland, the simulacra implicit in such notions of the "American dream" are not without flaws. Examining the "internal boundaries permeating everyday life" in these nontraditional settling communities calls for heightened attention to both overt and subtle ways of bordering- and distance-making at the crossroads (Lugo 2000).

Latinos experienced figurative border inspections and border crossings nearly 1,500 miles away from the geopolitical U.S./Mexico border. Their inclusion in the local and national imaginary was limited by false assumptions of criminality and exclusion from narratives of rightful belonging that discounted the contributions Latino Hoosiers had made historically and in present-day Indiana. Notably, battling denied belonging was not specific to small towns or urban settings; it was not a Republican or Democratic issue; it was not a midwestern, southern, or western problem. Twenty-first-century immigration politics exposed a contentious environment prevalent throughout all corners of the nation as people defined who had a right to claim belonging and who could be denied basic human consideration. A "possessive investment in Whiteness" justified why some residents, those rendered as White and privileged, had earned their rightful place in a national racial and ethnic hierarchy (Lipsitz 1998). This hierarchy depended on certain "ideological assumptions" engrained in the popular American psyche that conditioned certain unequivocal "truths" about Othered peoples (Santa Ana 2002). These stereotypical "truths" were repeated often enough that they took on the aura of fact. False binaries based on raced, ethnic, classed, and gendered negative associations confined belonging and marked undocumented immigrants with abject status.[21] For some residents of Greater Lafayette, the definition of resident, citizen, neighbor, or community member shifted to exclude anyone identified as Mexican or Latino and therefore plausibly undocumented. Undocumented immigrants were imagined as impatient, dishonest, and disrespectful of American laws and sovereignty. Given these "truths" about undocumented immigrants, the general American public deemed them, and any Latino suspected of being undocumented, to be outside the parameters of belonging. Evidence of this Othering and reliance on these dubious "truths" emerged periodically during 2006. Printed election materials, newspaper opinion pages, and spoken utterances related how presumed criminality, language, and ethnicity implied "exceptionality, or the status of living as a person exempt from particular rights" (Rosas 2006: 337).

At job sites non-Latino co-workers shifted and sneered at the presence of Latino Hoosiers, even if they were full-fledged citizens. Latino youth reported being accosted at schools and public spaces. Mixed-status families cautiously stepped out of their homes in fear of being separated as a result of rumors of deportation raids. This meant that young children with birthright citizenship lived with the constant fear that their parents or siblings could be taken away. Mothers faced paralyzing fears at the thought of being separated from their children or returning to a place of hunger and desperation from which they had escaped.[22] The rhetoric also took inspiration from past arguments that depicted Mexican women as poor, irresponsible, and the source of overpopulation.[23] Gendered demarcations of Latino men as threats and Latinas as "baby-makers" operated in racialized narratives that bifurcated who could be deemed acceptable to community. If a woman looked "Mexican" and was out talking to her children in Spanish, she was automatically assumed to be undocumented and her children a strain on social services. Latino men, on the other hand, were conscious of how the dominant population viewed their presence as economic threats and violent criminals. At times, non-Latinos avoided being in proximity to Latino men, avoided their gaze, and grimaced at the sounds of Spanish. Undeterred by the way they were perceived, Spanish-speaking residents kept on living and working in central Indiana.

Latinos sought ways to assert their "right to be different and [to] belong in a participatory democratic sense."[24] Ethnic belonging, as represented in this book, expands Renato Rosaldo's notion of cultural citizenship to more daily efforts to *participate* and *belong* as recognized members of local, regional, national, and transnational communities.[25] Instead of looking to typical avenues of citizenship, this volume accounts for the way participatory belonging was rebranded through cultural and lived contributions to community. Latino Hoosiers navigated their right to belong by refusing to give in to a rhetoric that narrowly defined the parameters of their acceptance. Latino cultural citizenship was evident in the immigration rallies across the nation; however, there were other, seemingly banal maneuvers of belonging that also demonstrated how Latinos constructed meaning and home in U.S. spaces. Individuals, families, and communities made use of public and private spaces where they could openly practice their transnational ethnic identity without compromising their local belonging. Fashioning their own sense of belonging through female *comadrazgo* [social networks], family, church, and entrepreneurial networks, Latino Hoosiers enacted their own feelings of home that challenged politicized exclusion. Openly speaking Spanish, scheduling *quinceañera* portraits in public areas of downtown Lafayette, and participating in ethno-religious processions on city streets all asserted their rights to belong. Though not purposefully planned to contest the politics of immigration, these organic displays of ethnic belonging still subverted the narratives that protested their presence.

Ethnic Belonging at the Crossroads

Ethnic belonging provides a way to acknowledge the simultaneous exchange of being Latino and feeling at home in Indiana. Ethnicity, nationalism, transnationalism, and local belonging are concepts traditionally placed in opposition to one another, as if emphasis in one denotes challenges to the others. Critically, the drive to be transnational—that is, to be able to navigate freely across borders without fear of deportation,

We ♥ Indiana message at Indianapolis rally. Photo by author.

criminalization, or being denied reentry—actually inspired immigrant arrivals to claim local legitimacy in the United States. Instead of being oppositional, ethnic belonging fuses ethnicity, nationalism, transnationalism, and local belonging. Developing ties to Indiana did not lessen transnational commitments to hometowns or families elsewhere. Similarly, strong ethnic ties to places like Mexico did not interrupt attempts to feel affinity toward Hoosier communities.

Ethnic belonging allowed for degrees of global flows in correlation with national belonging and accounted for the way Latino Hoosiers actually lived out their daily negotiations between both. For instance, marchers along the Indianapolis immigration rally held up signs that read "We ♥ Indiana" while loudly proclaiming in Spanish: "Aquí estamos, no nos vamos, si nos echan regresamos" [We are here, we aren't leaving, and if you throw us out we'll return]. A middle-aged Latino male might have shed a tear at the sight of his son playing American football in the high school game and yet still sang the Mexican national anthem during another sporting event. Children participated in Virgin of Guadalupe processions as well as represented their school in the annual downtown Christmas parade. Adults voted in November elections while preparing for their holiday trip to see family in central Mexico.

In daily examples, individuals straddled that border between transnational ethnic identity and local belonging to Indiana. These daily encounters built ethnic ties and fortified a collective identity needed for moments of public protest. To understand the activism which resulted in the pro-immigration rallies that challenged H.R. 4437, we must first explore the daily practices of ethnic belonging that inspired and sustained eventual participatory citizenship. Here, we may adopt and adapt the feminist adage that the "personal is political" in exploring the politics of everyday life. Personal interaction in the workplace, family celebrations, educational strategies in the classroom, and even attendance at sporting events lay the foundational consciousness and organizing networks for coordinated political expressions. Fashioning ethnic belonging provided families with the emotional commitment to assert themselves as legitimate members of local, regional, and national communities.

Instead of absorbing into the mainstream, Latino Hoosiers reconfigured what it meant to belong in this region. Latino residents of Greater Lafayette, regardless of immigration status, engaged their own position as civil partners in central Indiana and in that manner provided a more nuanced form of imagining themselves as legitimate citizen-actors of community. Latino Hoosiers continually pointed to their entrepreneurial spirit, home mortgages, and sweat equity as evidence of a commitment to this national landscape. Longtime Lafayette resident Hilda was brought to Lafayette as a baby; she was raised here, and though she lived in Mexico for some time, she returned eventually because, as she expressed: "aquí es mi tierra, mis primeros recuerdos son de Lafayette" [this is my homeland. My first memories are of Lafayette]. For many Latino Hoosiers their family, their job, their church, and, in other words, their life was located primarily in central Indiana. Even as Latino Hoosiers wove themselves into these landscapes, they did so without separating their Latino lives from their U.S. surroundings. The art of carefully balancing themselves as both Latino and Hoosier was written in their own narratives of success, a success that did not necessitate assimilation into the mainstream.

Organization of the Book

Chapter 1, "*Recuerdos de* Lafayette: The Making and Forgetting of the Past in Central Indiana," situates this book within a history of past encounters with belonging. Tracing the manner in which residents from this midwestern city historically positioned themselves in relation to Native Americans, Black freedmen, and earlier European immigrants exposes parallels of denied acceptance that would resurface in 2006. This chapter examines how the area's earlier generations perceived immigrants and people of color and how these marginalized communities negotiated their place within central Indiana. Exploring the palimpsest of history written, rewritten, or forgotten in the local imaginary, the chapter mines the way knowledges (plural) of the past influenced contemporary definitions of belonging. The presence of the past became critical in the anti-immigrant discourse of 2006 that channeled generational precedence against recently arriving Latinos to Indiana. In addition, this chapter explores how and why Mexican residents began settling in Lafayette, with a particular interest in recounting what life was like for Mexican "pioneers" in Lafayette during those earlier settlement stages in the 1960s.

Chapter 2, "Kneading Home: Creating Community While Navigating Borders," appreciates the complicated ways in which Latinos created community. This chapter includes discussion of the myriad ways in which Latinos sacralized their presence in this midwestern space. Whether through religious practices or familial networks, Spanish-speaking families needed community to provide a sense of home. Locating familiarity and comfort in central Indiana was difficult at times, especially when others, including those who shared the same religious faith, put up mental walls or shut real and metaphorical doors on Latino families. Illustrating an incredible resiliency, the Latino community created their own avenues of belonging. Publicly and privately, they sustained opportunities where their faith practices and ethnic lived realities could be affirmed.

Chapter 3, "Written Otherings: Policing Community at the 'Crossroads of America,'" places non-Latino interviews in dialogue with local print media to account for the ways by which an anti-immigrant sentiment infiltrated locally. Highlighting the impact of words and images on people's perception of Latino residents, this chapter describes how race, gender, and class saturated the politics of belonging. Specifically, it places respondents' voices, letters to the editor, campaign flyers, and media representations to consider not just the discourse itself but also its impact on people's perceptions. Through an analysis of written, spoken, and embodied communicative acts, the chapter explores critical moments of enacted discourse.

In other words, someone who spoke of "illegals" and ascribed undocumented status to perceived visual markers of Mexican identity projected racialized, gendered, and classed assumptions that were then used against Latinos. Thus, the language surrounding immigration and "legality" altered the way people interacted with their Latino neighbors. Moreover, because these conversations remained shielded by the cloak of legality, sovereignty, and terrorism, the actual racialized undertones that infiltrated the daily lexicon went virtually ignored. By eliciting a discursive analysis of how belonging was talked about, this chapter performs the necessary task of placing public discourse in context with respondents' voices to see how the national debate on immigration shaped personal perspectives and altered embodied distance.

Chapter 4, "Clashes at the Crossroads: The Impact of Microaggressions and Other Otherings in Daily Life," advances the previous discourse analysis by probing the lived moments of conflict and confrontation. Verbal and felt distances at work, on the street, at stores, and in schools illustrate the social borders and boundaries set up throughout the town. Responses from Latinas and Latinos addressed gendered differences that manifested in multiple microaggressions. From their perspective, Latino residents described an immense disappointment with the negative social climate molded by false assumptions. Moreover, the chapter integrates the experiences of second-generation Latinos who were also targeted with slurs, negative interactions, and traumatic moments of denied belonging.

Chapter 5, "'United We Are Stronger': Clarifying Everyday Encounters with Belonging," records the importance of daily lived experiences as a marker on community dynamics. Beginning with an examination of the seemingly innocuous assumptions held by non-Latinos, the chapter exposes how even the most well-intentioned person could accede to dangerously oversimplified views. Unlike other respondents, letter writers, or politicians, these residents felt themselves more open-minded to immigration and the Latino presence in general. Still, they often reverted to the dominant narratives prevalent in the politics of immigration that unfairly portrayed Latinos as monolingual or criminal lawbreakers. For Latinos, they enacted and embodied their own counter-narratives to these debates in their lived daily experience. In addition to forming critical community organizations or individually inserting a more complicated picture of the immigration debate, Latinos' interactions in the classroom and sporting events also lay the foundational consciousness for asserting a "right to belong." This ethnic belonging in seemingly banal activities built comfort, a positive self-image, and ties to their version of a Lafayette community. The political activism displayed in 2006 did not simply materialize overnight; layers upon layers of lived ethnic consciousness built solidarity, social networks, and the committed enthusiasm to march for social justice. At times, these more personal impromptu moments may have meant more to Latino Hoosiers than overtly demonstrated acts of protest.

The book's Conclusion, "The Politics of Belonging Wages On: How State-Based Legislation Affects Community in Indiana," relates how rigid definitions of community continued to undermine state and local notions of belonging. Widening the concept of community strengthens how people relate to one another as a collective and see value in one another's presence, but the resolve of certain politicians to continue to build their careers on anti-immigration legislation speaks to the importance of this book. In 2011, Indiana politicians followed the lead of other legislators in states like Arizona who continued to mark Latino residents with suspicion and worthy of policing. If unchecked, these local state-based actions dangerously maintain divisive rhetoric in the popular imaginary and block any opportunity to move forward together. The Conclusion provides a space to delve into ways in which individuals and local groups could reimagine community as an inclusionary concept. The narratives in this chapter provide significant lessons for other towns currently facing their own challenges. As the politics of race and divergent notions of belonging continues to afflict states like Arizona, Alabama, Georgia, Oklahoma, and even Indiana with draconian state-based bills on immigration, this Conclusion reminds readers of the case of central Indiana and what this community confronted. Appreciating the resiliency of Latino residents in the face of direct and indirect animosity can inform other areas of the country that are facing their own politics of belonging.

Whether in traditional Latino-settling destinations like Arizona or in southern states experiencing a rise in Muslim immigrants, the ethnic belonging developed by marginalized groups remains significant for combating otherwise inhospitable environments. I have no doubt that thriving counter-responses exist in all these spaces, but the question remains: What do we search for when looking for agency, activism, and oppositional politics? For Latino Hoosiers, their asserted agency materialized in daily refusals to give in to the rhetoric of exclusion. Many faced constant material and structural threats to their belonging and encountered negative borderings with fellow non-Latino residents, but they met these daily oppressive moments with equally persistent claims to ethnically belong. Living in Indiana meant confronting an imagined sense of community rife with tensions that presumed White residents as the norm. Layers upon layers of past conceptualizations of belonging riddled the contemporary landscape: the Ku Klux Klan control of state politics and anti-immigrant hysteria, the realities of settler colonialism, and the romantics of earlier European immigrants informed the construction of a twenty-first-century Hoosier identity. Yet these Latino Hoosiers continue to alter the changing face of the Midwest. Their lives and daily affirmations to ethnic belonging illustrate how change is made daily, tenaciously, and perhaps even subconsciously by those unwilling to consent to national and local manifestations of injustice. Regrettably, politicians still refuse to budge on comprehensive immigration reform while families continue to live in fear. Anxieties over deportation, separation from U.S.-born children, and evident reminders of their liminal, exceptional status persist. Still, these individuals and families remain. Daily they live out their lives, compartmentalize the fears, and find avenues to celebrate their humanity amid other Latinos who together make neighborhoods, towns, and regions slightly more bearable. This book celebrates their resolute spirit and acknowledges the pains undergirding their strength.

1

Recuerdos de Lafayette

The Making and Forgetting of the Past in Central Indiana

There is the most serious task of determining not what history is . . . but how history works.
—Michel-Rolph Troullot, *Silencing the Past*

Though it was dark and cold outside St. Boniface Catholic Church, the warmth and enthusiasm of Latino parishioners illuminated the sanctuary space with pre-dawn festivities to Our Lady of Guadalupe. At 3:00 A.M. on December 12, 2006 the Spanish choir began the events with Las Mañanitas.[1] After a few *alabanzas*, or traditional hymns, a Norteño band joined in with its accordion, drums, and unique sounds that melded secular music with faithful veneration. By 5:00 A.M., an Indianapolis mariachi band trumpeted in the mass to a sanctuary space at maximum capacity. At the altar, brown paper mounds, cacti, rocks, and flowers created a replica of the landscapes of Tepeyac, Mexico, where the Virgin Mary first appeared to an indigenous man. Walking into the church building on that morning, one could hear the sounds of Mexican music summoning Mexican Catholics to celebrate this holy day. Violins, trumpets, and guitars rang out in inspirational melody as parishioners sang church hymns and popular Mexican songs rewritten for this special occasion. Songs like *Amor eterno, Gema, Cielito Lindo*, and *La Guadalupana*, and chants of "¡A la bio, a la bao, a la bim bom ba. La Virgen, La Virgen ra ra ra!" reverberated across pillars and vaulted cathedral ceilings.[2] In addition to the music and celebration of mass, an interpretive dance performed by a Mexican youth group recognized the indigenous component to this commemoration. Plumed headdresses bounced up and down the aisles accompanied by the beat of a drum and the jingles of their bell-clad ankles.[3] Families and individuals, all gathered on that morning spiritually, culturally, and physically, prepared to observe this deeply Catholic

Mexican holiday. Hundreds of Mexican parishioners filled the Lafayette church space and worshiped their particular form of ethno-Catholicism.[4] Notably, the ethnic religiosity practiced in 2006 paralleled that of German immigrants in the same space a century earlier.

By 2006, walls originally intended for German worship became christened by Spanish prayers, Mexican music, and neo-indigenous performance. Founded by German Catholics who were seeking to preserve their particular religious identity, St. Boniface was established in 1853 as a sanctuary for religious, linguistic, and ethnic traditions. The German congregation named the sanctuary St. Boniface in honor of a monk known for converting Germanic tribes. Now, in the twenty-first century, St. Boniface hosted the celebrations of the Virgin of Guadalupe, herself credited with converting Mexico's indigenous communities. The parallels did not end there. Like Mexican immigrants, Germans spent the first sixty-five years of the parish speaking their native tongue and teaching it to their children. Regrettably, this history is not always recognized in popular national narratives that position European immigrants as rapidly assimilated. This romantic, if inaccurate, reconstruction of the past effectively silenced opportunities for comparative parallels between earlier Germans and present-day Latino families in the public imaginary.

At the height of the 2006 immigration debate, letters to the editor in the local newspaper narrated accounts of European assimilation that strategically challenged contemporary Latinos living in Indiana. In an effort to target those who spoke Spanish and proudly displayed their ethnic heritage, letter writers discursively set up an idealistic past where their immigrant ancestors legally arrived in and assimilated to this country. For instance, in May 2006 a letter writer proclaimed, "What did we do with the Polish, German, French, Italian, Russian, etc. immigrants. My ancestors were immigrants and they learned. I speak English and I do not celebrate the 'old' country's holidays." A few weeks later, a letter headlined "Grandpa spoke English, obeyed law" explained precisely how family lore replaced experiential knowledge of actual relatives. As this excerpt of the letter indicates, the result of this imagining constructed a past disjointed from the present.

> My grandfather immigrated to the U.S. from Germany. He had done so legally. Although I never knew him (he passed away the year I was born),

one of the few stories I have been told of him was that he became a U.S. citizen and did not teach his family the German language. . . . Anyone wanting to live in this country should feel the same as my grandfather. If you don't want to follow our laws, customs and particularly our language, then feel free to go back to your own country. I, for one, do not want my freedoms, my language, etc., controlled by someone who is here illegally. (June 11, 2006)

Conflating the use of Spanish with unsanctioned entry, the letter set up a dyad of belonging that included earlier immigrants and excluded contemporary immigrants. This "us versus them" positioning disavowed Mexican and the larger Latino population from belonging to *his* (the letter writer's) imagined national and local community (Anderson 1991). Of course, absent from this politics of belonging were the race-based privileges that provided European immigrants a path toward citizenship even if they too arrived through unsanctioned entry points (Sadowski-Smith 2008). Moreover, much-celebrated assimilation tales actually obscured the practices of maintaining ethnic identity, home languages, cultural traditions, and transnational networks among earlier European immigrants.

Appreciating how history was discursively used to establish legitimacy against present-day immigrants, I searched the archives and historical texts to understand what life was actually like in Lafayette's past. Peeling away the layers of history unearthed experiences concealed by distance, time, and all-too-convenient narratives. Seemingly imagined as a homogeneous space of romantic frontier settlement and industrial modernity, the reality of central Indiana expands beyond European ingenuity for commerce and trade. Bringing to the fore the social stratification of this Wabash River valley, this chapter examines the manner in which people of color and immigrants were remembered throughout Indiana's cycles of settlement and how their positioning affected contemporary notions of belonging. Through a deeper, critical eye at the historical record, I engage the narratives associated with American Indians, Black residents, European immigrants, and even the KKK in the making and forgetting of a Hoosier identity. Most notably, the Klan's early-twentieth-century rhetoric of "100 percent Americanism" provided disturbing parallels to contemporary anti-immigrant messages in 2006.

Within this paradigm of understanding the present through the past, I position early Latino, primarily Mexican, settlers as part and parcel of this community history. Too often relegated as "new" communities, places like Lafayette have had a longstanding Latino presence. Though certainly smaller than the influx of Latino arrivals in the 1990s, Lafayette's Latino "pioneers" reached as far back as the 1950s. It was the memories of one of these long-established Latino residents that truly influenced this chapter's focus on memory-making and constructions of self. Hilda, recalling her arrival in Lafayette in the 1960s at the age of two, said that her life journey had taken her as far away as Alaska and even back to Mexico for a few years. Given these multiple spaces of residence, I asked Hilda why she returned to Lafayette after being in so many other places since her childhood in Indiana, she responded, "Yo aquí me siento como que aquí es mi casa, como que aquí es mi tierra. Mis primeros recuerdos son de Lafayette. Aquí es donde empecé a crecer" [I feel that my home is here, that this is my homeland. My first memories are of Lafayette. Here is where I was raised]. Hilda identified with Lafayette and claimed a unique hometown experience; still, her memories were not validated in simplistic renderings of a Lafyatte past that excluded her family's early contributions. Ironically, Hilda's feelings of home and belonging were similar to the feelings of those who trafficked in the rhetoric of exclusion against contemporary immigrants. The *recuerdos*, or memories of Lafayette, were multilayered and needed to be unpacked precisely because these pasts were often used to pit residents of Lafyaette against one another, residents who otherwise lived on the same city blocks and simultaneously created a sense of home in this midwestern landscape.

Presumed to be new arrivals without legal or historical residency, Latino residents faced a battle for acceptance. Displaying selective narratives of the past kept Latinos out of the collective imaginary and sharpened comparisons with "worthy" assimilated European forebears. Tales of past immigrants positioned them as honorable, loyal pioneers and simultaneously discounted undocumented immigrants, and those racially associated with them, as criminals and cultural threats. The juxtaposition not only erased a century and a half of Mexican residency in the United States but also perpetuated a system of whiteness that privileged and sanitized European ancestry. As Guillermo Gómez-Peña states, "The U.S. suffers from a severe case of amnesia. In its obsessive quest to 'construct the future,' it tends to forget or erase the past" (1989: 22). This pathology of forgetting afflicted the way individuals framed one another in Indiana. Whether purposeful or unconscious, the concealment of critical pasts splintered the population and impeded opportunities for comparative dialogues. Descendants of ethnic immigrants or Black residents who experienced discrimination lacked the wherewithal to critically reflect on the xenophobia present in twenty-first-century Indiana. Notable exceptions included individuals like Pastor Walker. Born and raised in central Indiana, Pastor Walker had spent his entire life working in and ministering to places throughout the state. By 2006 he was head pastor at one of Lafayette's historically Black churches, a local institution for well over a century. Disappointed by members of his congregation and the general public who adopted an anti-immigrant stance, Pastor Walker was frustrated when he explained, "But most people are not students of history, they're students of the thirty-second sound bite and don't have a clue. . . . Sometimes civil disobedience is a necessary thing for justice. Well, how do you think we started this country? A doggone Boston Tea Party rebelling against a doggone king and an authoritarian rule. We forget. They [American revolutionaries] were all criminals." Pastor Walker referred to the Revolutionary War to highlight the parallels between undocumented immigrants and historic U.S. figures both fighting unjust authoritarian rule. Rather than blindly defend a defective immigration system, he tirelessly encouraged people within his congregation and several community organizations to acknowledge their intertwined histories as a means of engaging one another.[5] Comparing immigration reform to the fight against the British Empire and civil rights–era clashes, Pastor Walker located immigration activists within a national precedence of resistance. Indeed, immigrant activists typified a long history of revolutionaries fighting for the right to be recognized as contributing members of society.

The late Michel-Rolph Trouillot (1995) prolifically articulated that there was a critical distinction between "what happened" and "what is said to have happened" in the historical record. Unfortunately, the distinction between *what happened* and *what is said to have happened* is not so easily teased apart in the public imaginary. We may never know what truly happened in the past, but the sustained assemblage of particular narratives as historical truisms must be unpacked for what they miss, or for what is being conveniently erased. In central Indiana, partial accounts of the past framed how Latinos could be perceived and denied belonging in the twenty-first century. Parallels with earlier generations could have provided empathy and understanding; instead, renderings of assimilated ancestors supported the demonization of Lafayette's newest arrivals as separate and apart from previous immigrant residents. Seeking distance from the latest denigrated group in society meant conveniently erasing past ethnicity, unlawful settlement, or one's own exploitation. Indeed, this is not new in the United States. According to George Lipsitz (1998), the specter of race has historically pushed individuals into ignoring personal injustices in order to consolidate their privilege or invest in the dominant White category. The process of becoming White, however, had to be restricted in order for it to have power over those who could never be White.[6] While certain individuals could start to claim whiteness, racialized Others became relegated to socially and legally impaired subcategories. Thus, White privilege relied on omissions of *what happened* that were conveniently supplanted by manufactured narratives of *what is said to have happened* in order to sustain a system of inequality. The emphasis here is not simply on the erasure or creation of history but on how this act of forgetting elicits a particular response. Trouillot asserted the performative qualities of history by recognizing that there was something being done in the remembering or forgetting the past. Looking to not just what history *is* but how it *works* leads us away from a fight over positivist approaches and suggests a deeper critical eye toward what is being done with history, how history-making works toward certain ends.

The exclusion of specific uncomfortable details reveal much about what a community chooses to remember and how that choice alters life for individuals years after the first exclusion occurs. In the popular history of the United States, ghosts from Native massacres, land grabs, human enslavement, and ethnic persecution become displaced by stories of pioneering triumph, self-reliance, and assimilation. These stories of the past reverberate into contemporary feelings of entitlement for those whose forebears have been rescued. Conversely, forgetting details of marginalized communities suppresses their contributions and promotes even further silences. Harnessing the power to silence controls the narrative and determines how subsequent tales can be spun to maintain privilege. Forgetting, or ignoring, historic moments meant that contemporary anxieties about immigrant intrusion in the twenty-first century could overlook analogous examples of settler colonialism, illegitimate occupation, xenophobia, and ethnic immigrant resistance that muddied the argument against Latino immigrants. Thus, exploring the public history of Lafayette situated how pastness operated in present-day conceptualizations of belonging. Memories of the past could have created possibilities of empathy had they been allowed to surface; instead, idealized constructions of inherited belonging aroused feelings of animosity.

In 2006, multiple references to history shaped everyday discourses of citizenship and belonging to central Indiana. In the newspapers and online commentary sections, some residents deployed specific stories to sharpen the critique against undocumented or unassimilated Latino families. Even seemingly innocuous traces to the past scattered in preservation efforts of neighborhoods, battlegrounds, museums, names of places, and local lore shaped communal narratives of belonging and historical entitlement to the Midwest. For example, the myth of the vanishing Indian played an extraordinary role in placing European claims on local spaces. With the erasure of Native peoples, lore about pioneering families and brave "founders" could be utilized (Buss 2011). Even if Lafayette residents did not frequent museums or read about the past, area festivals or historic neighborhoods preserved who could be associated with legitimate belonging. To account for the written and experienced historical narratives of belonging, I looked to archives, history texts, newspaper stories, public celebrations, and vocalized allusions to the past. Placing these multiple accounts in dialogue provided a larger picture of the way the past informed contemporary visions of community and legitimacy in Lafayette. This chapter begins by looking at what the public imaginary overlooks, an established Latino presence in central Indiana that extended back into the mid–twentieth century. Recognizing Latinos within this geographic space in the 1950s and 1960s combats renderings that called into question the legitimate residency of this population. Still, twenty-first-century moments of Othering and denied acceptance must be contextualized much earlier than those of the twentieth century. The following sections present a more traditional chronological trajectory. For instance, the assertion of legitimate White presence is set against the constructions of a Native Other. In a state called Indiana, these musings of Indians revealed how residents saw themselves in the making or erasing of this region's first settlers. Moving toward Indiana's antebellum era, the next section follows the tension of that state's role in slavery, abolitionism, and the construction of White benevolence in its historical record. This White benevolence became critical in composing the idealized European immigrant and later White resident whose thorny relationship with the Ku Klux Klan was creatively amended in the public imaginary. I showcase how the popularized collective history summoned during the 2006 immigration debate, read against strategic omissions, was layered with problematic distortions.

Retracing *Los primeros Mexicanos en* Lafayette

I sat in Alicia's living room, looking through treasured albums of her initial years in central Indiana. Pictures of baptisms, first communions, birthday parties, and Christmas celebrations displayed a virtual living history of these families' interrelationships and how they began to count on one another for spiritual and social support. Then Alicia's hair was teased in a classic 1980s style while holding her goddaughter asleep in her arms above the St. Boniface baptismal font. Now a grandmother, Alicia proudly showed me pictures of her adult children, whom I now knew as parents themselves. Her only daughter's *quinceañeara*, one of the first in Lafayette, was particularly memorable because now, a decade later, she was pregnant with her second child. Pictures of her three sons and their birthday parties were throughout. Alicia laughed, recalling how she had had to make their *piñatas* because no one sold them locally during those years. Now in her custom-made home, Alicia looked at her younger self, almost as if to reassure herself that it had all been worth it. Trying times met with exuberant celebrations in the photographic chronicles of this early Latino community. With each page, she recalled different stories, different moments of survival. The time when the priest kicked them out of the parish, the *inquietud* [anxiety] of her husband starting his own car business while still working a full-time job, the barn fire that killed what few animals they had on their rural Indiana property, the family laughing, crying, struggling, and surviving. Pictures of religious and secular celebrations recorded Alicia's established family and sense of home in Lafayette.

Decades before twenty-first-century immigration debates turned the national gaze onto Mexican immigrants, "new" communities throughout the nation were already engaged in building belonging in spaces previously unfamiliar with a Latino presence. The considerable increase in Spanish-speaking Lafayette residents during the 1990s altered the landscape and garnered the attention of White residents who turned to unsubstantiated rumors to explain the growth. For example, a running narrative throughout the town placed sole responsibility on one employer rumored to have placed a billboard on the U.S.–Mexican border to entice undocumented immigrants to Lafayette. This story was related to me on multiple occasions when I spoke to White residents about their knowledge of the immigrant population. Further investigation of this anecdote revealed that contrary to popular opinion, news of any such billboard was never reported in the newspaper. In fact, upon contacting the business beat reporter often associated with this story, I was told, "That may be an urban legend. I've heard [the billboard] is there but we have never published a photo of it and I'm not sure one exists."[7] This urban legend, and its continual retelling in the local imaginary, illustrates how tales of recent pasts swayed the way non-Latino residents positioned their Latino neighbors as very recent and presumably undocumented. While the presence of Spanish-speaking residents increased substantially during the 1990s, the fact that the Mexican residents first arrived in 1956 and that some families were already third-generation Lafayette residents was virtually unknown to the majority of residents. Moreover, the complexity of other Latino residents, mostly Puerto Rican, did not register in the minds of those whose imaginary allowed room for only "job-taking" and "law-breaking" Mexican immigrants.

Recovering the historical presence of Mexican Hoosiers in Greater Lafayette meant turning to oral histories and memories from some of those whose intricate family networks spanned five decades in Lafayette. Long-established Mexican residents revealed their familial ties to one another in interviews and retold stories of their grandparents, parents, and extended relatives who had originally settled in the rolling prairies and cornfields of central Indiana. Individuals identified specific events in the late 1950s and early 1960s that resulted in their family's presence in this corner of Indiana. A migration chain from central Mexico to central Indiana triggered entire family relocations from townships near Colotlán, Jalisco, and Tlaltenango, Zacatecas. In later decades, the network broadened to immigrants from Aguascalientes, Mexico City, and Veracruz. Additionally, Latinos from Puerto Rico and El Salvador added to the Spanish-speaking community in this small city. Even Latino families who once lived in other, more traditional settling locations in California, Illinois, Florida, and Texas also chose to leave them and resettle in central Indiana. The result was an unusual mix of historically established and recently arriving Latino community that to some seemed to appear out of nowhere. Until now, the experiences of Lafayette's earlier Mexican residents were untold in community history books and newspaper stories. The narratives of those who remembered this earlier period and recounted how their families settled in Lafayette were significant in updating a past whose gaps created divisive strains on the present community.

According to several descendants of the original two Mexican residents of Greater Lafayette, the arrival and success of two brothers in 1956 eventually impelled entire families to leave rural municipalities in Mexico's Crossroads of Zacatecas where Jalisco, Zacatecas, and Aguascalientes meet. Individuals and families from this area in central Mexico established migratory networks to Lafayette, and by the 1980s individuals looking to migrate to the United States bypassed the southwest and went directly to central Indiana.[8] Instead of a billboard in a border city, Lafayette's positive reputation for stable jobs and a calm exurban atmosphere circulated to territories far from the U.S.–Mexican frontier.

Neither of the initial brothers was present in Lafayette at the time of the research, so I collected stories of the past from their children, grandchildren, and great-grandchildren who still remained in Lafayette.[9] The accounts from two sons, a daughter, and a nephew of these men were influential in retracing the experience of these initial Mexican residents. Most notably, Ricardo, the son of one of these men, provided an account of how his father and uncle came upon Lafayette and the circumstances that prompted the arrival of more friends and family. According to Ricardo, a certain Mr. Allen employed his father and uncle in his hotel and restaurant and ultimately hired the rest of the family.[10] Fabiola, Ricardo's wife, was present in the interview and briefly interrupted his narrative to add, "Ese señor los trajo de Chicago a los dos. Fueron los primeros Mexicanos en Lafayette" [That man brought them both from Chicago. They were the first Mexicans in Lafayette]. I asked Ricardo if he knew exactly how this Mr. Allen recruited the men to Lafayette, and he responded by noting that his father and uncle had arrived in Chicago in the 1950s in search of work:

> Pero no encontraron y traían poco dinero. Entonces llegaron a la iglesia de la Virgen de Guadalupe en el South Chicago. Allí había un sacerdote, y ellos le dijeron que buscaban trabajo. Dijo, ¿quieren ir a Indiana yo tengo un amigo allá? Dijeron si, pero no sabemos ni a donde queda. Dijo, yo los pongo en el bus [sic]. Según el padre le hablo a Mr. Allen 'Te voy a mandar a unos Mexicanos para que los pongas a trabajar.' Llegaron y aquí los estaban esperando. Y entonces así fue como mi tío Juan y mi apá vinieron aquí.

> But they didn't find [a job] and they had little money. So they went to the Virgin of Guadalupe church in South Chicago. They told the priest that they were searching for employment. He asked, "Do you want to go to Indiana? I have a friend there." They said, "Yes, but we don't know where it is." He said he would put them on a bus. Supposedly the priest spoke to Mr. Allen [and said] "I'm going to send you some Mexicans so you could put them to work." They arrived here and [Mr. Allen] was waiting for them. And that is how my uncle Juan and my dad arrived here.

Within a few years, the men sent home news about job availability in Mr. Allen's hotel and restaurant. In 1961, Ricardo's mother and older brother joined his father, and by 1966 Ricardo's entire family had been reunited in Lafayette. For immigration purposes, Mr. Allen sponsored these family members through their employment in his business. Significantly, a network of English-speaking Catholic midwesterners provided a link that spawned decades of flow and placed Greater Lafayette within Greater Mexico.[11]

Much as with earlier German immigrants, transnational communication related what life was like in Lafayette and kept networks alive between family and friends in Mexico. Relying on these networks, individuals and family reached this midwestern landscape many times not fully aware of the location or the exact route from central Mexico to Lafayette. For example, I interviewed Ricardo's uncle Don Osvaldo, who remembered his initial experiences in Lafayette from the 1960s. Don Osvaldo first entered the United States in the 1940s in search of work as a *bracero*, or a contracted temporary worker. Most of these early years were spent working for the Southern Pacific Railroad in the southwest. By the 1970s, he and his wife were raising their three children in Lafayette. The couple moved back to Mexico upon retiring, but the children all stayed in the place that was most familiar to them, central Indiana. In 2006, Don Osvaldo was in Lafayette with his children while he had knee surgery and healed. He spoke about his sixty years in the United States and remembered his first trip to central Indiana by noting the role of family in his experiences: "Pues como estaban aquí unas dos o tres personas de allá, me interesé por venir. . . . Me vine de contrabando no mas que llegue a San Antonio. De San Antonio llame para acá y de aquí fueron por mi a Tejas" [Well, since there were some two or three people from over there, I was interested in coming. . . . I was smuggled into the country and arrived in San Antonio. From San Antonio I called here and from here they went for me in Texas].[12] Unaware of and unburdened by the distance between Texas and Indiana, Don Osvaldo expected his nephew to honor their relationship and give him a ride to Lafayette. Indeed, Don Osvaldo's nephew and his wife made the day-long drive to Texas. At the outset, this story illustrates the communal nature of migration chains and male-centered employment networks; however, Don Osvaldo's case also complicates how labor competition and notions of belonging penetrate even these long-established relationships. Don Osvaldo related a divisive moment for these families that demonstrates how a politics of immigration and belonging created tensions and competition between relatives even in these early periods of settlement.

Though the presence of Mexican relatives and friends from hometowns in Lafayette provided familiar faces in an otherwise alienating environment, a reported desire to control whom employers hired and who consequently reaped the benefits of employer-sponsored residency created rivalries among Mexican families. For Don Osvaldo, the conflict proved devastating and traumatic. A particularly upsetting moment in the past revealed itself when I asked him if he had ever encountered racism in Lafayette. He responded by stating: "Mas bien somos mas racista nosotros que los Americanos" [In reality, it is we who are more racist than the Americans]. I asked him why, and he replied, "Es lo que yo también me pregunto, que por que. Mas bien es que nosotros nos creemos mucho. No mas porque tenemos uno bien trabajo nos creemos mucho. Y al otro, porque no tiene pues esta fregado y habla uno de él, 'Mira este no tiene trabajo por guebon' y envés de ayudarlos hablo uno de ellos" [That is what I ask myself, why. Really, it is that we think too highly of ourselves. Just because we have a good job we let it get to our head. And the other guy, because he doesn't have [a job], well he's screwed. We talk about him and say, "This poor bastard doesn't have a job" and instead of helping them we talk badly about them]. At this point, Don Osvaldo revealed a deep-rooted disappointment in family members who he felt had called immigration officials on him forty years ago. He still felt betrayed as he recounted, "Esa vez que me agarraron me deportaron mis mismos familiares. . . . Me deportaron los mismos de allá, mis parientes" [That time that they caught me, it was my own family who deported me. The same family members from over there in Mexico were the ones that deported me]. Don Osvaldo's voice was louder as he said, "my own family" with a slight pounding on the armrest of his wheelchair. Much older now, Don Osvaldo was hard of hearing and had gone through several knee surgeries to repair what years of backbreaking work in the United States had done to his body, and this betrayal was still prominent in his memory. This event, and its repercussions on his immigration status years later, is indicative of the power of belonging and the way divisive notions of who should have a right to live in community permeate even families whose members could have otherwise provided strength and support for one another.

Because of his age and illness, conversing with Don Osvaldo was at times difficult; still, this moment in his past was clearly retold with sorrow and dismay. On that ill-fated Lafayette winter's day in 1966, Don Osvaldo did not have a valid visa to be in the country.[13] He was followed home by immigration officials, jailed, and eventually deported to Juárez, Mexico. When he returned to Lafayette some years later, he heard that members of his family had been the ones to call immigration officials on him. Laura, his daughter-in-law, present at the interview, added that his current citizenship proceedings had been halted because of this incident. Apparently, in 1966 Lafayette's police department wrongly arrested

Don Osvaldo in order to hold him in a cell for his deportation. They did not have to arrest him, but the Lafayette police department did not know any better and as a result Don Osvaldo now had a record. As of 2006, this forty-year-old record stood between Don Osvaldo and his U.S. citizenship status. According to Laura, "Por que tuvo record que estaba en la cárcel tuvieron que mandar por los archivos, por que they were too old. They had to search for them para ver el reporte. Por eso no le han podido dar sus papeles" [Because he had a record of being in prison [jail], they [immigration officials] had to search for the archives because the case was too old. They had to search for them to read the report of the arrest. That is why he hasn't been able to get citizenship]. He was a permanent resident, but this one mistake by the Lafayette police halted his application from moving forward toward citizenship. Don Osvaldo traveled throughout the United States for sixty years without ever attracting negative attention beyond this one immigration incident. He worked and sacrificed his body to the benefit of U.S. farmers, restaurateurs, and the Southern Pacific Railroad. Yet, because of the actions of the Lafayette Police Department as well as what he suspected were some envious relatives, Don Osvaldo remained caught in the bureaucracy of the immigration system.

Regardless of who actually was responsible for Don Osvaldo's deportation, he did return a few years later with the documentation to be approved for residency in Lafayette: "Fui en la mañana y en la tarde me lo dieron. Pero eso fue en aquel tiempo" [I went in the morning and by the afternoon they gave it to me. But that was in those days]. In "those days," as Don Osvaldo mentioned, immigration rules were much different. Siblings, wives, and children benefited from the efforts of hardworking immigrants who found employment in order to position themselves and their families for legal residency. As families slowly reunited, older sons and daughters were put to work in Mr. Allen's restaurant.

Mexican women during these earlier years may not have been exposed to the confrontations between males in the workforce, but they did contend with other issues of loneliness, nostalgia, and domestic survival. In the 1970s and through to the early 1990s, Mexican women were not readily hired in the industrial sectors. With young children, these women faced snow and bone-chilling winds, new cultural environments, and new language difficulties as they attempted to establish their

own places in this new community. Church, along with religious affiliation, was a primary space for some of these women to meet and locate
their support networks. For those who arrived during this early period
of growth, Lafayette was a small town that offered plenty of work hours
for their husbands, brothers, and fathers but lacked amenities present
in other larger cities for women in search of communal support. Notably, adjustment to this cold and unfamiliar environment was made even
more difficult by the isolation from one another. Unaware of Latinos in
the vicinity, the women found the town remote, strange, and uncomfortable. The move to the United States presented a drastically different
linguistic and sociocultural climate from that of Latin America.

Alicia recalled her move to Lafayette as a moment of seclusion and
doubts about living in central Indiana. Having lived with her family in
a rural part of Mexico her entire life, immediately after marriage in 1974
Alicia was faced with being a wife, leaving her family and country, and
then adjusting to an environment in central Indiana that was altogether
foreign. As Alicia noted, "De mi casa nunca había salido. Te imagines,
venir asta acá. Todo totalmente diferente. La gente, puro inglés. Tiendas,
no había tiendas Mexicanas. No había para cocinar. El clima, la gente"
[I had never left my house. Could you imagine, coming all the way over
here? Everything was totally different. The people spoke only English.
There were no Mexican grocery stores. There was nothing available to
cook. The climate, the people]. Alicia missed mainly the presence of familiarity. In Mexico she was surrounded by siblings, cousins, and aunts
and uncles; she was familiar with the community and the culture; and
she spoke and understood the language that surrounded her. Lafayette
offered none of those comforts. Similarly, Margarita, also a Lafayette
resident since 1974, encountered the culture shock and the language barriers of which Alicia spoke. Unlike her husband, Octavio, Margarita was
accustomed to an urban atmosphere. She had been born in Mexico, but
at the age of seventeen she joined her family on the South Side of Chicago and lived there for a few years prior to getting married. Margarita
summed up her initial thoughts on Lafayette by stating: "No me gustaba,
era muy chiquito. Como llegue de Chicago yo quería vivir allá. Era chiquito por que no había Mexicanos con quien platicar y estaba lejos de mi
familia" [I didn't like it at all; it was too small. Since I arrived via Chicago I wanted to live over there. It was too small because there were no

Mexicans to talk to and I was far away from my family]. Unfortunately for Alicia and Margarita, their feelings of isolation and distance from the familiar occurred while neither woman knew of the other's presence. The men sometimes worked two jobs. This left women completely in charge of children and domestic activities in an unfamiliar environment in which they could hardly communicate. In addition to bouts of depression and loneliness, female immigrants also lacked a number of significant benefits available to Mexican stay-at-home mothers in larger and more traditional settlement locations. For example, as Margarita noted, "En aquellos tiempos comprábamos la masa harina y yo tortillaba. O íbamos a Chicago cada mes y comprábamos cajas de tortillas, chiles, y chorizo que no había aquí" [In those days we would buy the dough, and I would make *tortillas* at home. Or on monthly trips to Chicago, we purchased boxes of *tortillas*, *chilies*, and *chorizo* not available here]. Eventually an Asian food mart that catered to the international students of Purdue University began carrying some *tortillas* and chili peppers; however, the women noted that trips to Chicago were still necessary for larger quantities and more variety of basic Mexican staples. As mentioned earlier, Alicia playfully mentioned having had to make homemade *piñatas* for her children's birthdays.

In addition to family meals, women also noted the difficulties they faced when navigating Lafayette with their children. As children grew older, attended schools, and made friends with White Hoosiers, mothers often felt intimidated by the world their children were beginning to master. Interactions with school officials and other parents became sources of anxiety and discomfort. Alicia's and Margarita's husbands had a better command of the English language and could communicate more easily with the larger general public. This level of familiarity and ease with language did not come as readily for Alicia and Margarita. As Alicia noted, "Ya ves que una mujer no sale mucho, ósea de lo que son los niños o de el trabajo a la casa con los niños. El era que conocía mas" [You know a woman doesn't get out much, except for that which involves the children or straight from work to the home for the children. He was the one that was more familiar]. This imbalance left both Alicia and Margarita at a disadvantage; initially, the linguistic and cultural differences were paralyzing. For example, Margarita was often intimidated by the world that existed outside her front door. This unfamiliarity with the language and culture of central Indiana barred her from parental involvement in her eldest children's school functions. Recently, Margarita had become more involved in the extracurricular activities of her younger children, an action that did not go unnoticed by her oldest daughter. Margarita noted how she responded to her eldest daughter's criticism:

> Ponte en mi lugar, yo no manejaba y luego tu crees que me iba rozar con las otras mamas si yo era como una muda. Haber échate tu en un país y metete con la gente y haber si no te sientes tu como una gallina descabezada. Por que hacer el ridículo, si yo me sentía ridícula. No iba por que no quería ni por que no me gustaba. Es que me sentía fuera de mi lugar.

> Put yourself in my place. I didn't know how to drive and on top of that do you think I would go near those other mothers after feeling like a mute. You go to a new country and go among its people and see if you don't feel like a chicken with its head cut off. Why attempt the ridiculous; I felt ridiculous. It wasn't that I didn't want to go or that I didn't like it; I just felt out of place.

Margarita recognized her absence in the lives of her eldest children and regretted that they, like her, had to endure times of uneasiness.[14] Even English-dominant Mexican females shared this restlessness with living in Lafayette. Laura reported that well into the 1980s she, too, felt lonely and completely cut off from social interaction. Laura was raised in California and grew up speaking English, yet the lack of a significant Latino population heightened her nostalgia for her family and negatively altered her own experience as a newlywed. Indeed, during a visit with her parents in California, Laura called her husband with an ultimatum:

> Le dije a mi esposo, ya I'm sorry ya no regreso a la Indiana [sic]. Si tu me quieres a mi y a tu hijo tu te vienes aquí por que yo ya no regreso. No way. [En Indiana] yo me enferme de los nervios, me la pasaba todo el día llorando, no dormía por extrañar a mi familia y la soledad. I had no one to talk to. Ibas al mall y no veías una persona Hispana.

> I told my husband. That is it! I'm sorry but I'm not returning to Indiana. If you love me and you love your son you'll come here because I am not

returning. No way. [In Indiana] I got depressed and spent all day crying. I didn't sleep because I missed my family and felt lonely. I had no one to talk to. You'd go to the mall and you wouldn't see one Hispanic person.

A few weeks after this conversation with her husband, Laura soon discovered that while her quality of life would increase in California, the high cost of living and low employment opportunities ultimately tipped the scale toward Lafayette. Within a few weeks, Laura and her son returned to central Indiana determined to convince her siblings and parents to make the move as well.[15] It was in creating a collective that many women finally felt comfort and belonging to the region.

Spiritual continuity and the search for a Spanish Mass ultimately united the pioneers of Lafayette's Mexican community.[16] In the 1970s and 1980s a dozen Spanish-speaking Catholic families made up a small traveling congregation of worshipers, going from church to church seeking priests who could and would be willing to give a Spanish Mass. Octavio recalled that by the late 1970s, his older brothers went in search of a Catholic priest who could speak Spanish. They found a priest at the St. Thomas Purdue University Catholic Center who agreed to occasionally give Mass in Spanish. Some Latino families attended English Mass but preferred the liturgy in their native language. As Margarita noted, "toda la gente saborea mejor a su idioma" [everyone savors [the experience] better in their own language]. Alicia recalled the collectivity she felt with the few Latino families that traveled together to the parishes. She remembered Bible study gatherings at St. Thomas with other Spanish-speaking adult couples, praying the novena for the Virgin of Guadalupe and singing among themselves *las mañanitas* on December 12 in West Lafayette. Noting the involvement of these families, the Spanish-speaking priest at St. Thomas approached the bishop and expressed the need for a Spanish Mass in Lafayette. Alicia explained that a priest from Cincinnati, Ohio, came to Lafayette to give Mass once a month. Often only two to three families attended this monthly Mass, but the services continued. Officially, church records show that by 1982, a Mass was occasionally celebrated in Spanish at St. Boniface. In 1986, Latino Catholics were directed to join the existing parish of St. Boniface Church, where 130 years prior German immigrants had established their own Catholic church. Also in 1986, the diocese sent one of its Franciscan fathers to

Guadalajara, Mexico, to stay at the home of a relative of a Lafayette Mexican Spanish-speaking parishioner.[17] Octavio remembered that between
the years of 1984 and 1988 "Era la misma gente Mexicana que empezaba
a participar en la lectura, la comunión, y el coro" [The same Mexican
parishioners were the ones to participate in the lector readings, communion, and the choir]. The same families that began the prayer group
at St. Thomas were now actively involved in the framing of a thriving
Spanish congregation at St. Boniface.

Because of the intimate size of some of these developing Mexican
parishes, passive attendance eventually led to active involvement on
multiple levels.[18] According to Octavio, the quaint size of the Spanish-
speaking congregation resulted in a dedication by all Mexican members to create and sustain a linguistic, cultural, and spiritual home.
Yumey recalled that "the church was intimidating at first because it
was so small, people had to take over. That made it seem more like a
community." Especially in these early stages of settlement, the church
served as a center for communal exchange. The spiritual interactions
provided a sense of community for families in search of comfort and
social support in what otherwise seemed a lonely, cold environment.
Spanish-speaking Catholics formed a necessary collective and rallied
around their spiritual beliefs. Feelings of isolation gave way to community building and long-lasting friendships that continued well into the
twenty-first century. Families began celebrating personal and religious
milestones with one another, often forming tight-knit relationships that
offset the absence of their families in Mexico. Indeed, by the time I
returned on a quick visit to central Indiana in 2013, Alicia's albums included the wedding photos of her son with Yumey as well as the sweet
faces of her grandchildren. Unfortunately, even with third and fourth
generations of Latinos raising their families in Lafayette, the larger political debate on immigration continued to infringe on the acceptance
of this community.

Settler Colonialism and Indiana's "Small Towns"

Debates over immigration grew out of questions of settlement: who had
the right to enter, make home, and claim ownership to John Mellencamp's famed small towns of Indiana. This conflict between legitimacy

and settlement in the United States began much earlier than the twenty-first century and, especially in the case of Indiana, reaches as far back as the occupation of Indian territories by European settlers. Asserting who should have a privelege to settle or even cross into these very lands has been a contested topic for centuries. From settler colonialism to immigration politics, Indiana has continued to find itself in a battle for defining legitimate belonging and who could be allowed or denied access to these lands. Before it was a state, these lands were the Territory of Indiana, and before then they were lands inhabited by communities like the Miami, Wea, Kickapoo, Sauk, Fox, and other American Indian communities. Then the protest to foreign arrival came from Native communities displaced by nefarious practices of land acquisition. To legitimize their belonging, White settlers usurped Native ascendancy and created a narrative of legitimacy that erased the realities of forced incursion. As Charles Mills asserts, settler colonialism depended on imagining land as "empty and unoccupied" to envision and allege rightful ownership of territories (1997: 49). This unpeopling was both physical and metaphorical through the systematic erasure of Native communities from the national imaginary. Thus, the politics of belonging is a consequence of historically fraught turmoil over settlement and stories that determined legitimacy.

Investment in the notion that European predecessors held legitimate belonging fueled the claims some individuals held over others. Contemporary letters to the editor and anti-immigrant discourse relied on tropes of belonging that completely ignored Native communities and established generalizations of White residents as rightful protectors of *their* community. Convinced of their belonging, some of these individuals felt justified in denying others the opportunities to establish their own claims to reside. Indeed, a system of White privilege delegitimized people of color from being thought of as co-citizens. Undoing and complicating the longstanding imaginary has proven a difficult task, but one that begins with acknowledging how early roots of White supremacy affected the way people imagined one another in community. Simple co-existence is not enough. As bell hooks remarks, "[T]o build community requires vigilant awareness of the work we must continually do to undermine all the socialization that leads us to behave in ways that perpetuate dominion" (2003: 36). Looking at the way difference was imagined and fixed against people of color in Indiana unearths how White supremacy continues to control belonging and rejection in the twenty-first century.

By 1717, French fur traders had set up the Ouiatenon trading post on what was then the western frontier. Nearly a century later, a coalition of Native communities valiantly defended their lands from European encroachment in the Battle of Tippecanoe. Local fall festivals, schools and street names, and museums maintain some knowledge of this past, but like much of the Native history in this country, this past was sanitized and limited in order to maintain White supremacy. Fort Ouiatenon, for instance, was often recalled as a space of peaceful trade and cultural interaction between French fur traders and Native peoples. The Battle of Tippecanoe, though illustrative of the coordinated resistance against western expansion, was still recalled through the image of the victors rather than through those who contested settler colonialism. These two limited and limiting moments guide the grand narrative of what is known about the Miami, Wea, Kickapoo, Sauk, Fox, and other tribes that inhabited central Indiana.[19] Thus, local memorialization of the battle and Fort Ouiatenon portrayed Indians as either defunct noble tradesmen or vanquished adversaries. Dueling public narratives of noble savage or vanished threat dominated museums, public celebrations, and popular perceptions of the area's first residents.

Perhaps inadvertently, the efforts of the Tippecanoe County Historical Society (TCHA) to recover the past and share it with the community actually reinstated these troubling depictions. For instance, the annual outdoor festival "Feast of the Hunter's Moon" was TCHA's largest fundraising function. Described on TCHA's website as "a re-creation of the annual fall gathering of the French and Native Americans which took place [at] Fort Ouiatenon," this local Thanksgiving-like event took place on the grounds of what was believed to be the site of Fort Ouiatenon. As a quasi–frontier, pow-wow, and Renaissance Fair–styled event, the display of food, dress, crafts, and period entertainment only further romanticized a congenial past devoid of any campaigns of mass displacement and genocide. Celebratory of the relationship between French traders and Native peoples, the Feast obscured the exploitive nature of the fur trade and the less-than-symbiotic relationship between European traders and American Indian communities.[20] Conversely, the

TCHA-sponsored Tippecanoe Battlefield and Museum provides a stark difference in narrative from that of the Feast. Recounting the role of Tecumseh and that of his brother the Prophet at the Battle of Tippecanoe (1811), the museum is full of mixed admiration for the "great Indian confederacy" while still dismissive of the Prophet's leadership in the attack against American troops.

The effects of this museum depiction were evident in the work of a fourth-grade class in the city of Battle Ground, where the museum is located. The class, having done some research on the Battle of Tippecanoe and taken tours of the museum, received a grant from the Department of Education to organize an online tutorial of the battle. The website, "Tippecanoe and the Internet too," included maps, a timeline of events, and a description of some of the major players in the battle. Moreover, the website was listed as part of the museum's resources for teachers who were developing lesson plans on the "Native American" experience.[21] Moreover, included on the site was a statement that the TCHA had verified the accuracy of the students' work. However, the content of the website was disturbing, especially given the TCHA's verification and teacher supervision with this project. Most notably, the hyperlink for the Prophet included various descriptions written by students on his personal background, his role in the battle, his visions and his "drinking." In the descriptions by the students, the first narrative to appear under "The Prophet's drinking" read as follows: "The Prophet drank too much. . . . The Prophet drank at all treaties. The Indians drank at all treaties and parties. They usually drank Whiskey, Rum, and Liquor. Indians and the Prophet drank a lot!!!" A second student added, "He smelled, drank, and was lazy." By posting these remarks, students under the direction of a teacher, with a grant from the Department of Education, and the verified accuracy of the TCHA perpetuated these stereotypes to a virtual audience of educators and students. The question here is not regarding the historical veracity of a fourth-grade project; rather, the problem lies in the dissemination of ideological constructions of a past that subtly and overtly vindicate White supremacy in children as young as those in the fourth grade. Ironically, the "drinking" of "rum and whiskey" referred to by these students may be attributed to the European trading practices readily celebrated at the Feast of the Hunter's Moon. Yet, accounts of French and English debauchery were not so readily available to the students' perceptions of the past. While the role and personal behavior of the Prophet is contested, these tropes of a drunk or "lazy" Indian distorted and diminished the agency of allied Native peoples to combat, if unsuccessfully, the invasion of White settlers.[22] As a result, contemporary populations learned to easily dismiss or, more important, forget indigenous residents as tragically vanished or unmatched in intellect or self-control to White forces.

Beyond fourth-grade classrooms, historical narratives long juxtaposed primitive Indian pasts with progressive White modernity. Though seemingly innocuous to some, the museum exhibits, TCHA documents, and public commemorations like Feast of the Hunter's Moon glossed over Indian experiences by remembering through a process of simultaneous forgetting. The resulting erasures not only denied present-day American Indian experiences but also conveniently veiled the realities of displacement, expulsion, and ethnocide. The art of carefully finessing suppression through admiration can be seen in the work of nineteenth-century historians who collected stories that "focused on the character of the pioneer" (Buss 2011: 166). For example, in a prologue to an early history of Wabash River Valley residents, Sandford C. Cox stated, "And it may be that on the very spot where the prophet priest was wont to chant his orisons, and pour his nightly incantations on the wind, now stands a *magnificent* sanctuary dedicated to the worship of the *true* God. *Splendid* dwellings—temples of justice, and of learning—have *taken the place* of the wig wam and the gauntlet ground" (1970 [1860]: 7; emphasis added). The historical record that Cox elicited was not value-free. Easily dismissive of the Prophet and his spiritual following, Cox artfully glorified White "civilization" as *true, magnificent*, and *splendid*. Similar to Renato Rosaldo's (1986) fourteenth-century Inquisitor documents, the words of Sandford Cox must be read through a politics of power that informed how the victor was rescued in relation to the vanquished. Moreover, the online student narratives illustrated how these biased constructions continued to influence future generations. Centuries of exotic representations, silenced pasts, and dismissive tones solidified a hierarchy that favored White settlers and reinstated myths of legitimate settlement.

Often placed in opposition to White settlers, the written narratives of Indian communities elicited fear and further "justified" dispossession.

Because the Wabash River provided an avenue for trade, the Greater Lafayette area was strategically placed at the crossroads of encounters between White settlers and various American Indian tribes. Named for a venerated Frenchman and Revolutionary War hero the Marquis de Lafayette, this region always attracted residents of varying ethnic and racial backgrounds who prospered from the economic stability of central Indiana. Notably, the drive to acquire land and property rights led to underhanded maneuvers by early settlers who wanted to lay claim, legitimately or not, on these lands. White pioneering settlers blatantly used unsubstantiated fear as a way to scapegoat Indians. Marked as dangerous in the imagination of White settlers, Indians embodied the fears of living on the frontier. Thus, Sandford Cox wrote of an occasion in the 1820s when squatters used fears of Indians to secure land claims. Apparently, alarmed settlers feared that "the Potawatomi, Miami and Kickapoo Indians were massacring the White population on Tippecanoe river near the Pretty prairie, and on Wild Cat and Wea creeks, and that they were hourly expected at Shawnee prairie, where the inhabitants were gathering into forts, and making preparations to repel their murderous attack. . . . This morning our scouts returned, and brought the news that it was a false alarm; that the Indians were peaceable" (Cox 1860: 51). Apparently, a squatter unable to pay for his claim and fearful of other "land hunters" used the fear associated with Indians to buy time and dissuade further encroachment on his land from other White settlers. According to Cox, the man rode off on his horse screaming, "Indians! Indians! The woods are full of Indians, murdering and scalping all before them!" and these warnings "spread like fire among stubble, until the whole frontier region was shocked with the startling cry" (1860: 51). The tale is recounted in Cox's text as a humorous frontier account, a "Yankee trick . . . done up by a Hoosier," yet the tale indicated how early White settlers situated their indigenous neighbors. While the rumor was discounted as false, scripting Indians as dangerous threats or living in pre-modern wigwams created caricatures that seemed to justify inequality and land appropriation. Moreover, conveniently imagining a past wherein the indigenous population simply disappeared supported a popular narrative of pioneering forebears who merely made use of abandoned lands.[23] Once disappeared, indigenous communities that were forced out, killed, or endured in Indiana no longer mattered in the public imaginary. This layering of half-truths and constructed pasts silenced critical details that could malign White settlement. For instance, details of the forced expulsion of the Potawatomi that resulted in the 1838 Trail of Tears remained omitted in public commemoration activities of idealized pasts.[24] Framing American Indians as either violent threats or people who mysteriously disappeared veiled the insidious nature of White settler colonialism and left possible a rewritten narrative of innocent pioneering White arrival.

Abolitionists and Imagining the Righteous White Hoosier

A battle for belonging in Indiana raged on through the nineteenth century. With the Potawatomi forcibly expelled from Indiana's borders, other "pioneering" settlers claimed the right to pass through or live in the state as freed men and women. Historically relevant as "one of three recognized Underground Railroad routes that crossed Indiana," Tippecanoe County was a critical stop along the path to freedom (Woods and Martin 1992: 22). The significance of this space as a part of the Underground Railroad could lend itself to celebratory nostalgia, but instead contemporary residents remained unaware of the buildings, routes, and rural landscapes that once provided sanctuary to so many souls. Virtually silenced, historic Black residents of Indiana continue to be ignored in the history of the state. Present-day imaginings of Hoosier belonging completely erased the experiences of freed or escaped residents who, despite Indiana's proximity to southern states, also settled and made Indiana home for generations. Notably, a strategic silence in the public history about slavery in the United States illustrates how the people are "more enthusiastic about history that confirms rather than confronts revered popular assumptions about America" (Horton 1999: 20). Indeed, public history and commemoration sites often struggle with the way slavery is remembered in the American imaginary. This is no different in free states like Indiana where freedmen and escaped slaves seem to evaporate in retellings of the past. This is especially the case for a place like Indiana where the twentieth-century resurgence of the KKK left a particular stain on history. If mentioned at all, Indiana's early Black residents were acknowledged only in relation to White progressive Hoosier abolitionists who proved nobler than their southern neighbors.[25]

Leading up to statehood, White settlers in the Indiana Territory con-templated the role of slavery and whether to enter the union as a free state. States just south of the Ohio River wrote their constitutions to include slavery. With the country equally divided between freed and slave states, Indiana was faced with a decision that could have brought about dramatic national consequences.[26] Ultimately, Indiana banned the practice of slavery in its constitution. Maurice Thompson, a once–Confederate soldier–turned amateur historian of the state, collected stories and tales of Indiana's past published in nineteenth-century pe-riodicals and later collected into books on Indiana. In *Stories of Indiana* (1898), Thompson wrote, "Indeed, from the beginning of civilization in the great Northwestern Territory, slavery had but feeble foothold and when Indiana became a state freedom was fixed in her organic law" (1898: 96). Indianans were seemingly forward-thinking in their consti-tution, but the case for or against slavery was far from "fixed" along the southern border with Kentucky. As Thompson noted, slave owners "contended that a constitution could not wrest a man's valuable chattels from him without just compensation" (122). The enactment of fugitive-slave laws meant that the absolute freedom of African Americans was still contested—not necessarily agreed upon by all of Indiana's residents. Far from taking the moral high ground, the position of Indiana on slav-ery was more complicated than Thompson suggested.

By including a provision in the state constitution that Indiana would respect the fugitive-slave laws of southern states, early Hoosiers were able to position themselves as a free state while concurrently sanction-ing the "rights" of slave owners to seek out and own their "chattel." In fact, Indiana passed a statute in 1824, decades ahead of the Fugitive Slave Act of 1850, whereby "the master was thereby armed with state authority to hunt his slave in any part of the state" (Leslie 1947: 349). This statute barred the operation of the Underground Railroad on the premise that "the courts had held that a man's property could be re-claimed wherever found, and so to hide it from him was, technically, a kind of stealing" (Thompson 1898: 124). Rather than Indiana's having what Thompson termed a "feeble foothold," residents of the state have long struggled with extending full citizenship rights to people of color. When faced with the issue of slavery and whether a person of color should have the right to live "freely" in Indiana, the rights of White slave owners across state lines were privileged over those of Black Hoosiers living in and contributing to the state. For example, Thompson's collection included the story of John Freeman, who "was arrested as a fugitive slave, after having lived in Indiana for a long time as a free man. He had a respectable and much esteemed family, and was, at the time of his apprehension, a citizen thoroughly in touch with the best people of his neighborhood" (1898: 126). Indeed, though his neighbors considered Mr. Freeman an upstanding citizen, they felt compelled to adhere to the fugitive-slave law—ultimately condemning him to his original slave owner. For his part, Mr. Freeman was fortunate enough to find an abolitionist lawyer who volunteered on his behalf and successfully convinced a judge and townspeople that his standing in the community warranted further consideration of his freedom. The difference between how the law defined a person's worth versus that person's actual contributions to society haunted Indiana well into the twenty-first century, when the state's attitude toward undocumented immigrants would once again challenge the unequivocal "freedoms" so celebrated by Thompson in 1898. The case of Mr. Freeman unearthed how Hoosiers were called to obey flawed laws and how residents of the state confirmed or confronted legalities in the past. Thus, the empathy shown toward Mr. Freeman could have translated into the empathy possible for undocumented immigrants in the twenty-first century. Regrettably, stories about building bridges of understanding and collective resistance lie dormant in the memories of the past.

It is important to recognize, however, that Thompson used this story to demonstrate the influential role of abolitionists in the state and highlighted the compassion of Mr. Freeman's successful lawyer. Thus, the protagonists were not the freed and escaped slaves who negotiated their freedom in Indiana. Instead, Thompson's narrative used White abolitionists as a means of promoting the state's emancipatory image. Conveniently veiled in Thompson's tales were resentment that abolitionists and freed slaves faced at the hands of fellow Hoosiers. Secrecy and fear were not uncommon for abolitionists and freed Black families during the period of the state's adherence to fugitive-slave laws. At times, this opposition to freedom manifested itself in physical violence and harm. For instance, in Greater Lafayette, three Black families found themselves victims of arson as their homes were destroyed by a mob that suspected them of having been Underground Railroad conductors during the 1850s.[27] In addition to arson and intimidation techniques, Sandford Cox also described an attempted kidnapping and enslavement of two young black residents of Lafayette. In *Old Settlers: Recollections of the Early Settlement of the Wabash Valley* (1860), Cox tells of a White farmer, Mr. Weaver, who had taken in two orphaned sons of a freed black woman from eastern Indiana whom Weaver knew. One day while working the field, the boys noticed two men lurking around the property. Days later the men tried unsuccessfully to snatch the orphans from the farm. According to Cox, "Such a bold attempt to kidnap the little negroes, aroused the honest indignation of the old soldier, who had marched under Washington . . . armed in backwoods style, to reconnoiter, and, if possible, to arrest and bring to justice those who had made so flagrant an attempt upon the liberty of the unoffending boys, who were free born, and over whom he was determined the lash of the slave-driver should never fall, if he could prevent it" (1860: 32). Like Thompson, these Black Hoosier bodies became merely the vessels for telling the story of a righteous White farmer. Reading this passage, one could wonder how often these kidnappings occurred and what did it mean that men could so easily enslave Hoosiers in a supposed "free" state. Instead, for Cox, it is the farmer and his benevolence that merit attention. Clearly, abolitionists who confronted a system of White supremacy must be recognized, but focusing solely on their altruism maintained patronizing models of helpless, voiceless Black residents. In their attention to White abolitionists, both Cox and Thompson silenced the voices and experiences of those residents of color that appeared only parenthetically in their accounts. As a result of neglecting these experiences, Hoosiers of color remained excluded from historical and contemporary imaginings of belonging.[28]

Myth Making and the Idealized European Immigrant

By the twenty-first century, race-neutral notions of legitimate belonging veiled the long history of racism that informed immigration policies. Far from fair, race-based privileges in the legal system approved of some immigrants and rejected others for generations (Haney-López 2006). So cunning was the deception of White legitimacy that "the history of

European illegality could be quickly forgotten" (Sadowski-Smith 2008: 781). Dominant myths idealized European immigrants and scripted how their descendants imagined these immigrants as lawful residents who rapidly assimilated and held unyielding patriotism to their new country of residence. Individuals evoked these myths as counterpoints to present-day Latino immigrants. In these encounters, a righteous immigrant past was juxtaposed to a criminal undocumented present. Conveniently, the result placed descendants of European immigrants as rightful inheritors of an American landscape and granted them the rights to deny belonging to others. Critically, as Maurice Halbwachs has noted, "the past is not preserved but is reconstructed on the basis of the present" (1992: 400). Much like descendants of nobility in Europe who "creat[ed] for themselves historical rights," in the United States royal titles were replaced by family genealogies of immigrants who pulled themselves up by their bootstraps, assimilated, and succeeded in the glorified American Dream (Halbwachs 1992: 124). It was through this celebrated past that individuals situated their critique of contemporary immigrant communities.

In the process of rescuing certain European immigrant experiences, other stories of ethnic resistance, undocumented entry, and racialization were omitted. Unearthing otherwise repressed immigrant experiences from the archive can complicate the public imaginary of these pasts. For instance, Claudia Sadowski-Smith (2008) identified an era of immigration restrictions between the late nineteenth and early twentieth centuries when "the number of Europeans who came as undocumented immigrants far surpassed that of Chinese newcomers" (781). According to Sadowski-Smith, a "spiral of illegality" existed for European immigrants who, like immigrants today, bypassed the restrictions meant to limit their entry and entered without proper documentation. These restrictions included the 1819 Steerage Act, the Immigration Act of 1882, and the Quota Act of 1924. Enforcement of these laws was in place at controlled entry points. Of course, there were other, less regulated land borders where Europeans entered without detection. Notably, even though these Europeans were "undocumented border crossers," once they arrived there was nothing strictly barring them from applying for eventual citizenship (Sadowski-Smith 2008). Thus, European border crossers benefited from having racial capital in a system whereby their whiteness provided them a path toward citizenship regardless of how they entered. More important, because European border crossers faced no restrictions when applying for citizenship, the details of their arrival could be subsequently severed and forgotten by their progeny.

Where and how this history was recalled was important to the way the myth of the ideal European immigrant developed currency. In Lafayette, archival evidence provided incredible parallels between earlier generations of immigrant residents and more recent Latino experiences. Though historical similarities existed between past and present ethnic groups, the myth of an ideal European immigrant supplanted the possibilities for compassion. TCHA's repository of archives was used by residents doing genealogical research or the lone university student searching for signs of people of color and ethnic immigrants in Lafayette's past. However, the archives were of interest to only a few individuals. Instead, residents interested in historical tales often relied on the musings of local journalist-turned-historian Robert C. Kriebel. Kriebel's short, accessible columns in the region's newspaper provided much more approachable, albeit second-hand, knowledge of the past. Like Maurice Thompson before him, Kriebel had a curiosity for history that led him to disseminate stories of an earlier time to the public. In 1977 he began the popular weekly column "Old Lafayette" to make history accessible to readers of the *Journal and Courier*. The column ran until 2011 when Kriebel retired his role as the troubadour of Tippecanoe County's history. So popular were Kriebel's contributions that upon his retirement letters poured in to the *Journal and Courier* lamenting the loss of the "easy and informative read" that "gave us a window to our past."[29] In addition to the newspaper, Kriebel's archival research for the column resulted in the publication of five books on Indiana history. Unfortunately, as with his predecessors, these stories of Indiana were limited in scope and range of content.

These books and columns did provide some details of Lafayette's immigrant predecessors, but the accounts subtly promoted an image of immigrant forebears who eagerly accepted acculturation or were subsequently "handicapped" by their foreign status. For example, in *Tippecanoe in 2000: A Hoosier County Recalls Its Past*, Kriebel and other community historians described the story of six German nuns and their work to establish St. Elizabeth Hospital. The coffee-table book illustrated how "The nuns were eager to get started, but were *handicapped* by the fact that they could not speak English" (2000: 29, emphasis added). Undeniably, not having a command of English created certain obstacles for the nuns. However, the use of the word "handicapped" signaled an English-dominant hegemony. Thus, the historians ever so subtly denied or undervalued other languages by referencing only how German set these nuns back.[30] Absent from their assessment of linguistic disability was a historical context. Command of the German language during this time was an asset rather than an obstacle when St. Elizabeth Hospital was founded in 1875. By this point, central Indiana's German-speaking population was already active in promoting its own religious and educational institutions. German Jews, for instance, formed Ahavath Achim in 1849, and by the late 1850s St. James (Lutheran) and St. Boniface (Catholic) held religious services in German. Schools for children were set up where a German identity and language were nurtured. In 1858, five different German newspapers were publishing out of Lafayette, including the largest German newspaper in all of Indiana, the *Indiana Post*.[31]

Deterministic language that reinforced notions of progress through assimilation was not limited to the printing of *Tippecanoe in 2000*. Kriebel's 2002 column entitled "Commercial bakeries had German roots" also noted that "Lafayette's earliest settlers in the 1820s had *matured* from Irish and English roots" (2002; emphasis added).[32] Though Kriebel recognized European immigrant heritage in the town, stories like these maintained problematic evolutionary paradigms whereby descendants "matured" from their seemingly unsophisticated immigrant forebears. Overlooking the complexity of a bilingual Lafayette or the ethnic identities of Germans, these columns created gaps in the popular collective memory of the past. To some extent, Kriebel's stylistic language silenced more than it elucidated. The celebratory and approachable tone of "Old Lafayette" columns fed popular knowledge of the past, and these renditions were eventually reiterated in damaging rhetoric displayed in the same newspapers' editorial pages. Without knowledge of possible parallels, individuals could uncritically support anti-immigrant and anti-ethnic discourse even if it was virtually identical to the harassment faced by their forebears. Did early European immigrants to Lafayette truly give up their "'old' country holidays"? Did they perceive themselves as "matured" from the "handicap" of being foreign? And might they have had more in common with recent Mexican immigrants than is otherwise negated by their contemporary progeny? With these questions in mind, I began to examine other historical texts on the early immigrant communities of Lafayette. Though answers to these questions may not be readily available, some archival documents and even some of Kriebel's own pieces still managed to reveal some fascinating moments in the immigrant history of Lafayette.

In contrast to depictions that presented Germans as linguistically and culturally assimilated, the ability to communicate in German was a right considered sacrosanct in some German circles of Lafayette. As illustrated in an internal document circulated to celebrate St. Boniface's centennial, parents in the congregation actively fought for this linguistic right and voiced their displeasure when it was threatened. According to the St. Boniface centennial publication, in 1876 "Difficulties arose when two of the four sisters appointed to the school could not speak German. Many of the people loudly voiced their dissatisfaction. They took up the school question with the Mother Superior at Louisville [Kentucky] and asked to be assured that only German speaking teachers would be sent" (1999: 39). The families wrote letters that upset the Mother Superior. She responded by stating that perhaps she would no longer assign nuns from her order, the Ursuline Sisters, to Lafayette. The demands of parish families and resulting tensions with the Mother Superior demonstrated the vocal and active investment Germans had in their linguistic continuity. The Catholic diocese was willing to acquiesce, at least temporarily, to the German families—a decision made easier by the presence of three exiled German Sisters of St. Francis of Perpetual Adoration who agreed to take on the duties of the Ursuline Sisters. The order of St. Francis of Perpetual Adoration arrived in central Indiana in 1875 fleeing the *Kulturkampf*—a political moment in Germany that drastically limited the role of religious organizations and placed the church under governmental control.[33] Upon their arrival, the Sisters filled the role of teachers for St. Boniface and almost immediately began their charitable work with the sick and poor of the community. The health ministry eventually developed into St. Elizabeth Hospital. Thus, the contemporary suggestion that these nuns were "handicapped" because of a lack of English dismissed the actual service they provided to the German-speaking population. Indeed, far from a handicap, the parents of St. Boniface viewed the German Sisters as an advantage over the English-dominant Ursuline Sisters.

Rather than being disconnected from their homeland, Germans practiced an early form of what social scientists now term transnationalism. Before more advanced technology aided global communication
and transport, circuits of exchange did exist between immigrants and
their sending communities. Multiple German newspapers supplied information to German residents in their own language about local and
international news.[34] Indeed, Kriebel did briefly note that the Lafayette-
based *Indiana Post* had "regular correspondence from Berlin." Moreover,
communication between residents in Lafayette and Germany continued
well into the twentieth century. For example, the first transatlantic flight
of the *Graf Zeppelin* in 1928 carried mail from Germany to a Lafayette
household. More famously, the burned remains from the *Hindenburg* di-
saster included a letter to a Lafayette resident from German relatives. International mail and German-language newspapers were early means of
supporting transnational networks in places like Lafayette where ethnic
immigrants continued to nurture international bonds. Unfortunately, a
lack of attention to German American transnational flows could be reflective of World War I hysteria, the catalyst for the twentieth-century
suppression of German ethnic identity.

The first World War became a watershed moment for German Americans accustomed to practicing their religion and teaching their children
in a language other than English. According to St. Boniface's centennial
booklet, in 1877 "Sister Bonaventura introduced the English language
into the school, much to the dismay of some of the parishioners" (1999:
5). Unfortunately, the ethnic antagonism that accompanied World War I
defeated earlier efforts of these parents to control the imposition of the
English language. Scrutinized for their cultural affiliations to a country
responsible for the sinking of the *Lusitania*, Germans in Lafayette were
forced into declaring their allegiance to the United States by silencing
their ethno-linguistic identity. As with Japanese immigrants on the West
Coast during World War II, non-Germans were suspicious of public utterances in German.[35] As a result, St. Boniface parish was required to
make some drastic changes: "In 1918 Father Florian announced, first in
German, then in English, that a decision was made by the pastor and
trustees to stop the use of the German language in the church and the
school. This pronouncement was offensive to some of the staunch Germans, and as a result they left the parish" (1999: 7). Religious services

and school instruction conducted in German since the 1840s abruptly ended. However, the evidence of families' leaving the parish demonstrates that the transition from German to English was not always enthusiastically supported. Notably, the mainstream newspaper's account of the same event illustrated how popular print media altered moments such as these to fit a particular nationalistic purpose. Viewed through the prism of loyalty and patriotism, the actions of the church trustees was applauded by the *Journal and Courier* editor:

> I wish to extend congratulations to the trustees and pastor and congregation of St. Boniface Catholic Church over their decision here after to dispense with the use of the German language in either the school and the church. . . . [I]t is a big thing on [the] part of many of these people, who have grown old in their religious and school curriculum to thus at one fell swoop abandon, very likely forever[,] the use of the tongue of their youth. But they have the satisfaction of knowing that they have agreed to do that which the government would desire, and it is only another proof of their loyalty of one of the largest and most substantial congregations in the county. (St. Boniface 1999: 77)

While the editor recognized the sacrifice of the parish to "dispense with the use of the German language," he remained oblivious to the way in which this community had been systematically stripped of its linguistic heritage. The "decision" was reached by a select few and was apparently not agreed to by the entire congregation.

Calls to abandon the use of German came out of local and national anxieties over possible betrayal and espionage. This climate not only affected religious congregations and schools but also thwarted newspapers printed in German. James P. Ziegler's (1994) short bibliography of Indiana's German-language newspapers described this moment through the words of editors who were forced to halt publishing. Ziegler noted that "unfounded biases and prejudices" against German speakers ultimately led to the demise of newspapers across the entire state of Indiana. In 1918, papers throughout Indiana were forced to shut down. The fifty-year-old Evansville newspaper, *Täglicher Evansville Demokrat*, was forced into discontinuing its publication and noted in its last issue, "The circumstances force upon us a step which we truly only unhappily take"

(1994: 36). The staff ended this somber farewell by asking readers not to grow attached to other newspapers, saying that they were hopeful of a return, and in the end punctuated their closing remarks with "Until then, *auf Wiederseh'n*" [until we meet again]. The paper never returned to publication and, as Ziegler documents, neither did any of the other German-language newspapers. Notably, the Indianapolis newspaper the *Telegraph-Tribüne* used its last letter to its readers as a way to vent its frustrations against the bigotry present at the time:

> The decision to take this action has been arrived at reluctantly, but voluntarily. . . . As far as our own publications are concerned, we can say in the most emphatic manner that they have been loyal at all times; that since the entry of the United States into the war, true and correct translations of all war news published in our columns have been furnished the Postmaster. . . . Unfortunately, however, a pronounced prejudice has arisen in this country against everything printed or written in the German language . . . and because of this prejudice and because we feel that all causes for possible disturbance in our community should be removed, we have decided to take the step above suggested. (1994: 36)

Ziegler noted that the *Telegraph-Tribüne* published this message in both German and English and, he felt, geared the English translation for "people who harbored prejudice against all things German" (1994: 36). Unfortunately, the lack of attention to this period of de-culturation privileged the illusion of a seamless assimilation and in the process denied the nuances reflected in the above accounts.[36] Sadly, the dissenting opinions of German-language publications, church attendees, and parents of schoolchildren remained obscured by more sanitized content that portrayed passive, if patriotic, German American experiences. National pressures and local xenophobes in early-twentieth-century Indiana altered for generations how German settlers could live and would be remembered.

Of County Fairs and Klan Membership in Lafayette

Selective preservation of history displaced Native, Black, and White ethnic residents of Indiana, but it also conveniently concealed how politicians stoked the flames of hate and intolerance to gain power in the state. Sanitized constructions of history suppressed the role of groups like the KKK and omitted stories of oppression, exploitation, and lynchings from the popular imaginary.[37] During their reign, the KKK used religion, race, and ethnicity to determine how community was imagined and who could be granted the right to reside safely in Indiana. Thus, the political and social ramifications of the Klan on Hoosier belonging cannot be overlooked, for even as recent as 1994 the Knights of the Ku Klux Klan held a rally in Lafayette.[38]

World War I and the arrival of more people of color to the Midwest fed the anxieties promoted by the Klan. As a result of industrial demands from the war, the northwest corridor to Chicago's steel mills grew tremendously. These economic opportunities coupled with a debilitating socioeconomic environment for Black families in the South resulted in the Great Migration to places like Chicago and Detroit. Additionally, unrest from Mexico's Revolutionary War in 1910 and employment stability in the steel mills enticed Mexicans to settle in Indiana Harbor and East Chicago.[39] In addition, Indiana formed a part of the "German Triangle," a swath of the Midwest settled largely by German arrivals.[40] These demographic shifts added to fears of a country under siege by racial and ethnic Others. Using racism and xenophobia, the KKK set up an insular argument to strengthen its numbers and gain political power. Ideally positioning itself in public as an objective body of concerned citizens, the Klan shrewdly built its base of followers. Shrouded by the pretense of patriotism and national unity, Klan members, like Hiram Evans, were able to get away with hostile rhetoric that decried immigrants as "'ignorant and unskilled, covetous and greedy'; they maintain 'loyalty to the lands of their birth . . . they preach their own religions—mostly Roman Catholic or Jewish; they read their own newspapers, printed in foreign tongues; they deride America and its ideals'" [Moore 1991: 21]. This hate-filled rhetoric attracted Hoosiers who felt their power diminished by the arrival of newcomers who looked different and spoke a different language. Fueling resentment against the "horde of immigrant invaders," Klansmen used the language of victimhood to rally their call to arms (Moore 1991: 21).The Klan's own Grand Dragon, D. C. Stephenson, rose to power in Indiana during the 1920s through "social and economic intimidation, boycotts, slanderous propaganda and rumor, awesome spectacles, vigilante patrols, and—above all—the ballot box"

(Tucker 1991: 6). Thus, the KKK became a political stronghold in the state by promoting "100 percent Americanism" and disseminating antagonistic messages through religious revivals, parades, and newsletters.

During the Klan's control of the state, a significant amount of Germans, Catholics, and Jews resided in Lafayette. I sought to unearth the impact of the Klan on these Othered Hoosiers, but not surprisingly both the state and local narratives of this moment had been minimized by a general discomfort with this shameful era. As noted by D. C. Stephenson biographer William M. Lutholtz (1991), "The Klan period, squeezed in between World War I and the Great Depression, was covered in less than a paragraph and dismissed. It was as if most of the school textbook writers deliberately wanted to blot the story from the history of the state" (1991: xiii). As with the furniture of a long-abandoned home, draped white linens protected today's Indiana from exposing the demons of its past. Those sheets, and the men who wore them, remained concealed in the state's shame against the Klan. As Lutholtz noted, when the Klan is acknowledged at all, it is done through fleeting moments easy to overlook. In the case of Lafayette, mention of the Klan existed only through a rhetoric of righteousness and triumph over intolerance. In *Tippecanoe at 2000*, the Klan's impact in the area is covered in two paragraphs. The book itself is a historical celebration of Tippecanoe at the turn of the twenty-first century. Therefore, the celebratory narrative style seemed an odd place to mention the KKK. Why would these lay historians want to highlight the Klan in a book that commemorates the millennium? Rather than a critical recognition of the past, the inclusion praised locals who contested the Klan's influence. The section began by recognizing the "division, animosity, fear and resentment within the county's religious community, even in rural towns" but ends with admiration for Lafayette residents who obstructed a Klan parade in an Irish Catholic neighborhood (Kriebel et al. 2000: 156). As a contributing author to *Tippecanoe at 2000*, Bob Kriebel included this story verbatim in one of his 2007 "Old Lafayette" columns. In the column, Kriebel explained how the details of the parade were obtained from an anonymous letter written to the newspaper.[41] Relying on information from this anonymous letter, Kriebel mentioned that the Klan's local membership was never more than ninety and had "plunged to 35" before reaching no more than seventy thereafter (2007: 5B). Opposition to the powerful presence of the Klan should be acknowledged. However, these triumphant memories of resistance overshadowed the thorny influence of the Klan at the local and state level. Consequently, pointing to the insignificance of the KKK in Lafayette rescued the town as a beacon of tolerance and understanding.

Beyond the musings of a single anonymous letter, other historical sources illustrated a more complicated Klan presence in Tippecanoe County. Soon after the opposition to the Klan parade in the Irish neighborhood, the Lafayette city council voted to ban "masked parades" in the city limits, and Lafayette's Mayor George R. Durgan was one of few Hoosier politicians who refused Klan involvement in their campaigns, but other documents painted a different picture than that of racial progress. For instance, Leonard Moore's (1991) provocative historical analysis of the KKK accounted for a deeper presence than was recognized in more popular notions of the past. Even with resistant city officials, the Klavern succeeded in galvanizing support among central Indiana's Protestants. For instance, Moore notes, "In Lafayette and Elwood, Klan chapters played a similarly dominant role in community celebrations. Lafayette Klansmen purchased the Tippecanoe County fairgrounds in 1923 and successfully operated the annual fair despite considerable opposition from Mayor George R. Durgan" (1991: 98). That is, this significant public plot of land was purchased in the same year in which city officials protested the Klan parade. Additionally, Moore's archival analysis showed that the letter used by Kriebel for his column drastically underreported the Klan's membership numbers; instead of fewer than 70 total members, in 1925 Tippecanoe County actually had a membership of 2,500 residents or 20.8 percent of the population.[42] Unfortunately, these numbers and the history of the county fair grounds appeared nowhere in renditions of the popular past of Lafayette. These fairgrounds, still used for county fairs and major outdoor events, demonstrated the power that the Klan attempted to solidify locally and its ability to claim public space in central Indiana. The Klan's membership and the control of a major outdoor venue complicated the image of Lafayette residents who wanted to honorably protect the town from the Klan. Depicted as both numerically present and politically opposed, these seemingly contradictory narratives of the local Klavern related a town in transition, a town full of tension, a town whose residents were torn as to whom to accept as their brethren. Moreover, negating the role of White supremacy and ethnic intimidation during early-twentieth-century Indiana diminished the everyday struggles of Hoosiers who were deemed not quite "100 percent American." Without proper recognition or critique in the popular imaginary, the same rhetoric of assimilation and denied acceptance appeared almost a century later among the rolling cornfields of Indiana. Once more, politicians rendered particular residents unwelcome and used ethnic anxieties to rally voters to the ballot box.

Embarking on the Past to Address the Present

Highlighting critical connections between past and present battles of belonging revealed how cycles of injustices continued to reappear across time in the same spaces. Specifically, exploring the ongoing perceptions toward people of color and the ethnic experiences of earlier immigrants provided insight into how these pasts were documented or distorted in the contemporary popular imaginary. The chapter drew on archival documents, late-nineteenth-century county histories, public celebrations, online classroom resources, and contemporary newspaper columns to display how silences or careful renderings constructed specific historic narratives of community. These silences altered the way Mexican arrivals, European ethnics, and residents of color could be perceived and received in local notions of belonging. Generations from this past, contemporary Hoosiers still operated under certain assumptions about who had rightful claim to Indiana's communities. Past systems of inequality shaped the way certain individuals could be perceived as comrades, citizens, or even human beings. Layers upon layers of past atrocities and parellel ethnic experiences lay dormant while popular references to "legal" or assimilated forebears built up steam.

Partial accounts of early settlers also neglected examples of collective resistance against intolerance and prejudice. Beginning with the coalition of Native peoples led by Tecumseh and the Prophet, locals have united against attempts to physically and socially exclude them from their claim to community. The Underground Railroad traversed the Wabash River Valley and brought together runaway slaves with abolitionists to circumvent Hoosier laws that condemned escaped, or "illegal," African American residents. German immigrants practiced earlier forms of belonging that did not subsume their ethnic and transnational ties. Though contemporary immigrants may have crossed through identical pathways as other Europeans, a racialized politics of belonging bred resentment and rejection. By privileging certain voices at the expense of others, popular historical narratives did not provide locals with the knowledge to contest the all-too-familiar rhetoric of exclusion. Indeed, debates against supposed "illegal" residents conveniently overlooked that, unlike earlier European and Asian immigrants, Mexicans were not limited from entering or settling in the United States until 1965.[43] That is, some of the original Mexican families in Indiana actually had longer claims to Hoosier residency than many of those with European ancestry.

The seemingly disparate experiences of American Indians, Black freedmen, ethnic Europeans, and Mexican residents all point to layers of racial, cultural, ethnic, and religious forms of exclusion that defined community belonging for generations. Hegemonic tropes denied certain Othered peoples a proper place in the concept of community. Recovering the conflict and triumph of earlier residents who were perceived as too different, too ethnic, and not quite good enough to belong allowed for a palimpsest of past injustices to shine through. Without knowing this past, residents of Indiana continued to base their fears and anxieties on already historically fraught battles of race, ethnicity, language, and "illegality." In the process, Hoosiers replayed cyclical strategies that dismissed one population while bolstering another. By the twenty-first century, familiar layers of racism and ethnocentrism positioned long-established Mexican Hoosiers in the margins of belonging. Indeed, even descendants of previously oppressed Hoosiers used their acquired privilege against newly arrived Spanish-speaking residents. The next chapter will examine the ways in which contemporary Latinos living in Lafayette responded to these dismissals and established alternative modes of maintaining ethnicity while still demanding the right to belong.

2

Kneading Home

Creating Community While Navigating Borders

Soy un amasamiento, I am an act of kneading, of uniting and joining that not only has produced both a creature of darkness and a creature of light, but also a creature that questions the definitions of light and dark and gives them new meanings.

—Gloria Anzaldúa, *Borderland/La Frontera*

Residents of central Indiana were accustomed to chilly December evenings that marked the inevitable arrival of winter. Gray, dank weather patterns often limited open-air evening events. December 12, however, was different. As described previously, on this day Lafayette's Latino Catholics were up before sunrise to celebrate energetically the Virgin of Guadalupe. But, honoring the Virgin of the Americas also included an evening outdoor component. Every 12th of December around dusk, Guadalupanos in Lafayette gathered once more to pray the rosary in an outdoor procession. The *peregrinos*, or pilgrims, eventually arrived at the church, where their efforts culminated in a reenactment of the holy apparition. In 2006, cold drizzle and forecasted freezing temperatures would not dissuade families from participating in this ethno-religious tradition.[1] With coats and umbrellas at the ready, Lafayette's Latino Catholics patiently awaited the annual Virgen de Guadalupe *procesión* [procession]. Dawn festivities and wintry dusk pilgrimages were minor discomforts offered up in reverence for the Holy Mother. The final two-mile religious procession started at the area's most popular Latino grocery store and ended at the sanctuary of St. Boniface. Sixteen hundred miles away from the original site of the apparition in Mexico City, this group of Mexican Catholics in Lafayette venerated the moment that marked them as a chosen people. According to the faith, the Virgin

Mary herself selected a local Indian, Juan Diego, over the Spanish clergy to deliver the message of love and faith. Once prevented from practicing their ethno-religious holidays in this very same sanctuary, Lafayette's Mexican Catholics fought hard to maintain ethnic religious practices that blended faith with ethnicity. Decades earlier, Latina mothers defied the Church and formed their own ethno-Catholic collective. Their commitment developed into a deep ethnic presence embraced by the same Catholic Church that once literally closed its doors on them. Exhibiting a lived religion informed by rich Mexican traditions, these Catholics inserted their particular faith practices onto the religious landscape of the Midwest. In the famed words of Gloria Anzaldúa, they kneaded and remade a lived experience enmeshed with survival strategies that allowed for both Mexican and U.S. definitions of self, faith, and community. I use this notion of kneading to understand how people took faith and belonging to remake the definition of who had the right to exist. This chapter looks to public rituals and individual ties to faith to see how "space belonging" was given new meaning or how faith and space mattered for Latinos in the Midwest. Regardless of how they were received in the 1970s or in the twenty-first century, these families carried on, inculcating the next generation in a belief system that validated their very existence.

At the Mexican grocery store, a crowd gathered, willing to take the cold walk across town, praying and singing in Spanish to affirm their faith in the blessed Virgin of Guadalupe. A large image of the Virgin of Guadalupe was elevated to the back of a flower-lined truck bed. Flanked on either side by the Mexican and U.S. flags, the Virgin cast her gaze upon her followers as adults hoisted two small children up to her side. A young girl draped in a blue shawl and a little boy made to look like Saint Juan Diego re-created the sacred apparition. The procession was a time for the next generations of Lafayette's Latino Catholics to carry on the traditions set forth by their predecessors and showcase their own commitment to faith and identity. After weeks of practice, the *Matachine* dancers, made up mostly of teens from the *Grupo de Jóvenes* [Hispanic Youth Group], prepared to lead the procession of families in dance and prayer.[2] Mothers brought their children to dance or walk along while praying and singing traditional Mexican hymns. While waiting for the procession to begin, a group of mothers fondly remembered how these events were celebrated in their hometowns in Mexico. A woman from Oaxaca, Yanelli, told of entire neighborhoods lit up with candles as families awaited the procession to near their homes; the multitude of flames lit up the early morning December dawn sky and culminated with a town-wide festival to commemorate the event. One after another, women from disparate regions of Mexico nostalgically shared their experiences of Guadalupe celebrations in their hometowns.[3] This wintry afternoon in central Indiana differed from those times in Mexico, but they were grateful for the opportunity to worship collectively in a manner somewhat similar to those they remembered. Yanelli only recently arrived in central Indiana and was pleased to see some ethno-religious continuity in an otherwise unfamiliar, and at times unfriendly, town. She sounded eager and thankful to have another group of women, of mothers, to share this evening with. Moreover, her children now intermingled with the children of these other women as they shared in this tradition. Among the frolicking, Yanelli proclaimed, "Hmm, y ni quisieron venir" [and they did not want to come]. The setting may have been radically different from their natal parishes, but central Indiana's ethno-Catholics created their own new memories and new religious experiences for their Hoosier-raised children. While younger ones played to keep warm, the *Grupo de Jóvenes* anxiously practiced and awaited their long-anticipated contribution to the procession. Some of these young Catholics were raised in the St. Boniface parish and witnessed multiple cohorts of youth lead their community in veneration. Now it was their turn. With conch shell and drums in hand, the elder dancers and the head choreographer rehearsed with their feathered troupe.

Just prior to beginning, dancers gathered around the visiting priest from Mexico as he praised and blessed their participation. Unlike earlier resistance from the parish to Spanish prayer practices, by 2006 St. Boniface actively sought to engage its Latino congregation and annually coordinated visits of priests from Mexico to attend to Spanish-speaking parishioners. The visiting priest blessed the dancers with a prayer but followed with murmurs of concern regarding the weather. To the Mexican priest, the cold presented an obstacle for the procession. Unfamiliar with midwestern winters, he felt it was too cold to walk in the open air and suggested that the children, their parents, and others ride in cars

Feathered *Matachines* preparing for Guadalupe procession. Photo by author.

to the church. While some of us started to count cars and coordinate ride options, resistance grew among *Los Matachines*. Rosa, a member of the *Grupo de Jóvenes* at St. Boniface, addressed the priest's suggestion with opposition. As a veteran of previous *Matachine* performances in Lafayette, Rosa was adamant that the procession go on. She maintained that they had marched through worse weather in the past. At least, she added, there was no snow on the ground. Rosa's excitement and enthusiasm for the procession rallied the rest of the troupe. Others joined her in arguing that the procession must go forward. This was their memory, their part to play, and no inclement weather nor visiting priest would deter that. Much like Catholics in the past, Rosa and her companions asserted themselves against an authority figure of the Church. Overtly defying his suggestions, she stood committed to the right to enact ethno-Catholic traditions in this midwestern setting. It took some convincing, but the Mexican priest acquiesced and allowed the procession to continue. He, on the other hand, decided to ride in a car and met them at the church.

The procession drew inquisitive glances from passersby. Mexican parishioners prayed and sang in Spanish to the beats of *Matachine* dancers as they crossed streets, stopped traffic, and continued on to their sacred destination. Those along the route heard the cacophony of voices singing, "Desde el cielo una hermosa mañana. Desde el cielo una hermosa mañana, la Guadalupana, la Guadalupana, la Guadalupana bajó al Tepeyac" [From the sky of a glorious morning the Virgin of Guadalupe appeared in Tepeyac] and halted their daily activities to acknowledge this interesting display of religiosity. I walked alongside a few mothers as we all helped corral the children away from oncoming cars. A police escort accompanied the pilgrimage, but some drivers interrupted the procession to illegally turn into the crowd or accelerate past the parishioners, visibly annoyed at the traffic blockage. I counted at least fifteen cars that defied the parade route and came dangerously close to hitting adults and children along the way. Notably, of the reckless drivers I observed, every single one was White. I was visibly frustrated by the lack of consideration for what otherwise would have been a less-than-ten-minute delay. The mothers I accompanied were more worried about their children's safety. Still, they continued marching, praying, and inculcating their children in these familiar ethno-Catholic traditions. Navigating a world that no longer included patron saint *fiestas* that spanned village streets and culminated in a fantastic evening *castillo de cohetes* [fireworks show], these Mexican families rejoiced in any semblance of familiarity to the memories of their childhood. Providing their children with a taste for their own ethnic Catholic rituals provided some continuity in an otherwise distant, and at times cold, environment.

Sacralizing Public Spaces

This chapter recognizes how borders were navigated in central Indiana and highlights moments when Latinos chiseled away at barriers to make home. For Latinos, this meant kneading or weaving complex ethnic identities to enhance, not deter from, their midwestern experience. Lafayette families had assembled on December 12 to celebrate this transnational ethno-Catholic holiday on the streets and church grounds of this seemingly White Hoosier space for more than twenty years.

The Virgin of Guadalupe display in 2006. This picture was taken of the altar a few nights before Tuesday, December 12. By Tuesday morning, the flowers had overflowed and reached the forefront of this photo. Photo by author.

Celebrating collectively and publicly was a local tradition. However, when read against the political climate of 2006, this year's procession held enhanced symbolic meaning. On one level, the religious meaning and faith practices were similar to those in the past, but the 2006 public displays of ethno-religiosity amid a climate of anti-ethnic assimilationist debates revealed much more about the everyday politics enacted by these families. Notably, the public religious rituals of 2006 were not purposefully coordinated with the intent to contest the existing damaging rhetoric. Instead, the very assumption that they had a right to continue these events even as the country and local politicians chastised Latinos for not being assimilated enough was an act of asserted belonging. Perhaps unconsciously, the pilgrimages, the prayers, and the Spanish uttered on those streets were activist assertions of belonging, similar to the mass immigrant demonstrations organized months earlier across the country.

Certainly the *mega-marchas* and political demonstrations were different from these otherwise localized attempts to appropriate space. Not as overtly political, these religious acts and daily assertions were just as important for navigating boundaries and asserting a right to home. Though Chicago was the site of the earliest and one of the largest rallies for immigration reform, years earlier I witnessed another event in Chicago that resonated with the religious processions in central Indiana.[4] During the 2003 national tour of the *Tilma de Tepeyac* religious relic, a seventeenth-century statue of the Virgin of Guadalupe carrying a glass-encased piece of the *tilma* [cape worn by St. Juan Diego] visited Our Lady of Tepeyac Parish in the Little Village neighborhood of Chicago. To honor the presence of the *tilma*, a faithful procession of 200 marched and prayed a half-mile to the famous 26th Street Little Village arch.[5] Stopping just short of the arch, the procession listened as the parish priest spoke of the recent history of gang violence that was afflicting the very neighborhoods along the procession's route. He explained that the prayers and presence of the *tilma* had just sacralized this space. The idea that parishioners, by their presence and movement in a procession, could alter space, even if only spiritually, was a concept I returned to when observing the Virgin of Guadalupe celebrations of Lafayette in 2006. However, the context of time and place in this central Indiana procession refracted a different type of significance from that present in Chicago. The public enactment of this ethno-Catholic tradition during a time of heightened anti-immigrant, anti-Mexican, and anti-ethnic criticism brought new meaning to the spatial significance of a Virgin of Guadalupe procession.[6]

Boldly validating their right to practice their own brand of ethnic religious identity and undeterred by the political climate, Mexican Catholics continued to organize the December procession of Guadalupanos, the Christmas *Posadas*, and the highly attended and publicized outdoor *Viacrucis* [Living Way of the Cross].[7] These public displays of ethnic religiosity were critical both for those whose Lafayette experience always included these events, like Rosa, and for those recent arrivals, like Yanelli, who hungered for opportunities to be comforted by this new and at times inhospitable experience. Regardless of time spent in the area, witnessing these familiar traditions in public arenas provided a "degree of comfort, of security, some feeling of being 'at home'" (Bonus 2000: 64). Children raised in this negotiated environment developed their own sense of identity through a Mexican experience in Indiana. Critically, these unabashed acts of ethnic faith also inadvertently challenged the assimilationist rhetoric of the twenty-first century.[8] For instance, attempts to border and restrict ethnic differences gained national attention in late April 2006 when a Spanish version of "The Star-Spangled Banner" received considerable negative attention because it was perceived as a threat to American assimilationist rhetoric. The song's sole "threatening" feature was the use of Spanish. Indeed, the controversy reached as high as the Oval Office when President George W. Bush declared, "I think the national anthem ought to be sung in English. And I think people who want to be a citizen of this country ought to learn English, and they ought to learn to sing the national anthem in English." Weeks earlier, during Easter, Latino Catholics of Lafayette practiced their ethno-religious practices in very public ways and by December 2006 they were once again, on the street, proclaiming their religious and ethnic right to exist in these spaces. Significantly, the continuation of these Catholic celebrations challenges the ethnic public/private dichotomy which suggests that if ethnic ties exist at all, they have become confined to private spaces.[9] Instead of privately practicing ethnicity, Lafayette's Mexican Catholics participated in the public spatial display of a "vibrant lived religion that prized family-and-community-centered traditions" in the open areas of the city (Treviño 2006: 11). Not meant as a political act, these outward manifestations of ethno-religious identity still demonstrated how cultural citizenship was lived and belonging experienced in otherwise nonpoliticized events.[10]

Claiming Place, Making Home

By sacralizing and marking the streets with their own public form of religiosity, these Guadalupanos exerted their rights to exist publicly and without shame in the larger, more general, spaces of Lafayette. As public performance, these events had multiple discursive qualities.[11] Beyond the religious significance, reading these events within the climate of anti-immigrant and anti-ethnic attacks allows for an undercurrent of counter-hegemonic protests in the very act of continuing these established traditions. Outdoor performances of the Stations of the Cross and the December Virgin of Guadalupe procession both expressed the right of Mexican Catholics to, as Pnina Werbner suggests regarding Sufi public rituals, "celebrate their culture and religion in the public domain within a multicultural, multifaith, multiracial society" (1996: 333). In this sense, Latino physical appropriation of space became both spiritual and political. By inhabiting the physicality of Lafayette's city streets, these residents reclaimed their right to belong and in so doing responded to those who would otherwise limit their physiological navigation through national and local space. Public displays of religiosity in this context created a new kind of "memory-place" where religious performance gave meaning to place and not just place gave meaning to performance (Flores 1995). The movement of bodies and the cacophony of voices transformed and gave meaning, if only momentarily, to the spaces of belonging for Mexican residents.

For the purposes of this chapter, space is not merely physical landscape or architectural elements; rather, space is a socially constructed mode of analysis that recognizes how people inhabit space and the manner in which race, gender, ethnicity, and class are enacted in those places.[12] Thus, the importance of space appropriation cannot be overlooked, especially in situations where particular populations are otherwise excluded or ignored as proper inhabitants of local and national spaces. Indeed, Renato Rosaldo and William Flores refer to *sacred places* to illustrate how "it is in such sacred places that people have developed

Sacralizing in the name of Guadalupe. Photo by author.

community by coming together and claiming a place of their own, where they meet friends, develop romances, and make enemies" (1997: 79). Physical spaces take on sacred meaning though the memory and practices of individuals who forge attachment to the environment that shelters their social emotional lives. The concept of sacred places illustrates that people assert the right to claim spaces for themselves and are, by their very presence, active shapers in the meaning of local and national places. Simply put, "they are walkers, *Wandersmänner*, whose bodies follow the thicks and thins of an urban 'text' they write without being able to read it. . . . The paths that correspond in this intertwining, unrecognized poems in which each body is an element signed by many others . . ." (de Certeau 1984: 93). According to Michel de Certeau, a social imprint is poetically inscribed as people walk, live, and interact in space. For Mexican Catholics, sacralizing the cold, rainy city streets with their ethno-religious identity wove together a unique transnational experience that recognized both Mexican and Lafayette social spaces. In so doing, they not only inscribed their own signature on space but also interacted with the signatures of other past and present "walkers."

This layering of walkers, of multiple meanings imprinted in space, is otherwise recognized as multi-locality, or "the idea that a single place may be experienced quite differently . . . that space is socially constructed, and *contested*, in practice" (Rodman 1992: 647). Recognizing multi-locality becomes critical to understanding how multiple residents of central Indiana conceived of their local and national spaces of belonging. As the local 2006 letters to the editor indicated, some White residents protected spaces while some Latinos were "conscious and articulate about their need to be visible, to be heard, and to belong" in their sacred places (Rosaldo 1997: 37). As a result, sacred places were multi-layered and interpreted differently depending on the "walkers" who inhabited, or remembered, the spaces in particular ways. For Latinos navigating their own notions of belonging, these midwestern spaces became part of their sense of home. Daily and spiritual activities manifested into place-meaning for Latinos who fused their sense of selves within central Indiana. Notably, looking to the role of space, or place-meaning, in the lives of individuals comes out of a theoretical focus "to underscore the cultural processes through which places are rendered meaningful by looking at local knowledge, localized expressions, language, poetics, and performance. How do people encounter places, perceive them, and endow them with significance?" (Escobar 2001: 151). Thus, space becomes *place* at the point of meaningful attributions to an environment or physical feature in the landscape.

As previously indicated, place is not singularly defined, but complicated through multiple multi-layered meaning. The role of Latinos as walkers, affecting the palimpsest of place-meaning written onto spaces, is not new. Indeed, the field of cultural geography has paid close attention to the "cultural signatures" of Latinos on landscapes in order to appreciate how Latinos communicate their ethnic identity through uniquely manipulated space (Miyares 2004: 146).[13] Moreover, geographers attentive to the strategic alteration of spaces into ethnically empowered places use Homi Bhaba's theoretical framing of Thirdspace as a means to understand these complex maneuvers of mobile people across global space. Thus, cultural geographers look to the alternate spaces of ethnicity where "an intricate transnational world is woven. This Thirdspace comes from the duality of immigrant existence, a tension between a lived-in space . . . and a distant, remembered space. The reconciliation between these different worlds leads us to someplace in between" (Price and Whitworth 2004: 185). In these constructed Thirdspaces, immigrants create belonging through rearticulating home experiences in new spaces. The places in between allow for a duality of belonging to realities that exist somewhere between nations in carefully crafted places of comfort. But, as Ulla Hasager has so critically noted, "[T]his 'somewhere' does not mean that new homelands cannot be constructed, nor that it is impossible to belong in several ways to several places at the same time" (1997: 185). In other words, rather than a metaphysical Thirdspace or an ethnic simulacrum of a space somewhere else, Hasager asks us to imagine the possibility that mobile populations may indeed form new, and perhaps different, bonds to the spaces of settlement. These new affiliations do not sever emotional bonds to other homelands, nor must they be sites of tension or Phoenix-like eruptions of hybridity out of tumultuous encounters. Instead, Hasager reminds us that "human beings have the capacity of living sane lives with many different, even conflicting, models or perceptions of the world—and of homelands—at the same time. By understanding culture as a process, we might be able to embrace an understanding of a simultaneously continuing and changing multiple attachment to places" (1997: 185). In essence, conceptualizing a Thirdspace, as it were, requires that we first imagine a segmented and fixed first or second. Instead, Hasager and others prefer the notion of processes, of fluidity, that does not ignore power and institutional limitations but rather recognizes the ability of people, ever mobile, to be able to construct multi-faceted homelands in a variety of meaningful places.

This suturing of physical spatial analysis with socio-spatial meaning of home and belonging corresponded with the analysis of Latinos in Lafayette. My research project was initially intended to focus on the built environment and the Latino appropriation of economically abandoned spaces, but the political context surrounding immigration debate in 2006 yielded interview responses that redirected the research. Related to socio-spatial appropriation, the interviews and observations moved away from an analysis of altered physical space and shifted toward a closer understanding of how people daily navigated their socio-spatial notions of belonging. The politics of immigration altered the way Latino bodies were written and perceived out of the national imaginary. The research project then shifted to include the power of place for Latino residents. Theoretically framing this analysis within the discourse of space/place pushes us to think past the built environment to understand how meaningful places are endowed with significance for those protecting and those asserting a right to exist in local or national landscapes. Regardless of immigrant status or actual contributions to community, Latino families were otherwise denied legitimacy in political debates, media representations, and daily conversations that questioned their claim to belonging.

For immigrant communities, especially those branded with words like "undocumented" or "illegal," the power of place becomes incredibly important. Moreover, their very presence and visibility in public during religious processions, in their workplaces, while shopping, or even in their neighborhoods communicates the reality of their presence, welcomed or not, in the contested national imaginary. Returning to Pnina Werbner's analysis of the Sufi religious appropriation of London cityscapes, "marching . . . must be grasped as a performative act, an act of metonymic empowerment" (Werbner 1996: 311). Thus, the movement of this Sufi sect through public space could be read as a political performative act that conveys a sense of collective identity against larger social pressures to adjudicate difference in the name of acceptance. Still, Werbner would have her readers "distinguish between the mere pragmatic capturing of new spaces and acts of ritual sacralization, which are perceived to be essentially transformative of the substance and quality of a lived space" (1996: 311). The blessing of places means something more than the simple act of walking or traversing a particular space. Though I agree with Werbner that the sanctity of religious processions cannot be lost, I suggest that even the pragmatic capturing of new spaces become critical to claiming space. The mere presence and visibility of these immigrant populations altered spaces especially at a moment of heightened antagonism. Indeed, the sanctity attributed to an event is not what creates Rosaldo's sacred places. Instead, the sacredness comes in the ability to mean something or evoke a feeling of familiarity for people. As Kathleen Stewart has so poetically suggested, "places mark the space of lingering impacts and unseen forces, that the world speaks to people who find themselves caught in it" (1996b: 32). The power of sacred places becomes even richer with meaning when one considers how the border plays into the lives of Latino, and specifically Mexican, residents caught in the political and physical topography of the United States.

Whether they survived the Arizona desert, traversed the Río Bravo [Rio Grande], or tolerated the indignation of immigration officials at Customs, Mexican immigrants have long experienced the meaning of geopolitical barriers in their lives. Living in Arizona, I can personally attest that the progeny of immigrants find themselves inspected at formal and informal checkpoints throughout the United States.[14] Thus, even after generations of settlement, some individuals confront real and metaphorical borders that bar their acceptance as legitimate members of society. The geopolitical border between Mexico and the United States provides a physical and theoretical point of departure for understanding the Mexican Latino experience in Indiana. The "*herida abierta*" [open wound] of the border is truly a space of wounding pain, where deaths, crimes, and abuses occur from both sides of the divide (Anzaldúa 1987). The border is where national officials assert their power in place, where the nation defines placehood and peoplehood, where humanity is acknowledged or denied based on discriminatory practices.[15] Notably, this interstitial space also signifies incredible resiliency. As the front lines for geopolitical control, the borderlands are also a space of overlap where people, goods, and services interact in complex relationships that defy national limitations.

Queer feminist and border theorist Gloria Anzaldúa has spoken of the borderlands as a space of rich exchange and incredible anguish. For Anzaldúa, the borderlands were not limited to the actual geopolitical spaces between both countries. Instead, the borderlands encompassed a theoretical meeting of experiences where indigenous deities melded with Spanish culture, where languages vary and shift, where queerness exemplified *mestizaje* in being simultaneously neither and both. The borderlands formed a border culture that was birthed out of survival and poetic symbiosis. Indeed, Anzaldúa reframes this "zone of possibility" as Nepantla, or a dimension of overlapping layered spaces that require a process of "redefining what it means to be una Mexicana de este lado, an American in the U.S., a citizen of the world, . . . In this narrative national boundaries dividing us from the 'others' (nos/otras) are porous and the cracks between the worlds serve as gateways" (2002: 561). Instead of affirming a popular imaginary of the border as a decaying space, Anzaldúa rescues the bordered experience as a site, a gateway, of tremendous possibilities and resiliency. The border is not just a line drawn on maps or a space of national militarized protection. Instead, the border provides an analytical framework for understanding the actual lived experience of those who face the confines of increasingly dangerous border zones and still find ways to overcome and survive. Mapping the border zones of nation-states onto lived realities, border theory suggests that boundaries can be embodied and navigated by people who negotiate these bifurcated spaces daily. Instead of accepting a rhetoric that marred them with marginal outsider status, Latino Hoosiers survived by balancing their ethnic identities within central Indiana landscapes. Latinos daily navigated bordered limitations on their belonging by simply asserting their right to be in public space. Their ethnic displays of identity in public illustrated how Latinos navigated their belonging as part and parcel of an Indiana setting.

Spaces of Home

Sacralizing space and practicing one's faith publicly validated the right of Mexican Catholics to exist openly as ethnic beings in a predominately White community. Rather than a top-down model of religious instruction or reverent obedience, the Lafayette experience demonstrated how religious institutions were sites of comfort and strength beyond traditional ecclesiastical values. Lafayette's Latino residents located strength in one another's company and used sanctuary spaces as sacred places that rejuvenated their spiritual and ethnic sense of self. Confronted by moments of discrimination, snide remarks, or *malas vibras* [bad vibes], Latino Catholics found sanctuary in the spaces of the Church. In the past, the pulpit has been used to promote assimilation to newcomers.[16] In these scenarios, sometimes well-intentioned religious leaders promoted rapid acculturation to shelter their flocks from further social scrutiny. As discussed in the previous chapter, St. Boniface's German parishioners found themselves pressured into de-emphasizing ethnicity in order to assure local and national acceptance during World War I. For these earlier Germans and for the contemporary Mexican parish, their religious identities remained intimately interwoven with their ethnic selves. This is why some Germans chose to leave St. Boniface over acquiescing to national expectations. For many immigrants, the church meant much more than a place of worship. Especially for marginalized populations, the social bonds and shared sense of community in immigrant congregations provided incredible strength in overcoming the world beyond the sanctuary walls.

For families who felt isolated and lonely, locating the spaces of worship often meant discovering a support system for overcoming the obstacles of living in Lafayette. As Jorge Iber notes in his historical analysis of Mexicans in Salt Lake City, religious spaces provided a "psychic and spiritual 'home' where they could pray, gather as a community, and celebrate their heritage" (2000: 49). Religious services in Spanish granted Mexican immigrants in Lafayette the opportunity to find others who shared in their experience and unite under common circumstances.[17] Similarly, Jill DeTemple's work on immigrant congregations in Boston showcased how congregations offered coping spaces where "[i]ndividual suffering is expressed, and met, by communal voices, by communal hands. The silent and often isolated world of the immigrant in a major metropolitan area is, for the moment, dissolved" (2005: 219). In Lafayette, Latino families located spiritual centers where they could worship with others in Spanish and alleviate, if only momentarily, the trauma of displacement.[18] After Mass, parents visited with one another outside the sanctuary and discussed job opportunities, parenting, and economic and immigration concerns. Children looked forward to Sunday, eagerly awaiting the time to be spent with friends and relatives who, unlike White classmates, validated their linguistic, religious, and cultural identity. Indeed, when I asked Micaela, a daughter of Mexican immigrants, what helped her family initially transition when they first arrived from California in the 1990s, she replied, "I think the biggest thing is my faith. La Virgen de Guadalupe, being a part of *danza* [*Matachine* dance troupe] has been a huge thing. There's a huge Latino community at St. Boniface and that helps a lot." At the time of our interview,

Micaela related being involved in *danza* for eight years and recalled the importance of her church when combating bullying behaviors as a child:

> Especially as a younger person, you have to socialize. And honestly I had a really bad bullying situation at school, like all through elementary school and middle school. So for me, it was going to church with people who had to be nice because of the Church youth program that helped [with socialization]. Honestly, that's where some of your biggest friends come from, you know what I mean? *Grupo* [youth group] was great. I actually got really involved with it. The coordinator at the time was great. She's someone that I would talk to all the time about things. I guess here the summer gets really slow and the youth group and church gave us something to do during the summer.

Micaela's bullying started when she and her family moved to Lafayette from California. Now an adult, she recognized that the harassment was due in large part to her Latina features that attracted the negative attention of mostly White classmates and even the denigration of a few teachers/administrators at school. She credited the church, and specifically the youth group, for giving her a sense of identity beyond the taunting and lack of self-esteem present during her formative years. Meetings with *grupo* and joining the *danza* troupe (two separate, but related entities in their Church) created a sense of self-worth at a precarious time when Micaela lacked confidence. Critically, 60 percent of U.S.-born or -raised Latinas interviewed for the study identified their religious experiences as a positive escape from spaces like school or work where their Latina identities were not validated. Besides Micaela, other girls-turned-women expressed how the church provided a space for an alternate set of friends who not only spoke the language they spoke with their parents but also had direct knowledge of the gendered expectations and ethnic traditions specific to a U.S. Latino identity. The ability to find a group of other girls who faced similar situations was priceless for this generation of Latinas raised in traditional Mexican parenting. These women recalled stories of girlhood where they were limited from going out with their friends, dating, or staying out late. Mercedes, now a mother herself, remembered that the "typical teenage life" was outside the realm of possibility. However, their church and more specifically *grupo* provided an outlet for engaging one another in their similarities and justifying teenage outings that, though religiously grounded, gave these teens a place to congregate without fear of parental reprisal.

Church congregations maintained a sense of spiritual and communal belonging to newcomers and often provided Latinos with their initial social interactions in this new town. These social-religious networks framed a sense of community for those who felt alone and unaccustomed to Indiana's physical and social landscape. As Micaela recalled, "The temperature was different, but I think once you have your community set up, like through church, it makes it easier." Exploring faith through a concept of community recognizes the agency of immigrants who poetically navigated their belonging, contested barriers that denied them acceptance, and transformed the meaning of inclusion in places like Lafayette.[19] Indeed, Mexican Catholics were themselves the product of navigating religious borders even before their arrival in the United States. As the combination of Spanish and indigenous spiritual worldviews coalesced into a unique Mexican Catholic faith and practice, Robert R. Treviño (2006) insists, "By understanding ethno-Catholicism we can more fully understand the construction of ethnic identity, the formation of communities, the sources and processes of social change, the ways people find their place in a society, and some of the implications of gender relations—subjects that too often are studied without much attention given to the role of religion" (2006: 7). Notably, yoking ethnicity and belonging with faith is not specific to Catholicism. The social networks that result from religious centers transcended national, regional, and consanguineal difference to provide the first model for localized identities. For immigrants arriving in new socio-linguistic settings, challenged by racial and xenophobic bias and devoid of societal and familial networks, settling into a new community posed challenges that altered how they imagined community in Indiana. Mexican immigrants to Lafayette faced a cold reception in an unfamiliar environment. They enjoyed the employment possibilities but were unhappy with the lack of friends and family in this new town. As with other "new" destinations previously unfamiliar with a Latino presence, families found that central Indiana lacked the comforts of social, cultural, and religious networks affiliated with arriving at a destination.[20] Whether Catholic or Protestant, church engagement and active participation in a Spanish choir or Bible study provided a sense of spiritual agency that carried over to a sense of belonging. As far as parishioners were concerned, they belonged within the walls of their Baptist chapel or their storefront Mormon *rama* [branch]. And even when a Catholic priest challenged that belonging or right to congregate, families found friendships, solidarity, and "home" with one another regardless of spiritual space. Ultimately, these social networks helped ground many Mexicans by helping them adapt and adjust in ways not wholly in line with assimilation rhetoric of the past. Through ethnic solidarity and *ethno-spirituality*, these families defined what it meant to live and function in the area in ways familiar to them, making Lafayette work for them rather than abandoning themselves to Lafayette.[21]

Throughout decades of Latino settlement in central Indiana, the Catholic Church served as nucleus of community events. Even with the recent growth of Spanish Protestant congregations, St. Boniface maintained a central role in the lives of hundreds of the area's Spanish-speaking residents. The particular hardship of living in Lafayette created moments, such as those at St. Boniface, when friendships were solidified and relationships strengthened. As Margarita noted, "aquí es donde se encuentra la amistad" [here is where you find friendships]. Friendships grew out of a necessity to locate kin and relationships where there were none before. On Sunday afternoons, the same original families still took part in lector readings and communion or rocked their grandchildren at the Spanish Mass at St. Boniface Church. Their children, now adults, actively followed their parents' legacy and maintained active roles in the church. Recounted memories of a past before involvement in the church included periods of despair and isolation. Solidarity arose between families that united for Sunday church services where they found comforting ethnic collectivity among one another.[22] Through their resilient efforts, these "pioneer" families raised a Spanish spiritual center for Mexican Catholics in Lafayette and in the process provided communal comfort for hundreds of parishioners searching for that ethno-Catholic connection at the "Crossroads of America."

At these crossroads, Latino ethno-Catholicism melded with an Indiana setting to create traditions that would not be halted by snow or amended by a particular anti-Latino and anti-immigrant moment in national politics. Latino parishioners appreciated ethno-religious events like the Virgen de Guadalupe procession and other events like the Christmas *Posadas* and *Postorela* [Nativity play], Holy Week Viacrucis, and the organization of a church *kermes* [church carnival]. Ethno-Catholic rituals like these not only happened within a few months of one another but also provided a public expression of ethnic religiosity that affirmed a right to belong in these spaces. Beyond the importance of locating networks, the familiar practices in Spanish, the choir with particular Latin music beats, and the religious practices all coalesced to help families maintain ethnic identity. As one youth group participant recalled, "the music was *cumbia*. So it was fun music, it wasn't gospel music but fun music we're used to. I love going to St. Boniface, but I can't go to English Mass because the music is so relaxing. Yeah, like you need to have some spiciness." Participation and attendance in particularly "spicy" Latino traditions with familiar music stylings from Mexico created memories that some parents hoped would inculcate their children not just in faith practices but in ethnic identity as well. For instance, I asked another Latina Catholic, Dolores, to recall how she maintained ethnic identity for her children who, like her, had been born and raised in Lafayette:

> Pues si, hablando a los niños en español. Tratamos de, no vamos a la misa todos los días tal vez, pero el día de la virgen allí estamos. Oh también para navidad. Nuestra navidad en casa también hacemos posada y todos los niños se visten como San José y el mas chiquito es el niño Jesús. Hacemos como cosas así para que ellos vean las costumbres que ay también en México.

> Well, yes, we talk to the kids in Spanish. But we also, well we may not go to Mass every Sunday, but on [the] day of the Virgin [of Guadalupe] there we are. And also Christmas. Even in our own family Christmas, we also have the nativity play where all the kids dress up, like as Joseph and the smallest kid is the baby Jesus. We do things like that so that [the children] can see the traditions that are practiced in Mexico.

Indeed, the family was still heavily involved with coordinating events at St. Boniface. Though limited by time because of their three small children, Dolores and her husband, José, participated as much as they could in *grupo* and the multiple ethno-Catholic events throughout the year. As

José explained, he was going to be in charge of this year's *Posadas*, and though it was two months away, he already had twelve to fourteen children willing to practice for their Christmas nativity play. Like the teens in *danza*, this young generation of Latinos in Lafayette would soon perform their own ethno-religious memories in this midwestern space. During *Las Posadas* in Latin America, families pray a novena and host celebrations leading up to the holy birth wherein individuals travel house to house (in a kind of caroling tradition) asking for sanctuary as Joseph and Mary would have. After being denied entrance, they finally find a place willing to take them in. Throughout the route prayers and hymns are sung in honor of Christmas. Once someone finally opens the door to the traveling parishioners (the hosts of the celebration), food and games commence and the famous Mexican *piñata* shaped as a star is brought out to commemorate the importance of the North Star and delight in Jesus's birth. Much like Mary and Joseph in the *Posadas*, Latino congregants and residents of Lafayette searched for a place to call home, a place where they were welcomed, a place where their presence would not be marred by a government unwilling to recognize the value of human life above the politics of denied belonging. Prior to arriving in Lafayette, many of these families had attempted to make home in California, Texas, Florida, or even Chicago, but it was central Indiana where they finally felt that they could rest. The economic stability, low cost of living, and small-town calmness convinced Latinos that Lafayette was a good place to work and raise a family. For Latinos, this was their welcoming barn even if some innkeepers were not so keen on their settlement.

Comadrazgo and Sisterhood as Coping Mechanism

In interviews, immigrant women noted the importance of church as a gathering space of solidarity and mutual support, especially in the initial phase when they found themselves alone in an unfamiliar and overwhelmingly Anglo-dominated town. As Roberta, an Argentinian journalist, mentioned in her interview, "What I miss most is the public life. You know—people outside, people on the streets. People sitting in cafés on the sidewalks. People talking to their neighbors. Just stopping to have a coffee. You know, there are certain things of this culture that I still have a lot of time to adjust. I kept asking the first year I was here, not just here but in the U.S., they have these beautiful gardens and nobody's outside. Where are they?" Prior to her moving to Lafayette, Roberta's first experiences in the United States were in larger urban centers like Miami and New York. Arriving in Lafayette meant a huge adjustment to small-town midwestern living. Because she had lived and worked in the United States in the past and was a reporter for English-language newspapers, she did not face issues with a language barrier. Instead, what she felt most nostalgic for was a social life, a place outside her home walls where she could enjoy people's company. Moreover, the weather in Indiana did not help matters. When I asked if she ever felt nostalgic or if she missed Argentina when she arrived in Lafayette, Roberta explained, "Oh yes, at the beginning I would cry like every day. I was not working for the first time in my life. The very harsh weather. You know those gray days in a row, without sun, being inside all the time and the fact that I was with young children, that I knew very few people and we didn't have a lot of money. So, I think it was really hard." Indeed, more than 50 percent of the Latino participants interviewed mentioned the weather or, more specifically, *el frío* [the cold] as a deterrent factor in living in the Midwest. Vocalizing symptoms of seasonal affective disorder (SAD), Latino residents recognized signs of their winter depression as amplifying their feelings of loneliness and distress. Chela, Micaela's mother, expressed what so many others felt: "Me deprime el frío, no me gusta estar encerrada" [The cold depresses me, I hate being cooped up inside]. For women like Chela and Roberta, locating networks of support became crucial to their overall well-being. The cold, depressing winters only exacerbated their already isolating experiences. According to a brief psychological study by Mary E. Bathum and Linda C. Baumann, Latinas' "sharing the same type of loss and transnational experience seemed to help the women form new bonds in their new community" (2007: 172). In Greater Lafayette, women eventually located one another through religious networks and formed bonds of *comadrazgo*. Though Mexican ethno-Catholic religious networks are often referred to as systems of *compadrazgo*, Treviño (2006) suggests *comadrazgo* as a more appropriate term because "it has been women—the *comadres*—who have taken the lead in perpetuating this important Mexican American institution" (63). The *comadres*, or co-mothers, helped one another locate critical resources and services in town. More important, they provided friendship where there was once despair.

Trust and solidarity formed through prayer groups, support groups, and *comadrazgo* where women found they could depend on one another to get them through the bouts of loneliness, unfamiliarity, and nostalgia. These new-found friendships provided the social contact for which many of them hungered. Wives-turned-grandmothers sat across from me in their kitchens or living rooms and recalled the pain of arriving with their husbands in this initially inhospitable town. For Margarita, her affiliation with the church offset feelings of grief at leaving her family. As Margarita noted,

> No había nadie, por eso me sentía yo rara. . . . No tenia amistades, no conocía a nadie. . . . Íbamos a Santa María y luego a Santo Tomas y allí fui yo juntando mis amistades de un lugar al otro. Fue creciendo el circulo de amistades y entonces si me sentía mas en mi rancho o en mi ciudad.

> There was nobody. That is why I felt so strange. . . . I didn't have any friends, I didn't know anyone. . . . We went to St. Mary and then to St. Thomas and from one place to another [and] I started gathering friends. As my circle of friends began to grow, then I started to feel that I was in my ranch—well, my city.

For women who had little to no experience with life in the United States and whose husbands often formed their own networks in the workplace, church became one of the few avenues for female social interaction. Without this ethno-religious contact, women felt like *gallinas compradas* or, as Margarita explained, "Como que tu eres de este montoncito y te sacan a este montoncito. ¿como te sientes? Como gallina comprada. Así se siente uno como que no eres de esa granja [It is like you are from this little pile and they take [you] out to this other little pile. How would you feel? Like a purchased chicken. That is how one feels, like you are not from that farm]. Initially, religious activities in the Catholic Church offered the spaces where women could find familiarity, pray that their situations would improve, and locate one another. As described in the previous chapter, the entirety of the Spanish-speaking parish consisted of a few dedicated families who coordinated their own Spanish services and actively participated in establishing an ethno-religious belonging.[23] Oddly, the energetic involvement of large Mexican families displeased a parish priest who for some time closed the sanctuary doors to Mexican families that wanted to pray to the Virgin. Alicia arrived in Lafayette in 1974 as a newlywed and attended St. Boniface with her husband. Having never left her hometown in Mexico, she depended heavily on the contacts made in church to help her through the pain of unfamiliarity in a new country. With mixed pride, she recalled when the priest at St. Boniface literally closed the doors on them:

> Mira no nos quería para nada. Nos corrió de la iglesia una vez. Íbamos según nosotras a rezar a la virgen para Mayo, cada día queríamos rezar al rosario y el nos corrió. En un tiempecito ya nadie ayudaba. . . . Y es cuando nosotros dijimos, vamos si no nos quiere en la iglesia pues en las casas, que mas. No le gustaba yo creo que fuéramos allí con los chiquillos no se. Pues todas teníamos niños.

> Look, he didn't like us at all. He threw us out of the church one time. We were going to pray to the Virgin for May, we wanted to pray a rosary every day and he kicked us out. There was a time when nobody helped. . . . That is when we said, well then if they don't want us in the church, then in our homes, what else. I don't know, I don't think he liked us bringing our children. Well, we all had children.

In Mexico, Mother's Day is traditionally celebrated as both a secular and a religious holiday. Veneration to the holiest of mothers is often practiced all month long, as Alicia noted, and can consist of special prayer practices and rituals that evoke immense gratitude for the blessed mother. For Alicia and other Mexican Catholics, this was a moment to come together and commit time and adoration to the Virgin Mary in her sanctuary. This practice was not familiar to the English-speaking German-Catholic clergy assigned to the parish at that time and was certainly not appreciated for its deeply cultural and spiritual reverence.[24] Being discriminated against because of their role as mothers for the practice of honoring the sacred mother was insulting and resulted in a moment of incredible agency where these mothers and their families decided to defy the patriarchy of the church to practice their own forms of ethno-religiosity in their homes. Thankfully, by the twenty-first century the diocese reorganized the church and a new parish priest, a

Lafayette local himself, welcomed these ethno-Catholic practices and worked with Latino congregants to strengthen ethnic activities in the church. In addition, by 2006 the parish annually hosted a visiting priest from Mexico to help with the needs of Spanish-speaking Catholics.

Similar to the *comadrazgo* formed by ethno-Catholic Mexican women, a sisterhood flourished in a small Spanish-speaking Mormon *rama*, or branch, where about a dozen families, all recent immigrants to Lafayette, met and worshiped in a storefront church. The women held meetings both on Sundays and throughout the week with one another. The four women I interviewed echoed the feelings of Catholic immigrant women. Mago, after being in the United States for only six months at the time of our interview, revealed an immense gratitude to the women in her prayer group. When I asked her how the Mormon Church and the prayer group factored into her life, she explained that it was "un cariño y hermanidad, es una ayuda que nos damos mutua. Nos enseña a escucharnos, entendernos, y ayudarnos" [an affection and sisterhood, it is a mutual support we give one another. It teaches us to listen, understand, and help each other]. Likewise, in his history of the Mexicans in Salt Lake City, Jorge Iber recounts how Mormon parishes provide a social function that goes beyond spirituality: "the rama, and the contacts made there, provided spiritual comfort and much more" (2000: 28). These church affiliations and prayer groups offered women spiritual, material, and social support. The frequent gatherings and legitimate concern for one another allowed them to pull their emotional and financial resources together to help out an *hermana* [sister] and her family when she most needed it. Through these faith-based social networks Catholic and Mormon Spanish-speaking women were able to build community and a sisterhood that aided in emotional survival and resiliency, eventually strengthening their ties and justifying their settlement in an increasingly familiar town.

Familial Bonds at Church

Without biological family in the area, Latinos developed *cariño* [affection] for and ties to one another through church activities. Forming fictive kin networks through the church benefited entire families, not just the women. Men used these church-based networks for employment opportunities. As Micaela and Mercedes mentioned earlier, children also appreciated the church-based ethnic peers whom they lacked at school. Indeed, Chela knew the importance of these networks to her daughter and the entire family when she compared life in Lafayette to life in Van Nuys, California: "Aquí hemos tenido un poco mas como calor de familia. Aunque no sean nuestra familia pero hemos estado muy involucrados en la iglesia, y la gente de la iglesia nos a dado un cariño" [Here, we have felt more familial warmth. Even if they are not our family, we have been very involved in the church and the people from the church have given us affection]. For Chela, this involvement with the church was something that came out of her moving to Lafayette. She recalled going to church on Sundays in California but never staying longer than the hour that was required. After she moved to Lafayette in 1996, church became her only exposure to any semblance of community. Chela's despair lessened as her social network grew. She noted that at church a family friend "me presentaba con sus amigas y así fue rápido que no me sentí sola por que tuve amistades" [would introduce me to her friends and that is how quickly I no longer felt lonely because I had friends]. Social-religious networks grew out of this need for human contact, familiarity, and comfort. Moreover, the continuity and camaraderie developed from religious events offered immigrants new to the area a chance to meet with those who shared their migratory experience and ethno-Catholic identity. According to Mary Odem's work on Mexican Catholics in Atlanta, "[T]he experience of migration and dislocation heightened their need for religious practices and devotion" (2004: 38). Were it not for the church community that developed around ethnic, linguistic, and socioeconomic ties, Chela's quality of life in Lafayette would have been drastically diminished. Without the local presence of her immediate family, Chela was able to locate a surrogate grandmother for her children and a wealth of aunts, uncles, and godparents who filled a critical void created by immigration. One such extended kin to the family, Moisés, was married to their longtime family friend and worked with Micaela in leading the ethno-religious events at St. Boniface like the Viacrucis and the Virgen de Guadalupe reenactment play performed during Mass. Moisés too recognized the importance of community and building relationships through church experiences.

Beyond the religious rituals, Moisés also coordinated the youth group to surprise the mothers of *grupo* members on Mother's Day with midnight serenades at their homes. Expanding the novenas to the Virgin Mother that Alicia's generation affirmed, *grupo* also wanted to make sure their own Mexican mothers were celebrated in a traditional Mexican manner. They gathered those members who could play guitar and together visited each one of their mothers' homes to surprise them with roses and the customary rendition of *Las Mañanitas*. As Moisés proudly remembered, one year they started the serenades at 10:00 P.M. and did not end until 9:00 A.M. the next day. For Moisés and others, it was not just the space or the parish that made their participation important. It was the people, the feelings of familiarity and community bonds, which made the church a sacred place. As Moisés reiterated during a follow-up interview in 2012:

> No creo que no estoy pegado a alguna parroquia. Como cuando estaba en Chicago estaba en una comunidad y convivía con la gente. Entonces no estaba encariñado con la parroquia, estaba encariñado con la gente. Aquí es lo mismo, sigo conviviendo con la gente aun que no valla allí.

> I do not think I'm attached to one particular parish. Like when I was in Chicago, I was in a [parish] community and I rejoiced with the people. So I was not attached to the parish as much as I was attached to the people. Here it is the same, I continue to delight in spending time with the people even if I don't always attend Mass there.

The church provided a spiritual, sacred place to rejuvenate one's soul, but it also served as social scaffolding for families whose members hungered for belonging and familiarity. Locating kin networks, celebrating traditional ethno-religious holidays, and having the opportunity to spend recreational time with one another after Mass made these spiritual centers critical for immigrant belonging.

Spanish-speaking Protestant churchgoers also relied on one another for this social-spiritual support. The spiritual collectivity formed out of these congregations had the added effect of improving the social lives of all immigrants. Going to church services and spending time with their faith-based social networks offered a much-needed break from the monotony of the workweek. For many of these families, the work-week was demanding and strenuous on their physical and emotional well-being. These religious social interactions provided moments when congregants could briefly step back and actually enjoy the fruits of their labors. Church leaders planned familial events after Sunday services or visited with one another on the church grounds, at their homes, or in public parks. Indeed, the small but thriving Spanish-speaking Baptist community almost always held some outdoor events. Christian music could be heard in the background of families eating; playing volleyball, soccer, or softball with one another; and enjoying the recreational mo-ments spent with new-found friends. As Refugio, a recent Baptist con-vert, noted when I asked him about his involvement in the church, "En nuestra iglesia se siente uno como si es nuestra familia" [In our church, one feels as if we're part of the same family]. Refugio and his family arrived in Lafayette only a few years prior to 2006, and as a lifelong Catholic he began attending St. Boniface. However, by the time Refu-gio arrived, several hundred people were attending Spanish Mass. He and his family felt overwhelmed by the overflow of parishioners and what he perceived as the detached nature of the Catholic Church. He hungered for a smaller, more intimate spiritual encounter. St. Boniface still operated as a vibrant ethno-Catholic center for many Mexicans in town, but the population growth made it difficult for some recent arriv-als to penetrate the longstanding social networks that went back to those original "pioneering" families. Similar to those original Catholic fami-lies, the Baptist, Pentecostal, and Mormon churches along with other small Protestant Spanish-speaking parishes in town all served to unite Lafayette Mexicans under the auspice of building a spiritual, ethnic, and linguistic community.

In addition to female-led prayer groups, these Protestant congrega-tions also placed lay individuals in leadership roles with the youth min-istry, adult Bible study groups, weekend retreats, and much more. In some Spanish-speaking Protestant services I attended, individuals were encouraged to bear witness to their personal encounters with spiritual-ity, and many times this included reference to their immigrant expe-rience. During a follow-up visit in 2012 to the local Spanish Mormon *rama*, I noted that some families were missing while other new families had joined. The space continued to operate as a place at which to weave interpersonal support with faith-based practices. Though some of the families I met in 2006 were forced to leave because of economic and political forces that made it increasingly difficult for an undocumented family to reside in Indiana, the *rama* survived by replenishing its member base with new families whose members also hoped to find spiritual meaning and community connections among parishioners familiar with their Latino immigrant experience. When I asked one woman what she gained from attending services and maintaining an active connection with her Mormon family, she simply said "*me da fuerza*" [it strengthens me]. She continued to explain that while her husband battled cancer, she had no one to talk to, no one to help alleviate the stress of working and living with death at the door. "Ni sus hermanos," not even his siblings, would come around to see how the family was faring, she tearfully explained. It was only her sisters and the church that persistently came around, provided food, and checked on the family. During services she could bear witness to people who understood her in more ways than one. Her Mormon family not only spoke Spanish, they could also identify with the distress of navigating a foreign environment while trying to maintain one's emotional and physical health. The Mormon family, the connections, and the spiritual support strengthened her and her husband during this trying time.

Deteniendo el Movimiento [Impeding the Movement]

Notably, not all encounters with the Church were positive or even welcoming. Religion provided relief for immigrant families, but there existed a glaring Church absence in institutional support for advocating on behalf of Latino inclusion in the local politics of belonging. During the 2006 Indianapolis immigration rally/march, an interdenominational coalition of religious and community leaders in Indianapolis coordinated to bring thousands together on that April morning. Scattered throughout the white t-shirts and posters pleading for comprehensive immigrant reform were images of the Virgin of Guadalupe, a familiar image used to promote social justice. The Guadalupe banners present in Indianapolis echoed the civil rights–era images of United Farm Workers strikes and certainly early-nineteenth-century appeals for independence delivered by Fr. Miguel Hidalgo in Mexico. This use of the Virgen de

Guadalupe image historically weaves religiosity with reform. Indeed, liberation theologians used faith to justify social activism both in Latin America and during the refugee Sanctuary Movement of the 1980s. Even with this rich past and the presence of active religious leaders in Indianapolis, a deafening silence appeared to be coming from Lafayette pulpits. Rather than lead the charge, church officials shied away from voicing public objections to the anti-immigrant rhetoric. Latino churchgoers felt supported by their religious leaders, but it was clear that outward manifestations of support were few and far between. With or without the institutional assistance of their church, parishioners asserted themselves as active agents in the struggle for justice.

Church networks were one of many avenues to communicate details of the Indianapolis march and May 1st economic strike among the area's otherwise disparately located Latinos. Moreover, Protestant communities affirmed the struggles of immigrant families by encouraging members to reconcile their marginalized experiences through vocalized affirmations of God's blessings on their lives. Potentially, this practice could discourage participation in political debate, leaving struggles and pains up to God's larger plan. However, it seemed to have the opposite affect on individuals who felt their God was present in their lives and supported them regardless of immigration status. The leadership roles in Bible study sessions and opportunities to bear witness to traumatic obstacles helped followers locate their voice and cultivate the *fuerza* [strength] to confront personal and structural adversity. Asked to reflect on their interpretations of the scriptures and engage their faith actively, Latino Protestants developed a sense of autonomy and confidence among their ethnic peers. Religious studies scholar Jill DeTemple (2005) even suggests that this Protestant approach of encouraging individual spiritual affirmation leads to the potential "road to civic empowerment" for devotees who take the skills and confidence learned in the church and apply them to the larger secular environment.[25] Indeed, I observed this first-hand with individuals who initially struggled to lead their prayer groups but who months later projected a much more assured presence in front of their congregation. It was these individuals whom I waved to as we marched together on those Indianapolis city streets.

Catholics, on the other hand, had an uphill battle toward autonomy and direct influence over their church. Perhaps indicative of the silence from church leadership, the major Latino-serving Catholic church faced its newest Spanish-speaking congregants with trepidation. Once barred from praying to the Virgin Mary, Spanish-speaking Catholics were able to practice their ethno-religious traditions openly by 2006. Still, even with much improved tolerance toward ethno–Catholic Latino practices, the church remained under the command of its English-dominant congregants. Ironically, the same church that once battled its Mother Superior over English-only teachers now actively insisted that Spanish speakers use English to enrich their commitment to faith. The implementation of a Spanish Mass, though crucial for Latino parishioners, went only so far in enriching the lives that craved more. Cultural and linguistic barriers continued to suppress active involvement and created a tier system within the church. For example, Isabel, a Chicago transplant fluent in English who was raised in the United States, lamented the lack of understanding that Latino Catholics faced in the church:

> You don't know how much we've [Latino Catholics] prayed that we [Latino and non-Latino Catholics] would learn to live with each other. In [the religious retreat], we went through so much. They [Anglo Catholics] didn't want us speaking Spanish. . . . One day I had to take my children, and they [Anglo Catholics] couldn't understand. I live very far away, and they tried to kick me out. They told me, you cannot come in because you have your daughter. One thing about our culture, you always bring your children and that's not something that *güerros* [White folks] do. . . . I said to myself, "Why must I go through this; who are they to tell me what I could do?" Two [Latino] ladies saw me leaving with tears. They stopped me and [said], "Where are you going, Isabel? *Regrésate* [Return], *tienes que hacer humilde*. God is asking you to be humble, He needs you to turn back.

In recounting the story, Isabel even made a verbal slip by noting that she did not understand why she had to "humiliate myself." She accepted this call to return but never forgot how demeaning it was to be asked to humble herself to English-dominant participants. Similar to earlier generations of Latinas during Mother's Day, it seemed that bringing children to church once again led to rejection. The requirement to speak English during these religious retreats went one step too far for individuals like Moisés. Like Refugio, Moisés yearned for a deeper

engagement with his faith. Active in the ethno-religious rituals and in
several ministries, Moisés was invited to attend another religious retreat.
He had hoped the retreat would provide a space to engage the Bible
and other texts in a way not customary during Mass. His experience,
though different from Isabel's, was equally troubling. I had many conversations with Moisés, got to know his wife, and watched his children
grow through the years. Our initial conversations in 2006 involved the
role *grupo* held in his life as a means to solidify the foundations of the
church. He found that *grupo* enriched his life and that participation provided spiritual fulfillment. During a follow-up interview in 2009, I asked
Moisés about his involvement with the church. Still deeply active, he did
hint at some frustrations. When I returned to Lafayette in 2012, Moisés'
concerns were more concrete as he made the decision to attend Mass
elsewhere. Though he and his wife credited Mass times as the primary
reason for making the switch, I asked Moisés to reflect on the uneasiness
he revealed in 2009 and if those feelings had anything to do with their
decisions. Still hesitant about criticizing the church that had provided so
much to them, Moisés stated,

> I think it's la única comunidad que trata a los Hispanos como si los His-
> panos quisieran tomar control de la iglesia. Como que la iglesia ahorita
> esta controlada con pura gente muy tradicionalistas. Entonces viene un
> Hispano y trata de cambiar ciertas cosas y como que no les gusta perder
> el poder sobre su iglesia por que ellos piensan que es su iglesia.
>
> I think it's the only [church] community that treats Hispanics as if the
> Hispanics wanted to take control of the church. It is like the church is
> controlled by very traditional people. So that a Hispanic comes in and
> tries to change a few things and they do not like to lose control of their
> church, because they think it's *theirs*.

For Moisés, this presumption of ownership and control over the church
was ridiculous. The church does not belong to any one group, nor do
those in power own it. It is a collective, a community that should be cognizant of the needs of its entire congregation. Moisés, Isabel, and other
Latino Catholics felt that St. Boniface might be serving a majority Latino
population, but it was clearly under the control of English-dominant,

White individuals, some of whom could trace their lineage back to its German foundations. Respectful of the German heritage of the church, Latino Catholics did not begrudge non-Latino members their contributions. They asked only to be included in the larger decision-making strategies and be given some access to the structure of the church. Eva, with a thirty-year family history in the church herself, feared that the control was related entirely to funds and who was able or willing to tithe to their church appropriately. Indeed, Eva asserted, "It's not involvement—we don't lack involvement." In fact, as Moisés suggested, it is this involvement and enthusiasm from the Latino Catholics that was sometimes suppressed. He remembered taking part in a well-attended group called "Movimiento Familiar Cristiano" [Christian Family Movement] that gathered to form a collective of Latino Catholic families that wanted to come together in prayer and service. Moisés recalled, "el grupo agarro mucha la gente y la forma que trataron de detenernos fue no hacer retiros. Seguro de oración si, pero retiros no se puede por que tienen que hacer en ingles" [the group attracted lots of people, but the way they tried to impede us was through the barring of retreats. We were allowed prayer, but retreats we could not do because they had to be in English]. Though Moisés had been active in another Bible study group at the time of our interview, he felt that the lack of retreats in Spanish was detrimental to Catholic adults and youths who he feared were fleeing the church in large part because of their lack of engaging their faith.

This English-only requirement seemed to be the final straw for Moisés; though proficient in English and even attending English Mass elsewhere at the time of our 2012 conversation, he was saddened by what he saw as a clear disregard for the Latino community's spiritual needs. He remembered the absurdity of a retreat he attended at St. Boniface where English-only was enforced among clearly Spanish-dominant attendants:

> Era todo en Ingles, todo en Ingles. Y eran como 95 percent Hispanish [sic], y todo en ingles. Entonces cada uno teníamos que dar nuestro testimonio final, but for some reason lo teníamos que ser en ingles. I was like no thank you. Ósea, no llegue a ese punto pero, cuando vi todo que era en ingles y que herramos casi todos Hispanos.

It was all in English. It was like 95 percent Hispanish [*sic*] and everything was in English. So we each had to give our final testimony, but for some reason we had to do it [in] English. I was like no thank you. I mean I didn't get that far, but once I realized it had to be in English and almost all of us were Hispanic . . . .

Moisés trailed off, shook his head, and could not finish his statement. Though this had happened over a year before, he was still disturbed by the preference for English even when it was obvious that the people who attended were more comfortable, and could have gained much more, if they had been allowed to speak their native language. Moreover, his slip of the word "Hispanish" communicated that these were Latino congregants whose Spanish was their primary language. Especially because this retreat was advertised during the Spanish Mass, it seemed the whole experience was misleading and insulting to those who gave up their weekend to attend. The problem, he felt, was a lack of empathy with non–English speakers. Speaking about faith and spiritual concerns should not have to be translated or interpreted, especially when resources were already available for those more comfortable in Spanish. Moisés reminded me that the church had a Spanish-speaking deacon for some time now, plus they had also housed a visiting priest from Mexico. The deacon and the visiting priest could have easily led the discussion in Spanish. Instead, there seemed to be a flagrant contempt toward a population that was seemingly taking over "their" church, as Eva proclaimed, "ya son mas mexicanos y además mas joven mexicanos" [there's already more Mexicans and, more important, younger Mexicans]. The youth factor was incredibly important, as many of the non-Latino leadership seemed to be in their sixties or seventies, as opposed to the Latino Catholics, who averaged in their thirties.

Eva, like Moisés, was disturbed by the clear imbalance within the church structure. According to Eva, it was the fear of being displaced by younger and more numerous Latinos, but it was also the financial backing these older families provided the church. As Eva related, "lo que yo pienso que pasa es que ay unas familias muy influentes por que ponen demasiado dinero" [I think some families have more influence because they give a lot of money]. She acknowledged that there was certainly an issue with the amount of money that Spanish parishioners gave during Mass, "But the thing is, the thing is, si no ay crecimiento la gente no va dar nada. Si lo único que nos dicen es den den den, la gente mas se va proteger de su dinero" [But the thing is, the thing is, if there is no growth in services, the people are not going to contribute. If all they hear is give, give, give, the parish is going to react by protecting their money]. Her repetition emphasized the level of frustration she had experienced with the church she had grown up in. During my conversation with Eva I recalled that the bulletin given out after Mass had only one tiny section written in Spanish and it was only about how much money was given the previous week and how much money was needed. I asked Eva if they ever included other messages in Spanish, like announcements about catechism classes or talks, or even translated the message by the priest. She said, "el único mensaje es que nos den mas dinero, no mas para atacar" [the only messages are We need more money, and even that's only to attack us]. Though Latino Catholics pray and go out of their way to invite non-Latinos to their events, it seemed this exchange went only one way. Rather than a true appreciation of how Latinos rejuvenated and renewed the church at a time when their own non-Latino attendance was diminishing, there was only resentment for not contributing enough funds to the church's coffers. Even when they did try to incorporate the Latino population into non-Latino events, they limited, or impeded, the involvement of Latinos. As Micaela remembered during our interview, the first-year Latinos were allowed to sell tacos at the annual church Germanfest (celebration of Oktoberfest in remembrance of the church's German roots), and they got into trouble for outselling the brats (bratwursts) in the stall next door. According to Micaela, the following year organizers put in place a "taco limit" which stated that only so many tacos could be sold at the festival. Even if the vendors could make more, once they met their quota they had to stop selling and encourage people toward the brats stall. As Micaela joked, "It's silly, I mean everyone loves tacos. If they like them more than brats, that's not our fault."

As with the taco sales, it seemed the church's leadership felt it had met its quota with the Latino congregation and on more than one occasion suggested that Latinos find a new place to worship. Eva remembered one meeting at which the lead priest asked the Latino congregation if they might be willing to attend a different parish, as it seemed St. Boniface was facing dire budgetary constraints. Eva wanted to make sure she expressed how much pressure she felt the lead priest was under, "but I know, we know that he loves us, que nos apoya y todo. Pero a la vez se siente como atado a ellos y como que trata de balancearnos todos" [that he supports us. But at times if feels like he's tied to them and that he tries to balance us all]. Regrettably, this balancing act was not always successful. Latino Catholics felt indebted to their priest for all the hard work he did for them and for the care he seemed to show when no one else did. Still, other factors and other individuals made it difficult for Latino Catholics to feel validated as proper members of their church and local community. There existed a Spanish council to the church, but this entity lacked any power when it came to interacting with the non-Latino council. As Moisés remembered,

> Nosotros les dijimos al concilio Americano que era lo mejor que podíamos hacer. Y ellos dijeron que nos fuéramos a otras parroquias. Así, directamente así. Well, why don't you guys go to somewhere else.

> We asked the (White) American council what we could do to help. They said we should go to another parish. Just like that, very direct. Well, why don't you guys go to somewhere else.

Moisés introduced this statement by explaining that Latino parishioners were trying to work with the non-Latinos and searched for ways to unite as one church. This encounter was eye-opening for the Hispanic council whose members realized after this moment that there was not much more they could do to be welcomed into decision making at the church leadership level. Ultimately, this division translated into a lack of support during a political climate wherein Latinos were targeted as the enemy locally and nationally. Rather than be able to count on their religious brethren for encouragement and compassion, it seemed Latino Catholics faced barriers to acceptance even within the structures of their own church.

Friendship and Faith at the Crossroads

Mexican Catholics maintained rituals like the Virgin de Guadalupe procession, the Viacrucis, and Christmas *Posadas* even if they initially encountered resistance from parish administrators. Whether in the

1970s or in the twenty-first century, Mexican Catholics committed to ensuring that their faith practices would continue in this new country even if their particular brand of ethnicity was not always welcomed. Women, in particular, led the struggle to maintain ethnic practices. Choosing to gather in their homes rather than sacrifice their religious traditions, women coordinated with one another to ensure that their ethno-Catholic identities were fostered. These Spanish-speaking Catholic families endured the snubs of a former priest and felt the disapproval of an English-dominant church leadership, but still they demonstrated a willingness to form community and practice their ethnic identity despite repressive limitations.

Notably, faith-based community building among Latino Protestants also provided familiarity, social networks, and emotional strength for facing an environment that was not always welcoming to their presence. Like Catholics, Latino Mormons, Baptists, and Pentecostals all created their own sacred places where their spiritual needs were met and ethnic familial bonds created. Sacralizing space and practicing one's faith publicly validated the right of Latinos to exist openly as ethnic beings in a predominately White community. However, more than shared religious background brought these families together. Behind the traditions and religious ceremonies was a drive for making this town a more comfortable and familiar place to live in. Rather than a fleeting stop in a chain of labor opportunities, many of the Latino immigrants in Lafayette sought stability, tranquility, and home. Navigating the socioeconomic environment of central Indiana was difficult at times, but it also had its advantages. For the immigrants who consciously decided to stay and remain in this town, church and work were often the spaces where they first encountered others who, like them, had justified remaining in the area. Unlike work, Sunday services and ethno-religious events offered the opportunity for entire families to enjoy one another's presence. Children grew up together, attended religious classes, and formed their own networks of friends that carried through into adulthood. Some pioneer families were joined by the marriage of their children while others had children who married White Hoosiers. Regardless of exogamy or endogamy, Latino children were invested in their particular Mexican Lafayette identity as many chose to stay and continue to raise the next generation of Latino Hoosiers. Indiana-born grandchildren were raised in Spanish-speaking and English-speaking homes and were inculcated in Latino traditions and ethnospirituality that defined this new Hoosier experience. For Alicia, Micaela, Refugio, Moisés, and so many others, their memories before becoming involved with their church were recounted as periods of despair and isolation. Solidarity arose between families that united for Sunday church services and found comforting ethnic collectivity among one another. Navigating the borders present both inside and outside their sanctuary walls, Latinos found encouragement through their relationships with one another. This need for support would become increasingly important during the heightened immigration debate of the twenty-first century.

3

Written Otherings

Policing Community at the "Crossroads of America"

Racism can be the unintended consequence of everyday discourses and practices that perpetuate and reinforce an oppressive structure of power.
—Faye Harrison, "Expanding the Discourse on 'Race'"

In 2006, political attacks targeted undocumented immigrants and
marked Latinos as worthy of suspicion. The pain, the fear of being positioned as an internal enemy, hovered over undocumented families. Even
within the walls of their own homes, undocumented immigrants faced
anxieties about their situation daily. Veronica and Efraín had committed
six years to living in central Indiana, but they still could not escape the
anxieties of possible deportation and the fears of relinquishing all that
they had built. Both worked double shifts at their employment, they'd
recently purchased a home, and both held leadership roles in the only
Spanish-speaking Mormon *rama* in the area. Veronica and Efraín's children, though undocumented too, were stellar, award-winning students.
Prior to migrating, the family lived a modest yet comfortable life in one
of Mexico's premier tourist destinations. The consistent flow of tourists
and foreign investors meant Efraín always had steady employment. Yet,
even with these unique regional circumstances, the drastic income difference in the Midwest ultimately pulled Efraín and his family to this region.
According to Efraín, the difference between working in the Midwest and
working in Mexico was an impressive increase of 6,000 more *pesos* per
week. As many families intend, the plan was for Efraín to work in the
United States for a year and then return with substantial start-up funds
to open their own business. Paying for rent, utilities, and food along with
sending remittances to Mexico ultimately depleted his savings and made
returning in a year virtually impossible. The longer he remained in the

United States, the harder it was to return. Efraín earned in one week what would take two months in Mexico; the contrast between wages in the United States and wages in Mexico made returning unthinkable.

In spite of the financial stability, Efraín was alone in Indiana and longed for his family. He grew increasingly depressed. It was during one of his lowest moments when a missionary from the Church of Jesus Christ of Latter-day Saints arrived at his door. This missionary arrived through a transnational network of Mormons that had a presence in Efraín's hometown in Mexico where Veronica and her family were in the process of conversion. As it happened, while Veronica was in Mexico, she was able to communicate with the LDS Church in central Indiana, which agreed to check on her husband. She was worried his depression might be getting the best of him. Members of the LDS Church provided emotional strength and some financial assistance to the family. The built-in community and support structure of the LDS Church strengthened Efraín's resolve to bring his family to Indiana. Notably, Veronica and her children did not meet the financial requirements to apply for sanctioned entry into the United States. Beyond the monetary threshold necessary for even applying for an immigrant visa, the family members knew they did not meet other prerequisites for a green card. If Efraín returned to Mexico to reapply for legal status, he would face a ten-year penalty for previously entering the United States without visa and still knew he would not qualify for permanent residency. Emblematic of most who traverse the border without proper documentation, Efraín and Veronica needed to move al Norte [North], but their very economic situation hampered their visa aspirations. To become a permanent resident able to work in the United States required that one have (1) a direct family member who is a U.S. citizen and willing to sponsor his or her arrival (accompanied by a decade-long waiting period for the applicant), (2) an employer willing to pay a $580 employer application fee and able to show the very specific need for said applicant, (3) a valid case that meets refugee/asylum standards, or (4) an extenuating circumstance as part of special categories withheld for diplomats or foreign nationals from specific countries like Iraq, Afghanistan, and Cuba. In other words, even if he or she could gather the more than $1,000 just to apply, a working-class migrant with a citizen family member would wait more than a decade to be granted entry or more likely would not qualify at all for permanent-resident status. Faced with the latter situation, Efraín and Veronica made the difficult decision to attempt a clandestine crossing. Even with two children accompanying her, Veronica thought it might take only about a week to get to central Indiana for her reunion with Efraín, but the crossing unexpectedly took a month to complete. Veronica wept in recounting the stories of sickness, near-drowning, and countless threats to their lives as they made several attempts to cross the Rio Grande. Indeed, Veronica tearfully noted that "mucha gente sufrió casi para morirse por estar aquí" [many people have suffered and almost died to be here now]. Indeed, the family risked their lives to be reunited in Indiana, and now together they lived through constant fear of having their lives ripped out from under them again.

Through all of this, Efraín felt incredible support from his Mormon church while he anxiously awaited word of his wife and children. Moreover, several members of the non-Latino parish even donated household goods for the arrival of his family. He felt such comfort that Efraín not only converted to Mormonism but was eventually made pastor of his own Hispanic congregation. In the six years since their arrival, both Efraín and Veronica held steady jobs and felt blessed by the gifts they had received in recent years. Yet, in 2006 these feelings of joy gave way to intense trepidation regarding their future. Efraín and Veronica spoke about the minimal options being tossed around on immigration reform. They related watching the evening news with fear, wary of what would happen to them. When I asked about the latest discussions for immigration reform that required learning English, filing paperwork, paying fines, and meeting other requirements to adjust one's status, Efraín responded earnestly:

> Para progresar tiene uno que aprender el ingles. Lo que nos falta es la seguridad . . . esto es lo que nos deprime y nos desespera. Un día nos dicen que no se preocupen, se pueden arreglar y al otro día salen que ay otra ley que los policías pueden agarrar la gente, deportarla . . . entonces se va serrando el camino y uno se siente mal. . . . Esa inseguridad que no sabe uno que va pasar el día de mañana no nos deja desarrollarnos.

> To improve [one's life] one needs to learn English. What we lack now is security. . . . This is what depresses us and causes desperation. One day

they say don't worry, you'll be able to get residency, and another day they come out with a new law that allows the police to pick you up and deport you. . . . In this sense our road narrows and we become anxious. . . . That insecurity of not knowing what will happen the day of tomorrow doesn't allow us to progress.

Veronica was equally distressed. Fighting back her tears, she painfully noted that many immigrants had already given up so much to be in this country; to be told from one day to another that you need to leave was an awful feeling to have to carry with you every day. The family faced this worry together. Though both children had adapted well to their new surroundings, neither had the proper status to guarantee their stay in this country. Very active in their church and holding leadership roles granted by fellow Anglo churchgoers, the family was still aware of their clandestine position that kept them at a juridical and social distance. Uncertainty and insecurity followed them everywhere, penetrating their daily routine at work, school, church, and public spaces. In the last six years, the family traveled to Chicago and throughout central Indiana for church and entertainment. They held parties at parks and shopped regularly at popular stores. Yet in the back of their minds there was always that persistent threat of having the proverbial rug ripped out from under their feet. This pending threat altered how they spent money and navigated certain spaces.

The political atmosphere was saturated with animosity and stories like that of Efraín and Veronica. Tales of despair and angst among immigrant families grew day by day. Indeed, the 2006 political battle on immigration evoked familiar century-old fears that racially marked certain individuals as outsiders, or perpetual foreigners.[1] Nationally, the debate gathered steam in twenty-four-hour news cycles, conservative talk radio, and political campaigns. In Lafayette, I paid close attention to how the debate was localized in the media and its impact on interactions between local Latinos and non-Latinos. I collected dozens of newspapers, recorded the local news station broadcasts when possible, and interviewed Latinos and non-Latinos alike to see how the rhetoric of exclusion infiltrated small-town America. It was disheartening how quickly divisive discourse influenced people's perceptions of their Latino neighbors as criminal threats. Rendered unworthy and dangerous in the local newspaper, Latino research participants experienced daily subtle and overt assaults on their belonging. Latinos sensed a dramatic change in the local climate through an increase in insults hurled on the streets, at work, and in school. Additionally, vitriolic language in the newspapers' opinion sections appeared more frequently as the political debate raged on.

Under the guise of national security, Rep. Sensenbrenner's famed H.R. 4437 sought to criminalize all undocumented immigrants in this country, effectively marking them as potential terrorists and finally punishing those who "assisted" them.[2] Broadly defined, this bill would have held accountable not just undocumented immigrants and coyotes that assisted in the crossing but also legal citizens of the United States who supplied this population with food, shelter, or social services. On a 239-to-182 vote in the House, the bill was passed on December 16, 2005, and set off a chain of events that refocused the American public on an internal "enemy." Notably, this moment in immigration politics occurred just as Spanish-surname residents increasingly settled in regions unaccustomed to Latino populations.

Immigrants were no longer "over there" in California or Arizona but "here" in Wisconsin, Indiana, North Carolina, and elsewhere. In the Midwest, Latinos were particularly attracted by manufacturing and meatpacking industries in smaller towns. Economic opportunities in these new locations coupled with the tense anti-immigrant climates of the places like California and Arizona in the 1990s created an increased dispersal of Latino residential settlement across the country. Rep. Sensenbrenner and his supporters often cited these demographic changes to raise concern. However, a policy brief published in February 2006 through the American Immigration Law Foundation noted that such fears were overblown and misleading: "[T]he supposed threat from undocumented immigration [was] enough to rally voters and move levers of power even in areas where the actual impact [was] minuscule" (Paral 2006). Indeed, the strongest support for the bill came from representatives whose districts had virtually no undocumented population. According to Paral's research, ninety-six districts were known at the time to have the smallest amount of undocumented residents and yet seventy-one Representatives of the ninety-six voted in favor of H.R. 4437.[3] In Indiana, only two Representatives out of eight voted against

H.R. 4437. Regardless of location, support for the bill relied on unsubstantiated claims of economic drain, cultural threats, and employment competition. Fear spread among constituents who saw themselves as potential victims to the "terrorists, drug smugglers, alien gangs, and violent criminals" described by Rep. Sensenbrenner in 2005.

In this political posturing, Latino workers lured in by neoliberal policies embodied the fears of terrorism circulating in a post–September 11, 2001, United States. Still reeling from the attacks on the Twin Towers and the Pentagon, the national populace had its confidence further eroded by sectarian battles in Iraq and the failure to locate weapons of mass destruction. The United States was also on the precipice of an economic decline, and quality of life was diminishing for the nation's working class. Reduced wages and benefits coupled with daily reports of lives lost in still-unjustified military campaigns chipped away at the American psyche.[4] From this angst arose a familiar debate. Immigration was used as a convenient diversion from other, very real, very politicized "threats" to the nation. Rather than recognize these circumstances as the quintessential outcome of U.S. neoliberalism, working-class Latinos and non-Latinos were pitted against one another. Though both experienced simultaneous exploitation, politics focused on the specter of immigration. Using familiar tropes of a perceived Mexican Other, the national conversation on immigration targeted brown-bodies as threats to American authority. Undocumented status represented more than simply the lack of legal residency. Those assumed as "illegal" defied the jurisdiction of "rightfully" or "Whitefully" settled individuals to dominate employment, social benefits, neighborhoods, and the authority to determine who belonged.

The presence of an undocumented population triggered anxieties over demographic changes, what was called the feared Latinoization of the United States.[5] Moreover, the criminalization of these individuals reinforced concerns over personal safety. The very presence of Latinos elicited uneasiness among some of central Indiana's residents. Sometimes subtle, sometimes obvious, the political rhetoric at the national level influenced how Latinos were perceived by unnerved non-Latino neighbors. I spoke to one resident, Jane, about her apprehensions regarding immigration. In her thirties at the time of our interview, Jane had moved to Lafayette, Indiana, after living in the southwestern United

States. Heading into the interview, I was somewhat apprehensive about what Jane's reaction might be when she met me. Would my subject-position as a Chicana keep Jane guarded? Or would she try to ask my position on the subject as was done in other interviews? Speaking to non-Latinos on the subject of immigration often garnered further questions of what I, as some sort of insider, would do to stop immigration. In other scenarios I was either positioned as "a credit to my race" or my ethnicity was completely stripped away as in the words of one individual who awkwardly stated, "Oh, I never would have guessed you were Mexican" when I revealed that my parents were immigrants from Mexico. Anticipating possible discomfort, I sent Jane an e-mail describing the research and further reiterated the importance of gathering multiple opinions in order to understand the varying positions on the topic. I wanted her to feel willing to discuss her positions regardless of who I was or what I looked like. As I met Jane and asked about her personal background and relation to the area, I soon realized how brutally honest she would be.[6]

Jane and I met at Purdue University, where she worked and was in the process of completing a master's degree in education. We began our interview with idle chitchat about the graduate school experience. Jane was apprehensive at first, but as the interview continued her voice and body language grew increasingly vivid with assertive declarations against undocumented immigrants. With the pounding of her fist, Jane insisted: "Illegals, they *don't pay taxes*, they *all live together*, and they send all their money back to Mexico. *We get hurt*, the taxpayers. People *collect welfare* benefits and all kinds of social service benefits. They're *working under the table*, they *send all the money back* to Mexico, and they *all live in the same apartment*, 5–6 families to one" (emphasis added). Each sentence ended with an emphatic bang of her fist on the table, which reverberated to me and altered my note taking. The sound of her metal bracelets clanking against the wood surface communicated clearly that she was incensed. She punctuated her ideas with a final "We don't live like that; *they destroy* the economy of the community."[7] Throughout the interview, Jane's frustration was delivered with consistent intensity. Her rage was apparent and her resentment uncensored. The passion in Jane's voice was obvious as she revealed how damaging stereotypes permeated her feelings toward all Latinos, not just undocumented immigrants in general. Most jarring was Jane's use of the word "illegal." In this and in other interviews, the word was uttered with such maliciousness that it took on something more than a description of undocumented status. But what exactly did "illegal" mean in this narrative, and how was it relevant to the larger immigration debate in general and the acceptance of Latinos in Lafayette in particular? I sought to uncover these and other rhetorical arguments in political fliers, letters to the editor, and online responses to news stories. Jane's interview provided critical evidence of how community protection and denied belonging came to fruition for Lafayette residents who shared her position. Undocumented residents were viewed as the enemy, the "anti-citizen," not deserving of legalization or human empathy.[8] As Robin D. Jacobson relates in her analysis of California's Prop 187 supporters, "The presence of Latinos becomes illegitimate through supporters' notions of racialized proclivities toward crime. The undocumented therefore are criminals undeserving of the rights of membership, including social services" (2008: 58). For months, writers to the local newspaper's letters-to-the-editor page vented phrases like: "We are a Nation Built on Law," "They need to come here legally," "What part of illegal don't you understand," and "They need to be legal, period." The visceral reaction to undocumented immigrants, and those presumed to be undocumented, dominated the local and national discourse on immigrants.

A rhetoric of denied belonging in letters to the editor reached beyond the printed word. As I interviewed other White residents of Greater Lafayette, a pattern began emerging between individuals who reiterated, almost verbatim, some of the same language used in the debates against immigration. As previously mentioned, Jane did not withhold her level of discomfort with undocumented immigrants and the Latino population in general. Typical of the Othering projected onto Latino residents, Jane's assumptions were laden with gendered rhetoric of men as dangerous and women as strains on society. These metaphors of a country under siege by menacing Mexican males or hyperfertile women have long plagued the politics of immigration. In the early twentieth century, immigrant mothers embodied "the problem" of poverty, fertility, and undesirable immigration, and a century later the notion of "anchor babies" once more dominated conservative talk radio.[9] Jane made mention of male Mexican gang members in Arizona who, according to her, introduced guns into neighborhoods and were "the first ones to take up the weapons."[10] Fearing Mexican men through an image of armed threats placed Jane in the role of helpless victim and justified her concerns. Jane, and others, returned to this trope when placing male immigrants as always and already violent interlopers. Jane's experiences in California exposed her to narratives of female villains who abused welfare and fraudulently collected benefits. Notably, Jane admitted to only hearing, not confirming, these stories of Mexican women crossing over to have "anchor babies" and claiming taxpayer benefits. These narratives informed Jane's current view on immigration and her perceptions of an eminent danger in Indiana. Jane warned, "You don't know what could happen when a large population of *illegal aliens* moves into an area. . . . I watched it in [the Southwest] where I lived. . . . Most of the houses were shacks falling apart, tin roofs, no water, no electricity. You would think it was a *Third World Country* and it was two miles from $100,000 homes . . . and it's going to happen here because that's where they go" (emphasis added). I interviewed Jane because I wanted to speak directly to individuals who were actively engaging the local public discourse on immigration in the editorial and letters-to-the-editor sections of the local newspapers. Unsurprisingly, the anxiety and fear Jane spoke of was echoed in a letter-to-the-editor she had written a few weeks prior to our conversation. Like the modalities of fear used in the letters to the editor, spoken utterances against undocumented immigrants relied on positioning immigrants as threats to the rule of law and as threats to "American" culture.

Like Jane, other letter writers positioned their conceptualizations within legal, not racial, concerns. Indeed, they often used the word "illegal" to reference the undocumented population. Speakers and letter writers dismissed the possibility of racism involved in such expressions and instead formulated rhetorical strategies of innocence to preface their very racialist statements.[11] Using what Bonilla-Silva (2006) aptly termed "rhetorical shields" or "discursive buffers," individuals like Jane prefaced their statements with phrases like "I am not racist, but" in an attempt to deter any suspicion of racism given what they were about to utter. Notably, if the speaker/writer did not already recognize that their statement was potentially racist, he or she would not need such a disclaimer. Declarations of righteousness often led into statements such as Jane's "I am not a racist, and this has nothing to do with race. It has to do with the kind of person you are." According to Jane, this was not a racial issue but a legal one. But did an otherwise misdemeanor offense warrant the outright condemnation of a person's decency? If the "kind of person you are" relied on frames derived from phenotypic and linguistic markers, then the word "illegal" must be understood by framing it as a racial slur. When someone used the word "illegal" in such ardent tones, it indexed negative connotations that represented undocumented immigrants as lawbreakers, criminals, abusers of social services, villains, competitors, impatient cheaters, and uncivilized Third World working poor.[12] Moreover, because "illegal" was often used to refer only to Latinos and mostly Mexicans in the United States, the word took on the elements of a racial slur that denigrated anyone brown, Spanish-speaking, and/or Mexican. In addition, the delivery of the word with a grimace or in a deep, drawnout guttural voice, such as those uttered in interviews, revealed how this word was transformed into a hostile epithet.[13] For Jane specifically, her spoken narrative accompanied by banging fists and intimidating tones illustrated the intensity of what she was saying when she uttered phrases like "those people," "illegals," and "Mexican."

Unfortunately, words like "illegal" continue in the contemporary lexicon because of their cunning concealment as seemingly race-neutral adjectives, describing a situation. In practice, the manner in which the word "illegal" appeared in written and spoken communication suggested race-based inflections of disdain, anger, and antipathy toward an entire population. For instance, unless Jane directly spoke to the people she suspected of "illegal" status, which she did not, how could she know whether her Spanish-speaking neighbors were undocumented? Notions of illegality went beyond simply describing someone's immigration status and instead ventured into racial indexing. The use of the word "illegal" in reference to a person or group of people stripped immigrants of their human qualities and converted the word from a modifier that described something to a noun that embodied *that thing*.[14]

In practice, the slippery slope between "legal" and "racial" political discourse was often traversed. Without much effort, the boundary that divided "legal" and "illegal" blurred in that all Latinos were perceived to possess negative qualities.[15] Similar to what Allison Davis (1965) explored in southern racist ideology, speaking Spanish or "looking" Mexican through dress, skin tone, or other phenotypic features represented "symbols of derogation" or derogatory characteristics that branded one as a threat.[16] Using the "legal" argument was a strategy meant to distance oneself from the racist label, but in reality it was often painfully obvious that racial markers, or "symbols of derogation," were used to determine juridical status.[17] Indeed, contempt eventually shifted from legal to cultural arguments. For example, even as Jane proclaimed that hers was not a racial but a legal argument, it did not take long for her dichotomies to collapse. Toward the end of the interview, Jane expressed her contempt for all Mexicans encroaching on her space regardless of legality by complaining,

> They are coming here and transplanting Mexico here. I find it offensive. . . . Everyone is always trying to be P.C. [politically correct] but to me I see this and I look at it as if it's somebody insulting my culture, my heritage. I mean my family has been here forever. . . . You're blasting your Mexican music out of the house that's falling apart. You know you've got your buddies out there partying, wearing your gang colors and you got your guns on your hips—you know that's *offensive to me*. (Emphasis added)

In this representation no mention of legality was given; all Mexicans were viewed as violent gang members disrespectful of homes and neighborhoods. When I followed up this statement by asking about her current neighborhood conditions, Jane responded that so far she had been only annoyed by loud "Mexican music" but feared being run out. She felt threatened that "Mexicans" in her apartment complex would diminish the quality of the area. Jane identified herself as struggling to maintain a middle-class lifestyle that placed her children in local upscale apartments. As a single mother and a Purdue student, Jane could barely afford the apartment she and her children currently resided in. Jane's flight away from ethnic neighbors had occurred several times in her past, and she acknowledged having chosen central Indiana for its whiteness. According to Jane, conversations with co-workers revealed like-minded decisions from a couple who had fled California for the same reasons. Positioning themselves as victimized racial refugees, Jane and her co-workers created a scenario that justified fear and outrage against an encroaching Latino Other. The reported 12 million undocumented immigrants and population estimates for Latino growth fueled this indignation and added to the anxiety and fear of a racial and cultural takeover. Framing themselves as protectors of justice and the "American way," individuals were able to hide behind anti-immigrant discourse that relied on threats of powerlessness to veil a true investment in social privilege and economic power.[18]

Jane's concern with her own insulated comfort prevented her from seeing that branding all Mexicans as gang members and positioning them as always detrimental to a neighborhood was itself extremely insulting and racist. Like other pejoratives used to denigrate minority groups in the United States, "illegal" has been birthed from a history of hate and fear. "Spic," "Greaser," "Wetback," and now "illegal": A legacy of xenophobic moments has supplied the American public with the language with which to condemn Mexicans. But now in this race-conscious twenty-first-century United States, where bigotry is quietly swept under the proverbial rug, hate-based racial categories have, in the words of Frank Reeves, become "sanitized."[19]

The linguistic shift was more than just an issue of semantics. When Jane and others uttered the word, there was a dramatic shift in octave from their natural voice. This changed the tone of the conversations and created a marked difference in the way they spoke about the immigration debate. In its written incantations, the word signified abject subjects unworthy of human empathy. The word "illegal" came to project an onslaught of negativity directed at undocumented immigrants in general and Mexican immigrants in particular. In this manner, the word was not simply describing the status of individuals. Rather, it became a forceful pronouncement of contempt.

Jane was vocally outspoken about her assertions and took the time to express these fervent positions in the local newspaper. Others may not have been as public with their commentary, but this contempt toward undocumented residents (and Latinos presumed as such) was expressed in various ways through actions and snide remarks. The specter of immigration relied on oversimplifications and divisive hearsay to fuel apprehension about Latino residents. An analysis of written communicative acts demonstrates how particular negative associations functioned to deny belonging to central Indiana's Latino population. For residents who wrote, read, or trafficked in the anti-immigrant language, the self was often defined against, and above, the undocumented Other. Relying on a discourse of legality justified a blatant dismissal of undocumented residents and ascribed criminality to cultural and racial markings that had nothing to do with immigration status. Thus, regardless of actual immigration status or the generational presence in the United States, Latino residents faced an internal border that barred them from being thought of as rightfully belonging. This bordered analogy illustrates how Latinos were assumed to be Mexican, regardless of actual country of origin, and as such belonged south, or outside, of an imagined border between the United States and Mexico. Like the geopolitical border, spatial surveillance and linguistic assaults accompanied how Latinos-*cum*-undocumented Mexicans continually felt policed in spaces many miles from traditional borderlands.[20]

Narratives in the newspaper positioned Latinos as unwelcome or, as Leo Chavez (1991) noted, "outside the imagined community" for simply exhibiting attributes (skin tone, Spanish-language skills, etc.) that might be considered "undocumented" or "illegal." Drawing on Benedict Anderson's (1991) often-cited work on national imagined communities, Chavez exposed the fissures of such national imaginaries through the experience of Mexican residents who represented differences and not shared comradeship within community. As Judith Butler and Gayatri Chakravorty Spivak (2011) note, "[I]f the state binds in the name of the nation, conjuring a certain vision of the nation forcibly, if not powerfully, then it also unbinds, releases, expels, banishes" (4–5). Notably, Anderson championed the use of print media as a means of connecting national residents into a shared sense of collectiveness across distance. I examined newspaper editorial pages, letters to the editor, and even the Internet to see how community was imagined against Mexican residents. Print media, election materials, and spoken Otherings divided specific individuals from "legally" claiming belonging to the imagined nation community. Once again, regardless of actual immigration status, Mexican residents, their descendants, and Latinos assumed to be Mexican were racialized in an "outsider" status simply for how they looked or for the language they spoke. Internal fissures that deemed some residents more worthy of "belonging" than others limited Anderson's notion of a "deep, horizontal comradeship" in the imagined national community.[21] Perceived as always and already foreign, or as part of a separate national community, Latino residents were pitted against their own neighbors. This discourse resulted in hierarchal rather than horizontal relationships.

An "Honest, Intelligent Discussion about Immigration"

On April 21, 2006, while attending the first meeting of the Mayor's Commission on Hispanic Affairs in Lafayette, Lupe, a Latina member of the commission who worked in downtown Lafayette, addressed the committee and asked that they "be aware of the negativity near [her] place of employment." Lupe pulled two fliers out of her briefcase. Both had been left on car windshields downtown. The message on the fliers was very upsetting to both her and other commission members. One flier came from an organization naming itself "Team America: A Political Action Committee (PAC) Dedicated to Securing Our Nation's Borders," founded by U.S. Representative Tom Tancredo (R.-Colo.).[22] The other flier asked, "Have we ceded our country" and in quality color resolution provided a picture of the Mexican flag flying above an inverted American flag. The flier declared, "*Illegal aliens* have given ample proof of their intent! If they *didn't obey or respect our laws* until now, you're foolish to expect it to be any different if they are legalized! In fact, they will lose *what little respect they had for America.* Now is the time to contact your Congressman. Do it today while there is still time!" (emphasis added). The image on the flier referenced a moment during the 2006 Comprehensive Immigration Reform (CIR) rallies. The placement of a Mexican flag over "Old Glory" made the rounds with political pundits, conservative talk shows, and newspaper editorials across the nation. The image confirmed suspicions about ethnic Others unwilling to assimilate to "American" culture. The snapshot of protesters usurping the American flag with a Mexican flag was read as an affront to post–September 11 patriotism, especially during a time of war. Too often ignored were the American flags that were carried in the late March demonstrations or the overwhelming display of red, white, and blue in the April rallies held throughout the nation. Effectively silenced were the voices of eloquent Latino youth who spoke to media outlets about the impact of anti-immigrant legislation on their futures and family cohesion.

¿Have we ceded our country?

PLEDGE OF ALLEGIENCE?

Illegal aliens have given ample proof of their intent! If they didn't obey or respect our laws until now, you're foolish to expect it to be any different if they are legalized! In fact, they will lose what little respect they had for America.

Now is the time to contact your Congressman. Do it today while there is still time!

You may contact them through C-span, loudobbs.com, or directly through the following;

> http://www.senate.gov/
> http://www.house.gov/
> http://www.whitehouse.gov/

NO AMNESTY- NO GUEST WORKER PROGRAM!!

Visit: www.noillegals.com   **http://www.alipac.us/**

Flier left on cars downtown.

Criticizing what was interpreted as a flagrant disobedience of "our laws," the flier set up a clear "us" versus "them" binary aided by the use of the term "illegal aliens." Notably, the image of the flagpole had come from an event at Montebello High School in California. The flagpole image was a product of an impulsive student protester from a neighboring school. The fact that this flag image represented an isolated event taking place more than 2,000 miles away from Lafayette misled local Hoosiers into a sense of local urgency and outrage. This vagueness may have led recipients to guess that this incident had occurred locally and that their Latino neighbors in Lafayette were capable of such transgressions. The description on the flier, specifically the alien designation, marked the entire population with foreign, intergalactic qualities whose democratic right to protest should be stripped. The flier referenced Lou Dobbs and also provided the web addresses for the U.S. Senate, the House of Representatives, and the White House. Below the flags, the flier concluded with, "NO AMNESTY—NO GUEST WORKER PROGRAM!!" and listed the web addresses for Alipac and noillegals.com. Alipac was a PAC (political action committee) based out of Raleigh, North Carolina, and noillegals.com was an Indianapolis-based website for the group Americans for Legal Immigration. The website provided a platform for those interested in the anti-undocumented cause in Indiana.[23] On its home page, noillegals.com boasted that the information on the site was "Not intended to be 'Politically Correct'[;] its Goals is [sic] to be 'Factually Correct' . . . We ask that you use this site to gain 'The Wisdom' you will need to change the path America has been on far to [sic] long and to obtain the ability to have an honest, intelligent discussion about immigration." Ironically, the website's quotation marks around "factually correct" and "wisdom" signaled the reality of how knowledge was constructed and consumed by this online community. Lacking the facts about the actual immigration process, such as how long it took someone to receive proper permission to work in the United States or the reality that many undocumented immigrants have entered through valid and legal visitors' visas, the site was indeed constructing a particular kind of "wisdom" for its readers. Members of the Commission on Hispanic Affairs were appalled at the fliers and viewed this distribution of propaganda as an unacceptable intimidation tactic against the greater good of the Lafayette community. Rather than an "intelligent discussion about immigration," these fliers and the affiliated website spread falsities and misrepresentations that fueled distrust of the Latino Hoosier population.

In addition to fliers left on cars in public parking areas, Lafayette voters were inundated with media messages and political mailers that warned of a threatening undocumented presence. With the 2006 congressional

Election materials sent to author's home.

election season in full swing, some politicians used the national debate on immigration in their campaigns. The hotly contested local race for State Representative between incumbent Democrat Sheila Klinker and her Republican challenger, Jack Rhoda, demonstrated how local Lafayette elections absorbed the national immigration debate. Having represented Lafayette and the surrounding area since 1982, Klinker was a fixture in local politics. Still, even with her popularity, Republicans had long sought to defeat Klinker. In 2006, this meant taking advantage of the caustic environment that positioned immigrants as violent criminals who were abusing social services. Rhoda's campaign exploited the moment and sponsored ads that portrayed Klinker as soft on immigration and suggested that she "voted to allow illegal immigrants to receive state benefits and welfare." Klinker's actual position was not to support a bill that would otherwise deny undocumented immigrants and their children emergency and subsidized health care. Rhoda failed to mention that thirty-two of his fellow Republicans voted against the bill because of fears of how denying health care to this population could affect all Indiana residents in the possibility of an epidemic. In fact, the bill was overwhelmingly defeated, 74–19, in 2006. Additionally, Rhoda's ads claimed that Klinker "allow[ed] illegal immigrants to take more than $700 million in state tax dollars." This estimate included state funds that went toward teaching English in public schools and state aid set aside for Latino residents. Though Rhoda's campaign later acknowledged that it could not be sure how much of these monies actually went to undocumented residents, that did not stop it from running the advertisement and misleading the local electorate.

By omitting critical information, campaigns rallied antagonism against political opponents and simultaneously cast Latinos in a negative light. Republican election committees ran their Lafayette candidates (Jack Rhoda and Connie Basham) as tough on immigration. In addition to Rhoda's campaign against Klinker, Basham's election committee sent mailers that depicted a menacing individual with barbed wire overlaid across his face. Basham's campaign against Joe Micon engaged in overtly racialized tactics of fear. Notably, both Rhoda's and Basham's campaigns used identical imagery to position their opponents on the wrong side of immigration. The same attacks against Klinker were recycled verbatim against Micon. Though local Lafayette politicians had virtually no impact on national immigration policies, conservatives continued to use the national debate to affect local politics. Basham's flier is particularly disturbing for its use of familiar racist tropes to raise alarms about immigration. The watermark on the flier depicts a dark-skinned male "illegal alien" ready to take your health care, and the large bold NO at the bottom right corner marks a signal to the audience to put a stop to this man and defend yourself with a ballot by voting "alien"-friendly Joe Micon out of office. The added barbed wire furthers the image of a country under siege and in need of better protection from these menacing, dangerous men. Here, masculinity and brown skin were joined with violence to induce an electorate to vote based on fear.[24] The other side of the mailer depicted a family running as water flowed beneath them.[25] On this side of the flier the narrative shifts from menacing dark male to a virtual flood of immigrants crossing into the United States. The family image returns to earlier 1990s gendered assaults on women and fertility rates. This mailer illustrates how the House Republican Campaign Committee and the Committee to Elect Connie Basham strategically used two all-too-common tropes against immigrants in their aim to reach voters.

Basham's mailer with flier showing family.

Both attempts were unsuccessful and garnered their own counter-response from voters who felt it unfair to use a federal issue to run against local politicians who had nothing to do with the national debate.[26] Indeed, Klinker's established history of serving this district of Indiana enhanced the trust voters had in her decisions and actually worked against what some deemed desperate attempts by Rhoda's campaign. Similarly, Joe Micon's activism in the local Urban Ministry, a faith-based organization aimed at helping local children and families, positioned him above the fray of Basham's attacks. Still, the immigration debate continued to play a role in local identity politics.

Presumed Illegality amidst Tragedy

In July 2006, the tragic death of an eight-year-old boy during a traffic accident tugged at hearts throughout Lafayette. On a summer afternoon a driver swerved to avoid an oncoming vehicle, jumped the curb, and struck a boy who was riding his bicycle on the sidewalk. The story made headlines in both print and broadcast media. The local newspaper included an image of the driver hunched over in grief with the following caption: "The driver of an older model Chevrolet Impala is comforted by two unidentified people Wednesday after he struck a young boy riding his bicycle."[27] Overcome by his part in this young boy's death, the driver was initially suicidal in jail and a year later expressed his remorse to the family and pleaded guilty at his trial.[28] Beyond the suffering of all families involved, this moment marked a moment in the local politics of belonging fueled by the national debate on immigration. Almost immediately after the accident, online commentary on the local newspaper's web page seized on the driver's Spanish surname. Though the story included only the details of how the accident occurred, the commenters quickly made inferences about the driver's citizenship status and politicized this somber event within an anti-immigrant agenda. Noting the exchange about the driver's status, the newspaper updated the story the next day revealing that he was indeed a U.S. citizen, born in Los Angeles, "moved to Lafayette when he was 13 years old and attended Jefferson High School," and promised its readers that the "police will confirm if this is accurate."[29]

The driver's native-born citizenship was a detail worth ignoring for those who would continue days, weeks, and months later to use this case as proof that something should be done to control immigration.[30] Notably, an examination of online commentary and letters to the editor exposed how the racialization of the driver was symptomatic of other publicly stated presumptions that Latinos in general, and Mexicans in particular, were always perceived to be foreign and dangerous.[31] Mercedes, a Mexican Hoosier born and raised in the area, knew both the boy's family and the driver of the vehicle and expressed uneasiness in attending the funeral because she was Mexican: "Te imagines [could you imagine] what they must think." She was concerned that the parents of the young boy might grow resentful of all local Mexicans as a result of this horrific incident. The parents were rightfully distraught with grief for their son, but their pain did not automatically lead to anger toward immigrants. Unlike the Internet commenters, this family never once publicly denounced or even questioned the perceived immigrant identity of the driver. The national immigration debate, the Internet obsession, the search for an enemy to blame in this scenario seemed the furthest thing from the family's focus.

Beatriz, a local business owner, also wanted to express her sympathy to the boy's family. She attended church with the driver's mother—their children were friends—and after the accident she felt for both families altered by it. Moreover, Beatriz did not want to defend the driver's actions, but she felt that the comments around town had unfairly used him for politics: "This was an accident, it had nothing to do with immigration." As it happens, the already tense national debate on immigration filtered into this small city and informed the way Mexicans were perceived as criminal threats first and people second. As this incident revealed, even U.S.-born Mexican Americans could be written off as threats to the imagined collective. The insensitive commentary on this little boy's death sparked conversations around town as the incident kept coming up in interviews with Latinos who noted that immigration maintained a subtle presence in the public and with co-workers. Twenty-first-century popular lexicon would call this trolling, or the use of online commentary sections by those desperately willing to make their voices heard through incendiary, anonymous attacks. However, this type of trolling is not specific to this era or this kind of medium. It is important to remember how traditional media outlets speak to and encourage trolling behavior by the very choices they make in depicting a story or a political moment.

In 2006 the local newspaper's opinion sections inundated Lafayette residents with anti-immigrant messages that limited the way community and belonging could be imagined (Anderson 1991). The opinion section of the *Journal and Courier* included subtle and overt caricatures of immigrants, couched in arguments against undocumented entry, that undermined dogged denials of racism. Righteous arguments in letters to the editor, guest columns, and Rapid Response community sound-off pages fiercely defended the right to denounce perceived interlopers, but in the process the authors exposed a racial slippage implicit in their narratives.

Familiar tropes of a country under siege or overrun by undesirable immigrants reentered the national and local imaginary. Framing this debate as a "legal" issue did not subdue deep-seated antipathy toward racialized, gendered, and classed immigrants. The specter of immigration placed Latino residents, regardless of immigration status, as "rejected and abject subjects" (Gonzales and Chavez 2012, 256). This abjectivity meant that authors could invoke particular tropes to cast doubt about Latinos in general and undocumented immigrants in particular. The written and spoken rhetoric of 2006 positioned immigrants as threats to national sovereignty, White privilege, "American" culture, the rule of law, and civilization. Certain phrases found in the letters repeated these five common themes. The accompanying table shows the themes and the specific way in which letter writers referenced a particular phrase to use against undocumented immigrants and Latinos in general.

Immigrants as:	
Threats to Sovereignty	*Threats to White Privilege*
References to soldiers, war	Undocumented Immigrants as strain on Social Services
Feeling Conquered	
Feeling Overrun/everywhere	Undocumented Immigrants abusing the system
Creating an Us versus Them Structure	
References to "Our Country"	Undocumented Immigrants do not pay taxes
Using the language of protection	Undocumented Immigrants depress wages
Threats to "American" culture	*Threats to the Rule of Law*
Latinos speak only Spanish	Undocumented Immigrants disobey rules
Latinos unwilling to assimilate	Undocumented Immigrants Have No Driver's License
Mexicans transplanting Mexican culture here	
Latinos destroying culture	Undocumented Immigrants Have No Car Insurance
Latinos causing tension and turmoil with cultural differences	Undocumented Immigrants break the law
	Undocumented Immigrants are criminals
	Undocumented Immigrants bring drugs
	Undocumented Immigrants bring Violence
	Undocumented Immigrants bring Gangs
Threats to Civilization	
Demeaning humanity of undocumented immigrants	
Using the word "illegal" as noun	
Referencing the undocumented population as "it"	
Latinos as pre-modern	

Authors of letters to the editor were particularly adept at using these modalities of fear in their criticism. For instance, a letter entitled "Illegal immigration a problem here" appeared in late March 2006 as part of a cluster of five letters that focused on immigration. This letter turned my attention on the newspaper's opinion section to see how authors articulated their positions on the debate. The publication of these letters in a widely distributed newspaper provided some credibility to the opinions expressed and disseminated in their message. Their arguments could read as convincingly logical to those unaware of the complexity of the debate. These letters held such a dominance over local interpretations of the debate that even when the occasional counter-letter appeared, a follow-up letter immediately challenged and dismissed the complexity in the counter-arguments as illogical and threatening to local and national interests. In total, I collected 113 letter-to-the-editor entries between March and December 2006 that referenced immigration. The author of the first letter, "Illegal immigration a problem here," pleaded with his audience to recognize the dangers that undocumented individuals supposedly brought to Lafayette:

> Wake up, Lafayette. Your so-called representatives are hard at work giving away *your jobs* while your local officials are looking the other way. We have *many illegal* immigrants here, and our police, our city councils and the people that hire them look at the illegal issue here like it does not exist, and it sure does. What was a *great city is no more.* Our jobs are being exported and are *taken here by illegals.* Hire illegals and you break the law. Pretending it [undocumented immigrants] isn't here—that should be illegal, too. It is good for some, but don't wave anything but an *American flag* in front of me. My father, his father, your sons are *fighting for America*, not Mexican President Vicente Fox. As many others, Lafayette seems more concerned about secondhand smoke. The smoke is already in our faces. By voting all the politicians out, let's *take our country and city back*, not leaving it at the hands of people that are here illegally. (March 31, 2006; emphasis added)

It is important to note that a rebuttal letter, "Danger of hysteria about immigration," was published in the next edition of the paper. Written to dissuade growing resentment, these written defenses of immigrants as humans worthy of consideration were few and far between. Authors like the one quoted above maintained a steady stream of animosity in the newspaper. The letter's frantic call to "take *our* country and city back" evinced a level of urgency, desperation, and victimhood. But what exactly was this author reacting to? Who was the intended audience? And who were the presumed "us" in the call to action? Playing off threats to sovereignty and personal safety, the letter used soldiers and a lineage of *men* "fighting for America" as a framing mechanism against external attackers. The entire letter was a call to action that portrayed a takeover and the need to defend the local and national community. As a result, this war trope was used to remind readers of the current war against terrorism and rallied against another impending foreign "threat."

The assertion that "we have many" undocumented immigrants came up in multiple letters as a way to raise suspicion against residents who may not have been immigrants or undocumented. Indeed, even hard, quantifiable evidence of only a small Latino presence did not dissuade those willing to make arguments of a community or nation "under siege." For instance, in the decade between 1990 and 2000, the Latino population in Tippecanoe County rose from 2,078 to 7,834.[32] And in 2006, the *Journal and Courier* reported a 21 percent increase in Latino residents since 2000.[33] Even as the county's Latino population was estimated to have grown, by 2005 the Latino population still represented only 6.8 percent of the total population in Tippecanoe County.[34] Clearly, these numbers indicated a change in the population that occurred most dramatically in the 1990s, but even with this growth, the White (non-Hispanic) community still maintained a majority with 84.2 percent of the total population. Regardless of actual numbers on the ground, some individuals in Lafayette voiced their frustration with the growing Latino population, who they were convinced were all undocumented and therefore criminals. Moreover, the economic climate of Lafayette at the time of this letter's appearance did not warrant such call to action. In 2006, Lafayette's local economy sustained itself at a better rate than most American towns'. With an unemployment rate of 3.5 percent, Tippecanoe County was faring better than the national average at 4.4 percent. In this regard, the Mexican population may not necessarily have been detrimental to local job security and employment availability. However, a reality of economic stability did not suppress the fears of economic threat. Framed in such a way, Lafayette was represented as a city on the verge of dystopia, overrun by an undocumented population endowed with the power to alter White American nationalism and wipe out job security for the "true" residents of this town.[35] Placing letters like this one in relation to one another exposed the particular tropes that perpetuated local constructions of social borders.

While meant to be attention-getting, these letters responded to and reinstated seeds of anxiety planted by national figures such as Representative Jim Sensenbrenner (R.-Wisc.), talk show host Lou Dobbs, and political pundit Pat Buchanan. From a top-down approach, these individuals based their careers on creating a politics of fear and mistrust of the Other. As agents of resentment themselves, local letter writers attempted to spread the message and further convince others of the maladies that lay ahead. In effect, these letters occupied a public space—the newspaper—to air grievances, spread falsehoods, and present seemingly logical arguments against a presumed undocumented Latino population. Unfortunately, with a consistent message in the opinion section of the newspaper this image of Lafayette-under-siege gathered strength. With this barrage of negativity, readers were exposed to the immigration debate only through this kind of filtering, and as a result, social space, and the role of Latinos within it, was interpreted through this skewed lens.

Those who spoke of "illegals" and ascribed undocumented status to perceived visual markers of "Mexican" identity applied racialized, classed, and xenophobic images to individuals. Simply put, the letters to the editor, the election materials, and the vocalizations in public were not just about expressing opinion. Notably, the performative aspect of language allows for the notion that "words can wound" and that certain types of language are not simply free expressions of opinion but should be thought of as "verbal muggings of people of color" (Hill 2008: 49). Perhaps not as sharp or as explicit as racial slurs, the rhetoric in these letters did carry the power to enact negative change against a particular community. As the above letter suggested, there was an intent to the writing, a wake-up call, to convince a public of the dangers and prevent any sort of immigration reform from happening. Understanding these letters as discursive performative acts illustrated the ability of these communicative spaces to alter social reality in Lafayette.[36]

The discourse surrounding immigration influenced the ways in which citizenship and belonging could be imagined for Latinos in central Indiana. Spoken and imagined assumptions against Latinos-as-immigrants barred some residents from seeing their Latino neighbors as contributing members of society. Images of criminality were woven with imagined references to words like "Mexican," "Hispanic," and "immigrant." The habitual thinking of a particular ethnic group with the descriptor of "illegality" instinctively assigned criminality to anyone phenotypically identified as Hispanic. The intent, it was argued, was not to be racist; rather, the problem was strictly legal and its resolution was in the nation's best economic and security interests. Veiled by an affiliation to safety, sovereignty, and terrorism, words like "illegal" were commonplace. In this framing, "illegal" became coded with a generalized discontent with anyone suspected as undocumented who fit the imagined Mexican profile. Anti-immigrant imagery was also embedded within intersectional insinuations to gender, race, and class. Specific assemblages of violence and other criminal activity against gendered, classed, and racialized bodies situated how violence was projected toward men of color.[37] Words such as "gangs," "drugs," "danger," and "jobs" signaled specific fears toward immigrant men. Women, too, were perceived as exploiting social services—birthing anchor babies—and a drain on society.

Letter writers made inferences against Latino residents based on what they perceived from the national media. Claims of a language takeover, challenges to American patriotism, and criminal associations at the national level resulted in ascribing such negativity to Lafayette's local Latino population.[38] For months, the *Journal and Courier* was appropriated as a space in which to hold virtual anti-immigrant rallies.[39] Invading households and minds daily, these letters and online commentary fed into one another and promoted resentment and suspicion against Latinos. For example, the following two letters not only presumed the "illegality" of immigration-rally participants but also illustrated tropes of a country under siege with dangerous (read: Latinos) and exploiters of social services (read: Latinas):

> "Send illegal immigrants back"—As I watched television, once again, I saw the streets *filled with people who are breaking the law* even being in this country waving Mexican flags and saying they do not have to *comply with the laws of this country.* They overload *our social services* and expect *free medical care* while *driving without a license* or insurance. They say they are making a political statement. *Most of them are illegal* and can't vote anyway. . . . Somehow they have the idea [that] they are vital to the economy of this country. All they do is *lower the average wage* for everyone. The economy did just fine before they arrived and it will survive if these *criminals* are arrested and sent back *where they belong.* (May 22, 2006; emphasis added)

"Don't let illegals *conquer* U.S."—*War* is not the only way to *conquer a nation.* Sadly, our government officials are opening the door and laying out the red carpet for our *conquerors.* Our towns are being *flooded* with illegal immigrants, and they will destroy *the culture* we have. I moved away from the West because I was sick of the problems associated with illegals: *crime, drugs, increased taxes* and many other related problems. So I came here, and lo and behold, here they come, too. It seems that U.S. Immigration and Customs Enforcement had a perfect opportunity to deport *a bunch of illegals,* but they blew it. *America has its own people to take care of;* let's not take care of *others,* too. As a nation, we must not allow America to be *conquered.* (June 15, 2006; emphasis added)

The majority of letters and commentary relied on a few common premises: All Latinos were Mexicans, all Mexicans were undocumented recent arrivals, they were all Spanish-speakers who refused to learn English, legal entry was only a matter of waiting patiently, and undocumented immigrants were criminals and a strain on society who needed to be deported. The repetitive nature of these letters reinforced these assumptions and strengthened the resulting anti-Latino message. Notably, both letter writers reacted to the coverage on massive immigration rallies and built their case that "our towns are being flooded with illegal immigrants." A majority of media attention focused on rallies and marches in larger traditional Latino-settled locations like Chicago or the U.S. Southwest and not the Indianapolis march. Still, these writers asserted that what was occurring nationally had to be going on locally. Any brown-skinned Spanish-speaking resident signaled undocumented status, and undocumented status was perceived as carrying negative attributes. These assumptions affected how local Lafayette Latinos, regardless of resident status, were treated in public, at school, at their place of employment, and even in their own neighborhoods.

Primarily, the letters reflected what Pierre Bourdieu noted as a "quasi-magical power to name and to make exist by virtue of naming" (1985: 729). In presuming that Lafayette had "many illegal immigrants" without citing any evidence to support such claims, the author of "Illegal immigration a problem here" was in effect *naming* or labeling all Latinos in the area as undocumented. Therefore, the growth in Latino residents over the past forty years was presented as a direct reflection of the *problem* with undocumented immigration and thus justified such bills as H.R. 4437. Without verifiable evidence indicating the number or percentage of undocumented peoples in the area, authors were simply relying on the suspected illegality of anyone phenotypically exhibiting perceived Mexican characteristics and/or speaking Spanish. Indeed, by naming illegality and defining it as associated with conquering residents, the authors of these letters planted the possibility of doubt that all Latinos were automatically suspect as dangerous threats. To that end, these letters, online commentary, and the visual representations broadcast on television screens all contributed to the racialization and surveillance of Latinos in Lafayette.

Beyond assumptions about legal residency, the utterance of Spanish was also heavily policed in public sneers and written letters to the editor. Proficiency in English became a commodity worth more than simply ease of communication. It reflected conformity and acceptance of American nationalism. Letters continually referred to the use of Spanish as proof of immigrant refusal to adapt and assimilate.[40] One of the most commonly held misconceptions was that Spanish speakers adamantly refused to learn English. A speaker who uttered Spanish was assumed to not have a command of English. Often the actual attempts by Spanish speakers to acquire and use predominantly the English language went ignored.[41] Efraín, for instance, revealed his willingness to learn. What he lacked was the time available for learning English and the confidence that these language skills would actually benefit him. He voiced a wish that his employer would have courses, even in basic English, for employees during break time. Many, he argued, would volunteer in a heartbeat if it meant they could learn English skills that would be beneficial and worthwhile in their daily lives. Efraín accurately deduced that if he was in danger of being kicked out tomorrow, there was an obvious choice between spending three hours in class or three hours at work. Given a chance to adjust his status, Efraín validated that he would be the first to give up several hours of work a week to take English classes.

Like Efraín, many Spanish-speakers worked full-time jobs, yet they managed to squeeze in time for language classes and honed English skills at home with their children. Indeed, even with age, work hours, and anxiety related to undocumented status taken into account, language acquisition is never an overnight process and is a difficult task for adults regardless of life situations. The ability to speak English correlated with an individual's suitability to the United States. This linguistic prerequisite was evident on April 13, 2006, when the letters "Learn English if you come to live here" and "No desire to become Americans" appeared in the *Journal and Courier*. The author of "Learn English" replied to a previous letter attempting to provide the perspective of Hispanics in town and wrote: "In response to a letter to the editor headlined 'Listen to the voice of Hispanics' how can we when many of them *do not speak English*? They want to come here for a better life. That's great. Come here and learn the English language and *the rules of the U.S.*" (April 13, 2006; emphasis added). This linguistic dichotomy placed bilingual Latinos who could effortlessly communicate in both languages outside of the imaginary. For even if full proficiency was attained, the use of a language other than English framed the speaker in such a way that the latter superseded one's command of the former. The "elevation of the English language," or linguicism, played a crucial role in the anti-immigrant discourse present both within the *Journal and Courier* and throughout the social sphere of Lafayette.[42] A resulting socio-linguistic hierarchy positioned all Spanish speakers beneath English monolinguals so that once more Latinos remained always and already "outside of the imagined community" (Chavez 1991). Placing English above Spanish situated American monolinguals in a conveniently higher social order. A model of linguistic superiority adopted by the author of the letter "Bilingual effort hurting America" (April 11, 2006) suggested that the acquisition of more than one language could destroy a society:

> America is being destroyed. *It* is proceeding methodically, quietly, *darkly*, yet pervasively across the United States today. The Lafayette Police Department, by sending three officers to Mexico to learn *its* culture and how to speak "en Español," is merely one small example of how it is being done. . . . [N]o nation can survive the *tension, conflict, and antagonism* of two or more competing languages and cultures. Histories of bilingual and bicultural societies that *do not assimilate* are histories of *turmoil, tension and tragedy*. (Emphasis added)

In this letter, immigrants were racialized ("darkly") and deprived of human qualities or consideration in the reference to the problem ("it" and "its") and not the people. Moreover, learning a new language and respecting another culture were viewed as worthless endeavors threatening the fabric of society that this author held dear.[43] The efforts of police officers to work with local Spanish speakers rather than against them were seen as threatening and destructive to the author, who found his own insular views in danger. Critically, the author failed to recognize how his own intolerance actually fueled the very "tension, conflict, and antagonism" within "bilingual and bicultural societies." The mere presence of multiple languages does not spontaneously result in the turbulence described in the above letter; rather, it is the creation of difference through the devaluation of language and subsequent hostility toward the people who speak it that truly produces such violent turmoil.[44]

Spanish use became emblematic of anti-citizen tendencies. A native Spanish speaker's very presence not only challenged the linguistic dominance of English but also threatened the sovereignty and stability of the nation-state.[45] In "No desire to become Americans," the author described Spanish-speaking protesters as unable to embody proper citizenship standards: "Has anyone considered that those who are waving another country's flag are *only using us* and have *no desire to learn English* and *melt into our culture*? Or become a citizen?" (April 13, 2006). Relying on assumptions that marked Spanish-speaking marchers as "illegal" foreign threats, this author interpreted democratic activism as somehow un-American. Though they were exhibiting a right to petition the government and address grievances, the civic participation of Latino protesters was read as an affront to national sovereignty. Residing in the United States "illegally" and then asserting the rights to protest the government was the height of arrogance. Taking a defensive approach, authors asserted their right to protect *their* country from such intimidation. For example, the letter "Senators refusing to enforce laws" warned,

> This *flagrant disregard of the sovereignty* of the United States, of the right (and duty) of the citizens of this country to decide who can live here and who cannot, and the *arrogant*, in-your-face flouting of our laws demonstrates far more convincingly than any argument I might present why people who have entered this country illegally and do not understand

that we are a nation built on law are certainly *not ready for citizenship* and should not be granted amnesty. Ignoring our laws is the first step down a *long, slippery slope* that could produce *dire consequences* for this country. (May 4, 2006; emphasis added)

Similar to the author of "No desire to become Americans," this author positioned the undocumented population as unworthy of citizenship. As before, civic participation and a right to protest were filtered through words like "arrogant." Read as pushy or arrogant, undocumented Latinos thwarted the rights of "true" Americans who had somehow earned their privileged place in the nation. Granting undocumented immigrants "amnesty" would, according to the author, unleash a national unraveling of laws, order, and privilege of "citizens of this country to decide who can live here and who cannot." Moreover, contesting the validity of these immigrants as deserving members of society served to further White virtue, or what Jane Hill noted as "the idea that Whites are highest in the hierarchy because their qualities deserve this arrangement" (2008: 21). Undocumented immigrants represented a challenge to state powers and White virtue; paradoxically, this otherwise vulnerable population was imbued with powers to undermine the nation and White privilege in general. Simultaneously stripped of their humanity and feared, undocumented peoples were deemed unworthy of empathy and understanding. Fantastical negative qualities overshadowed any contributions they offered to society.[46] Ironically, risking life and limb attempting to cross the border and the endless work hours already provided to the U.S. economy were reinterpreted as a defiance of the much-romanticized American bootstrap ideology. Social mobility through legalization was not something to be earned; rather, it was bequeathed onto the individual through the "proper channels" and waiting patiently and orderly in line.[47] These letters never presented the somber reality that led to the thousands of deaths in the Sonoran Desert or how and why immigrants would "choose" the "illegal" path. The absences of this critical information conveniently fueled the narrative that positioned undocumented immigrants as impatient, dishonest criminals.

Undocumented residents were barred from acceptance and denied citizenship because they were an Other form of being, an Other form of residing, an Other form of existence that challenged the popularized notions of equality in the United States of America. Notably, the basis of their Othering, the notion of illegality, was an enigmatic truism that lacked any serious engagement with an otherwise complex immigration system. All the discussion, reminders, and angry exclamations of the law overlooked the restrictions and policies that caused unsanctioned entry to begin with. Instead, immigrants were often described as "*sidestepping the law*" or "*sneak[ing] in the back door.*" Authors asserted that "anyone coming here and seeking citizenship needs to *go through legal channels.* They need to *learn English, learn our laws*, work and *pay taxes*" (April 30, 2006, June 30, 2006, and July 20, 2006, respectively; emphasis added). Authors deployed multiple criminal modalities to condemn those who could "not take the time to fill out the *proper papers* to get some type of citizenship" (May 3, 2006; emphasis added). Notably, the measures that granted legal access or the socioeconomic restrictions that barred certain people from entering were topics never discussed, argued, or even mentioned in these narratives.

Ironically, residents of the state of Indiana experienced their own bureaucratic frustrations with the Indiana Bureau of Motor Vehicles (BMV) during the summer of 2006. While the state's computers were being updated, lines at the BMV were inordinately long. At virtually the same time that some residents complained of undocumented immigrants losing their patience, letter writers complained about waiting in lines "from desk to entrance" and visits to the BMV "taking a day of their lives" (July 30, 2006). The paradox between state and national bureaucratic wait times was lost on readers. Indeed, when I spoke to White residents and tried to explain the number of years it could take a family from Mexico to enter through "proper" channels, I always encountered disbelief, and to some extent doubt, that the process could take a decade or longer and required significant financial commitments from would-be migrants.[48] Of the 24 non-Latino interviews I conducted, only two of the interviewees actually had any knowledge of the complex immigration system. None of the 113 letters referencing undocumented immigration actually expressed how difficult it could be to attain "proper papers." Instead, letter writers insinuated a supposed ease of legal entry. It was repeatedly alleged that all one needed to do was simply wait, patiently, to be granted proper entry.

In the words of one author, "they are breaking the laws of the U.S. to be here. They need to *go back home* and come back *the right way* like so many others who *wait their turn*" (July 13, 2006; emphasis added). Notably, this letter writer also asserted that "home" for undocumented immigrants was anywhere but here in the United States. What of those immigrants whose entire life was here in the United States, whose work and life consisted of dual notions of home, whose sense of familiarity was defined solely by the countries they left, but also by the places they inhabited?[49]

Instead of critically examining the process, it was easier to condemn the working-class populations that literally risked their lives to work for meager wages in the United States. Moreover, choice was individually located so that undocumented immigrants were positioned devoid of the socioeconomic political structures that made "legal" entry so incredibly difficult. The role of the United States itself in the global neoliberal policies that pushed migrants out of their own economies and pulled them into local low-wage labor was conveniently absent. Moreover, the actual employers who exploited these workers were left all but innocent in these condemnations. Though laws existed that barred the hiring of undocumented immigrants, those who violated these laws never had their worth stripped and identity solely determined by their extralegal acts. Though they too broke the law in hiring someone without proper residency, owners, managers, temporary agencies, or contractors were never themselves branded with the term "illegal." White virtue protected the employers who had somehow earned a right to exploit and simultaneously vilify brown-bodied working-class people.

Perceived in binaries of right or wrong, illegal or legal, immigrants and Latinos more broadly were not given the benefit of fluidity that White U.S. citizens practiced on a day-to-day basis during such illegalities as traffic violations, discrepancies in their tax returns, and other such outlawed behavior. The general public's blind acceptance of immigration laws as sacrosanct actually obscured the injustice implicit in these laws. As Suzanne Oboler (2006) noted, "[T]here has always existed a glaring difference between the letter and the spirit of the law—that is, the laws enacted by the state and often discussed as 'reality' by members of white and privileged sectors of our society—and the actual lived experience of people of color, including the distinctive experiences of immigrants" (2006: 9). Critical Race Theory (CRT) and Latino Critical Race Theory (LatCrit) critique the legal system and examine how legal discourse has been used to subjugate entire populations. Patricia Williams (1991) and other CRT scholars have noted how laws can be used for unjust causes. For instance, in the United States slavery and Jim Crow laws were allowed because, as Williams (1991) noted, "the law said" they were acceptable. In this circular argument, unjust actions were justified by unjust laws that excused the injustice. According to Williams, "the law becomes a shield behind which to avoid responsibility for the human repercussions of either governmental or publicly harmful private activity" (1991: 140). In 2006, immigration laws were sanctimoniously defended and Latinos assumed as always and already foreign.[50] Allegations of cultural terrorism and war metaphors were often cast against "Mexicans" as the notion of illegality developed into a racial and classed category of belonging in social space. Indeed, whether recognized or not by the architects of these policies, the anti-immigrant rhetoric of 2006 consisted of elements of what Virginia Dominguez (1998) calls "racialist talk" or underlined implications that set certain residents of the United States as racially non-White and marks their descendants as unable to assimilate into a national homogeneous collective.

The pervasive process of dehumanization implicit in words like "illegals" became ever-important in the cloaking of whiteness and anxieties over loss of social and economic supremacy.[51] Rhetorical devices were "increasingly strategic" to avoid the label of racism and instead use "the law" as a means of condemnation.[52] Arranging unsubstantiated claims as facts and using voices of victimhood and desperation, these authors created seemingly credible arguments that attempted to justify such hysteria. Performing the role of victim, these authors veiled their actual dominant role in local and national power structure. The appeal of these letters relied on unfounded fears of powerlessness and takeover. In sheer numbers, the control of Greater Lafayette rested firmly in the hands of English-dominant White Americans. The governments of both West Lafayette and Lafayette were devoid of people of color. The schools lacked faculty, staff, and administrators of color. Far from the tower of Babel, a slight growth in Lafayette's Spanish-speaking residents had virtually no impact on institutional decision making. Contrary to their message, these anti-immigrant actors exhibited much power in their ability to rhetorically alter reality and in so doing convince readers of an impending danger.

From Talk to Action

This atmosphere of animosity contributed to feelings of discomfort for Latinos who were denied a place at the proverbial table but whose services in the "kitchen" led to the economic growth and stability of Greater Lafayette. By exploring the ways in which local suspicions became written and vocalized in this particular location, this chapter tackled how belonging was imagined through limited conceptualization of community. However, there is still the question of how this vilification was acted upon throughout the multiple spaces of community. Subtle visual and verbal descriptions continued to "Other" individuals as nativist arguments penetrated the local discourse and affected the way people interacted with one another. Relating these discursive attacks illustrated how these persistent messages appeared in both print media and vocal indignation, but the true damage came in how these preconceived notions became acted upon at schools, the workplace, commercial spaces, and even places of worship. The next chapter reveals how race, ethnicity, and language informed the ways Latino bodies were patrolled in public spaces. The national debate trickled into daily confrontations between Latinos and non-Latinos. These interactions revealed how all Latino Hoosiers, regardless of immigration status, were treated as suspect.

Chapter 4 demonstrates how unfiltered resentment toward Spanish-speaking brown-bodied people manifested in 2006. Latino respondents noted that in the months following the marches and debates, they often overheard co-workers, customers, and friends making snide comments about Latinos and undocumented immigrants. Though not all non-Latinos acted this way, it appeared that those who resented a Latino presence felt it acceptable to make highly opinionated and deeply racist remarks in public spaces throughout the town. For Latinos who heard the insults and had the confidence to respond, these moments became tense and often intimidating because those expressing both subtle and overt racist statements were their bosses, co-workers, or customers who perhaps unwittingly used their powered positions to assert their opinion and seek the approval, or test the reaction, of Latinos. The continual presence of these overt acts marked non-Latinos too, as it was feared that the anti-immigrant and anti-Latino perspective was representative of non-Latino White residents. Microaggressions tied to White supremacy were so pervasive that Latinos began to fear how any White Hoosier might react negatively to their presence. Thus, this policing of who belonged to the community actually injured both Latinos and non-Latinos alike.

4

Clashes at the Crossroads

The Impact of Microaggressions and Other Otherings in Daily Life

The politics of belonging includes also struggles around the determination of what is involved in belonging, in being a member of a community, and of what roles specific social locations and specific narratives of identity play in this.
—Nina Yuval-Davis, "Belonging and the Politics of Belonging"

On any given weekend, Wal-Mart's automatic doors seemed to welcome customers of various socioeconomic and ethnic backgrounds. Latino and non-Latino residents often co-existed while searching for alluring deals that promised American capitalism in that ostentatious bright blue packaging. Indeed, residents of central Indiana exemplified Wal-Mart's ideals to provide "customers of various ethnicities and cultures access to merchandise related to their cultures."[1] Whether reaching for the *tomatillos* [small green husk-covered produce used in *salsas*] or tomatoes, Lafayette residents stocked their carts, waited in line, and traversed the expansive parking lot among one another. During interviews conducted in 2006, Wal-Mart was repeatedly identified as a space of both interaction and evasion. Latinos and non-Latinos continually referenced Wal-Mart's otherwise banal spaces as locations where they encountered one another. Often overlooked or rightfully dismissed as a site of globalization, the big-box stores that live out Sam Walton's vision of mass consumerism have become the market squares of twenty-first-century lives.[2] Like it or not, the aisles of Wal-Mart can tell us something about the shoppers who frequent and traverse these spaces daily. Indeed, during the contentious environment of the 2006 immigration debate, these locations of interaction revealed much about how belonging was enacted, embodied, and denied to particular shoppers.

Wal-Mart has carved out miles of parking space, aisles of groceries, clothes, and home décor in many American towns. Wal-Mart's arrival is not always welcomed in some upper-middle-class neighborhoods, but more often than not Wal-Mart entices droves of shoppers to seek out bargains. It was this promise of "Great Value" that attracted Latinos and non-Latinos to shop here and often provided the only means of interaction outside of the workplace or school. Wal-Mart was one of the first things Maggie, a White female of Lebanese descent, mentioned when we discussed her opinion on immigration. Notably, Maggie was a graduate student and lecturer at Purdue University. She emphasized her own Lebanese heritage and exposure to international students as a way to build up her global, more metropolitan, perspective. After some small talk about the 2006 Israeli–Lebanese conflict, I asked Maggie, "What do you know about immigrant history in Lafayette?" and she responded with "I probably notice more now because of all the publicity with illegal immigration." Maggie followed up, explaining her reservations by adding that "When you hear of crime committed in Lafayette a lot of time [the criminals] are Black or Hispanic. . . . It might be racist, but it's *more natural* to feel more threatened" (emphasis added). When I asked her whether she had ever felt intimidated by the "Hispanic" population locally, she responded with the following story:

> I was parking over by Wal-Mart and from the side of my eye I thought I caught a [*slight pause in voice and then awkwardly begins speaking again*] I was going to park and thought I saw a group of guys standing around a car that were Hispanic. So I decided to drive a little further away and park away from them. My son got mad at me and called me a racist because I felt a little threatened. . . . It turned out it was a family. . . . So I said why even confront it, why not just avoid it. . . . I take a defensive approach in living my life. It's street smarts, and maybe it wasn't the right thing to do but it *didn't hurt anybody*. They didn't see me look at them and think "I'm not going to park here." They couldn't have known. (Emphasis added)

Maggie's notion that it was "more natural" to feel threatened by men of color justified, in her mind, the maneuvering tactics she used in the parking lot to avoid this Latino family. And while she is forthright in recognizing that "maybe it wasn't the right thing to do," she still couched the action in terms of a "natural" or logical response that shield a larger critique of what it means to perceive a group of Latinos loading groceries as a threat.[3] Maggie justified her avoidance in order to distance herself from being branded a racist. But the act of consciously going out of one's way to physically avoid a racialized person's presence is not natural. Rather, this action was cultural, for it reflected a learned response steeped in racism and a history of privilege.[4]

In an atmosphere in which Latinos were continually criminalized in the media and in social conversation, the repeated association with criminal behavior affected Maggie's thoughts and actions toward this population. In Maggie's case, Latino and Black males could *never* be safe, for they were *always* feared for their supposed criminal potential. Branding these men as innately dangerous, Maggie stripped away their human qualities. In excusing her avoidance of men of color, Maggie was in fact acting on an unfounded suspicion of guilt that positioned her as innocent victim and all Latinos as potential predators.

But was Maggie truly innocent in this social exchange? Was she being "street smart," as she claimed, or was she perpetuating the racial paranoia intrinsically tied to her social order as a white female? By citing negative media attention, Maggie attempted to justify how she positioned racial Others in terms of their supposed criminal activity. However, in probing these claims further, I found interesting disparity between Maggie's conjecture and actual criminal reports. According to a local court case manager, "Tippecanoe County Court Services sees 4,000 cases annually and of those only 200 are Latinos."[5] Maggie conditioned an awareness of Latino and Black criminality over and above the actual predominance of White lawlessness. Looking to the history of heteropatriarchy and White supremacy, Andrea Smith (2006) uses the imagery of pillars to explain how racial and gender privilege is buttressed by pitting otherwise subjugated groups against one another in separate, but integrated, logics of slavery/capitalism, genocide/colonialism, and Orientalism/war. Integrated in these logics is the maintenance of heteropatriarchy and White supremacy. With regard to Maggie, it is important to recognize her own Lebanese background and the fond memories referenced earlier in the interview. For Maggie, hearing Lebanese spoken at home by her mother and grandmother could have provided empathy for Spanish-speaking families. Instead, Maggie operated under what Smith notes, borrowing on Edward

Said, as the logic of Orientalism or the marking of certain people as always and already a foreign threat. Viewed as perpetually foreign and criminal, Latino men were obvious dangers threatening to hurt her.

Here, it is critical to take issue with Maggie's notion that her avoidance did not "hurt anybody." Quite the contrary, this distancing demonstrated how immigration politics harmed and disrupted mutuality between residents. Maggie's actions in the parking lot illustrated how the politics of immigration altered daily maneuvers and created distances between residents of the same town. Unpacking the performative aspect of belonging, I look to what was *done* with the concept of belonging and how it was denied to certain gendered and phenotypically identifiable Latino residents. Embodied through stereotypical images of an Other, anti-immigration rhetoric became concretized in very real interactions between folks in this town. The negative assumptions engendered by the immigration debate resulted in an embodied rejection that was classed, racialized, and gendered in spaces throughout Greater Lafayette. Seemingly innocuous snubs, bad looks, avoidances, and verbal encounters actually translated to a felt sense of denied acceptance for many of the area's Latino residents. These felt distances were the result of what can happen when a nation, a town, or a community is inundated by a discourse of animosity toward a racialized immigrant Other. In researching the impact of a contemporary politics of immigration, I focused on how Latino and White residents interacted with each other. More specifically, I wanted to hear from Latino residents about their impressions of denied belonging. How did they interpret the way immigration politics affected their daily encounters with non-Latino residents? If Maggie assumed the Latino family "couldn't have known" about her fears and anxieties about their very presence, I wanted to talk to Latinos and see what, if anything, they did know, or rather feel, with regard to non-Latino responses to them.

The felt experiences here are critical, for they reveal the way denied belonging was enacted and interpreted in even nonverbal encounters. Spaces were controlled and policed by silent tensions, or *vibras* [vibes], that one felt in entering a space where they were unwelcome. As Consuelo noted, "Entras a un trabajo y sientes tu el rechazo" [You enter a job, and you could just feel the rejection]. Consuelo and others felt that their mere presence generated hostility from non-Latino, mostly White, residents who clearly did not want them in particular spaces. Beyond one's brown-body, speaking a language other than English also resulted in particular negative reactions. Octavio, a long-time resident of Lafayette, lamented: "uno va donde quiera, y uno habla Español y luego luego le dan la mirada . . . pues uno lo siente luego luego. Se siente en las vibras que no les parece bien" [It doesn't matter where you go. If you speak Spanish, right away someone gives you a bad look . . . you feel it right away. You feel those vibes that they don't like it]. Both Consuelo and Octavio had lived and worked in Lafayette for more than two decades. Still, even though they always sensed some apprehension from non-Latino residents about their presence, they both expressed how the contemporary immigration debate turned otherwise curious stares into outright rejection and disdain.

The *rechazo* [rejection] and *vibras* felt by Consuelo and Octavio were by no means isolated. Latino respondents consistently revealed moments of denied belonging manifested in sneers, vocal assaults, or body movements that signaled discomfort toward a local Latino presence. Racialized and gendered scripts commingled with dominant narratives of immigrant illegality to frame how Latino residents were read in particular spaces. Regardless of century-old Latino neighborhoods or a long history of Black settlement, Indiana, like much of the Midwest, continued to be imagined through a White majority. This imaginary played out in the responses to an increased in Latino presence in otherwise nontraditionally Latino destinations. Residents of places like Greater Lafayette did not need a census to reveal what they already knew to be true: Demographic shifts were changing the face of the Midwest. No longer a temporary presence associated with the migrant labor stream in the rural surroundings, Latino families increasingly settled in Greater Lafayette. Beginning as service workers in a local hotel and then moving into the industrial sector of town, the Latino population rapidly grew in the 1990s. Mexican restaurants, grocery stores, and Spanish religious services provided some of the first signs of this growth. Though there were early signs of ignorance and inquisitive stares, it took the 2006 national debate on immigration to inspire a sustained and seemingly collective sense of uneasiness toward Latino residents. Rather than outright physical attacks such as those reported in other parts of the country, respondents revealed examples of microaggressions that when woven together affirmed an environment of distrust and distance.[6] This chapter looks at the sometimes subtle, sometimes overt moments of hostility between Latino and non-Latino residents of Lafayette.

Far from inconsequential, the avoidances and snubs may look different from obvious familiar expressions of racism, but their wounds continue to inflict pain on communities. The civil rights movement (1950s–1970s) publicly exposed the injustices of racial discrimination, segregation, and second-class citizenship, but indirect forms of *rechazo*, or microaggressions in the form of rejection/avoidance, endured into the twenty-first century. Indeed, as psychiatrist Chester M. Pierce noted in 1974, ". . . one must not look for the gross and obvious. The subtle, cumulative miniassault is the substance of today's racism" (Pierce 1974: 516). Critical engagement with race recognizes that white supremacy did not evaporate after the civil rights era. It simply evolved into subtler and perhaps unconscious acts that still communicated superiority over people of color. These microaggressions, or what Peggy Davis called the "stunning, automatic acts of disregard that stem from unconscious attitudes of white superiority and constitute a verification of black inferiority," can manifest themselves against other disenfranchised groups though an equally intense positioning of power (1989: 1576). Whether conscious or unconscious, overt or subtle, the preservation of hierarchies through raced, gendered, and classed demarcations metastasized over time into deeply harmful microaggressions. Perpetrators like Maggie might imagine these acts as minor, "natural" responses toward differences, but these behaviors conveyed so much more than simple avoidance or safety precautions. Instead, the scholarship on microaggressions illustrates how detrimental these moments can be for people of color when they absorb these encounters as a general deprecation of their worth (Perez Hubner et al. 2008, Solorzano et al. 2003, Sue et al. 2007).

It is important to note that not all microaggressions are the same. It is critical to understand the different forms they can take in order to explore their place in the quotidian struggles that people of color endure. Derald Wing Sue and colleagues identified three major types of mcroaggressions that contribute to an overall denigrating system for people of color. They are as follows:

Microassault: verbal or nonverbal attack meant to hurt the intended victim through name calling, avoidant behavior, or purposeful discriminatory actions.

Microinsult: communications that convey rudeness and insensitivity and
   demean a person's racial heritage or identity.
Microinvalidation: communications that exclude, negate, or nullify the psychological thoughts, feelings, or experiential reality of a person of color.
   (2007: 273–74).

Whether consciously or unconsciously, various forms of microaggressions came up repeatedly in participant narratives. Especially during the 2006 national debate on immigration, interactions in ordinary
spaces like Wal-Mart became saturated with race and power. Microas-
saults, microinsults, and microinvalidations worked simultaneously to
diminish the experience of Latinos in Greater Lafayette.

Microaggressions explain how multiple registers of antagonism can
transform otherwise mundane moments. In other words, socially unacceptable examples of outright racism have been replaced by seemingly
banal acts that still communicate a level of discomfort and prejudice
present just beneath the surface. Interview responses and observations
made in 2006 indicated the role places like Wal-Mart played as the setting for microaggressions. Initially, I was made aware of Wal-Mart's role
in the research through the experience of Brandon, a doctoral student
at Purdue University. Brandon was giving a talk to a room of undergraduates at the university on the subtle yet pervasive role of racism. To
illustrate his points about the way local Black residents felt dismissed,
dehumanized, and distanced because of the color of their skin, Brandon
referenced Wal-Mart and the multiple times he entered the store's automatic gates only to be consistently reminded that race still indeed mattered. Brandon mentioned moments of microaggressions at the checkout
counter when cashiers consistently refused to hand him his change and
instead always opted to place his money on the counter. The subtle yet
persistent avoidance of a cashier's touch when placing his change on the
counter rather than in his hand marked the moments of disdain that he
felt daily throughout Lafayette. This avoidance of touch spoke to how
race marked individuals and influenced evasive tactics based on race.
Thus, in Brandon's case, the seemingly banal moments of avoidance like
those employed by folks like Maggie did not go unnoticed. Instead, these
moments suggested to racialized residents that their mere presences
still provoked discomfort. Though sometimes subtle, this White anxiety

over the presence of racial Others was equally troubling to Pastor David Walker, the president of Lafayette's NAACP chapter. When asked how he would describe race relations in the area, Pastor Walker responded: "Well, let's see, how could I put it. The best I could describe is, well down south in Mississippi you knew folk didn't like you. They let you know they didn't like you, but you knew you had to work together to survive: 'I don't like you, but I need you.' In the North, here in Lafayette, it's not like that. People smile in your face, they're your friend, they're going to help you, but they'll cut your throat at the same time." Both Pastor Walker and Brandon related how they, as Black men, interpret their social location in Lafayette. Local microaggressions grounded in very real feelings of denied belonging were not limited to Black bodies. Indeed, Latino residents revealed subtle and overt moments wherein they too felt racially positioned as outsiders and threats to Lafayette. Seemingly mundane moments of intolerance weighed down Latinos, but one microaggression seemed to fuel another as snide commentary and adverse reactions to Latinos became commonplace in 2006. Though there were White and Black Hoosiers willing to speak out against the negative atmosphere taking hold, consistent daily injuries at the hands of those comfortable with dismissing Latino residents stung deeply. Denying Latinos an equal footing in the community left scars that were difficult to heal.

Looking to daily otherwise ordinary events revealed a deeper understanding of what it was like to live in this small city during the immigration debate. I continued to inquire about how and when people interacted with one another to try to understand how these interactions revealed the complexity of a community undergoing demographic transition. Unlike in other Latino settlement locations, the residential pattern of Greater Lafayette's Spanish-speaking population was more widely distributed throughout the town. Residential concentrations were primarily determined by income and social capital. Those affiliated with Purdue University as faculty, students, or office staff primarily lived on the west side, closer to campus. Additionally, the south side had experienced a substantial growth in new housing developments that attracted a growing middle class. The north side of town held the older residential, industrial, and commercial centers; renting to lower-wage workers was commonplace in this area. Ultimately, this meant that the majority of Greater Lafayette Latinos were not concentrated in one area of town. Certainly there were pockets—mobile home parks or apartment complexes—that housed more working-class Latino families. Still, according to personal observations confirmed by three area Realtors, the majority of Latino families branched out to various neighborhoods and even to rural properties in their search for homes. This meant that there were opportunities throughout the day for possible interactions with non-Latinos that could reveal what those daily encounters meant for building camaraderie or community in the area.

Locating the space of interaction was important to understanding how this diverse community came together or segregated themselves from one another. In order to see whether people were aware of one another's presence, and if, where, when, and how interaction took shape meant asking people directly for moments where they might run into one another. Because I went into the research project with a focus on immigration, I began asking about history. I wanted to gauge how much locals knew about early European immigrants in this area. I also knew of contemporary non-Latino immigrants in the area affiliated with Purdue University or major businesses (German engineers affiliated with the Caterpillar plant or Japanese upper management with Subaru) and was curious if participants would reference these immigrants.[7] In the early questioning I asked about immigrants in general and avoided making references to Latinos in particular. I asked and paused for answers between each question:

What do you know about immigrant history in Lafayette?
In what neighborhood, businesses, or areas of town would you say one can
    encounter or notice immigrant populations?
Where do they live, work, or shop?

I was attempting to build up to specific questions about Latinos, but it was obvious that the political climate influenced how individuals interpreted "immigrant" to mean always and already Latino. Much like Maggie earlier, more than 60 percent of the non-Latinos interviewed made the immediate leap from the term "immigrant" to the "Hispanic" population by the first question. The others were unaware of history and did not know. When the contemporary questions came up, only one non-Latino participant, an employee of Caterpillar, even referenced local non-Latino immigrants. The automatic association with the words "immigrant" and the presence of Latinos was not completely surprising given the national and local media attention that often made the connection for them. I asked Latinos a different yet related set of questions to elicit their possible encounters with non-Latinos:

¿En una semana típica, que es su rutina? [In a typical week, what is your routine?]

¿Donde trabaja, donde compra la comida de la semana, donde a comprar ropa/zapatos, donde va para divertirse? [Where do you work, purchase groceries, buy clothes, shoes? Where do you go for entertainment?]

After listening to their varied responses, I would follow up by asking Latinos if they ever interacted with or encountered non-Latinos in these spaces. Latinos were also asked to discuss their knowledge of immigrant history. Interestingly, Latinos consistently interpreted the history question by acknowledging their ignorance of European immigrants in the past. They often did not know or could not say what immigrants were in the area before them. Notably, unlike non-Latino participants, Latinos were more willing to claim unawareness of the past than automatically tie the word "immigrant" to Latinos. Additionally, Latinos had much more to say about their interactions with non-Latinos and communicated multiple moments of tension, or "small acts," that revealed how the national and local immigration politics altered social space during 2006. This chapter maps these various accounts to understand how Latinos themselves perceived their locality and interactions with non-Latinos during a time when the nation itself was contemplating immigration and Latino belonging. As did the rest of the country, Lafayette found itself at the crossroads of defining community during the 2006 national immigration debate. The following narratives reveal where those crossroads converged and how people dealt with one another when existing in the same locations.

(Re)claimed Belonging at Wal-Mart

Both Latinos and non-Latinos were asked to reflect on their daily routines. Once more, Wal-Mart played a dominant role as a space of interaction in their responses: 70 percent of all respondents mentioned frequenting this space on weekly grocery trips. Thus, Wal-Mart provided a space where people from different social, cultural, classed, and racial backgrounds inhabited the same location. Yet, far from a panacea of American capitalism where consumers amiably converged and differences dissipated, references to Wal-Mart were anything but cordial. As Brandon and Maggie illustrated earlier, the social space of Wal-Mart was layered with multiple registers of belonging related to race, gender, language, and ethnicity. Indeed, Wal-Mart became a space worth protecting for those whose images of community did not include Latino Spanish speakers. The following letter to the editor appeared in the local newspaper a week after the 2006 May Day economic boycott during which Latinos across the country attempted to avoid work and commerce to demonstrate their contributions to the larger U.S. economy. Rather than reflect on the financial impact of Latino expulsion, the letter writer celebrated the absence with the following statement:

> I was surprised to see that life in America was *normal* last Monday when Mexicans decided to "strike." It was refreshing to be able to go to Wal-Mart and not have to hear utterances of the Mexican language [*sic*]. . . . The key word here is illegal. Illegal Mexicans seem to think that they can *scoff at the laws* that govern this country, they wave their flags in America's face, make a mockery of the national anthem, refuse to speak the spoken language and have the nerve to actually demonstrate. Homeland Security and the U.S. Citizenship and Immigration Services should have been at these marches and deported everyone there who did not have legal papers to be here. Companies that hire and support these illegal immigrants should be prosecuted. Far as I am concerned, last Monday's actions was nothing but a disgrace. (May 08, 2006; emphasis added)

According to this letter, "the Mexican language," or Spanish, had no place in Lafayette and certainly should not sully one's shopping experience at Wal-Mart. Moreover, demonstrations showcasing "illegal Mexicans" en masse asserting their rights to belong were akin to terrorists and, according to this resident, did not deserve to be in *his* country, *his* city, or *his* Wal-Mart. Months later, in November, the author of "Why should I learn Spanish to shop?" wrote a letter describing his anger when finding a toy in Wal-Mart's aisles that uttered Spanish words (November 26, 2006). After speaking to the manager and being told that Wal-Mart was simply responding to its customers, this author became enraged at the official marketing policies meant to attract Spanish speakers: "I live in America. Why should I have to learn a foreign language to shop in the great state of Indiana? One question for the store: Who was the clientele that made you who you are today? Answer: The English-speaking American (black, white, red, green and purple)." The answer to the question posed by this letter is much more complicated than the writer suggested. First, Wal-Mart's profit margins are not solely dependent on monolingual English-speaking Americans. Indeed, Wal-Mart's corporate goals expand the store and its merchandise to various customers. Moreover, the writer of this letter presumes that Spanish speakers, or those willing to purchase Spanish-speaking toys, are not truly authentically American. It was this revulsion toward Spanish speakers that spoke to larger fears of Latino infiltration.

Carmela, a U.S.-born self-identified Chicana fluent in both English and Spanish, was all too aware of how spaces like Wal-Mart could be policed against people who looked, or spoke, like her.[8] Conscious of the benefits of being bilingual, Carmela and her husband, also Mexican-American, did all they could to maintain Spanish in their household. The family went to Spanish church services and the children were often spoken to in Spanish to familiarize them with the sounds and use of the language. When I interviewed Carmela in 2006, she spoke of a recent trip to Wal-Mart that disturbed her. Apparently, Carmela was corralling her children, as mothers often do, and asked them in Spanish to help her retrieve certain items from the shelves. In one of the aisles Carmela heard two women comment to each other in a judgmental tone: "Look at these Mexicans with all these kids." The women, unaware that Carmela could understand everything they were saying, felt comfortable voicing this highly racialized and gendered critique that framed this Latino mother as hyperfertile and irresponsible.[9] Like Maggie's physical avoidance in the parking lot, the insult directed at Carmela was made at a perceived distance. The women assumed that neither Carmela nor her children spoke English and therefore they "couldn't have known" about the insulting comment.[10] Carmela, however, did speak English and being devoutly religious was grateful for the four blessings her children represented. Proud and confident, Carmela turned to face these women and in perfect English firmly said, "Yeah, we have a large family, don't we!"

By defending her family, Carmela hoped to startle and educate these women about their own false assumptions and unfair accusations. After relating this story, Carmela lamented the behavior of these women and the possibility that other Latinos in the area did not have the language skills or confidence to confront such slurs. She wondered how many other times Spanish-speaking families felt this kind of resentment at places like Wal-Mart where money, not racial/ethnic markers, was supposed to be the preferred marker of exchange. Indeed, this argument was often made by other Mexican families who referenced their economic contributions and the fact that, as one respondent put it, "when you see Mexicanos shopping we always have full carts with meat and other expensive items. Our being here sustains the economy." Still, it was evident to Carmela that financial contributions did not dissuade intolerant notions that she and her children were drains on society.

In the case of Wal-Mart, it was ironic that those shopping in its monolithic, transglobal arenas were in fact claiming local ownership and protecting this global company from encroaching outsiders. Indeed, those who would support the building of real and metaphorical walls to keep people out of the United States were directly adding to the market shares of companies that made an art of manipulating international laws and boundaries to fit their own capitalistic dreams. Wal-Mart functioned as a damaging force on the local economy, undercutting and overselling local small businesses, but it was fascinating to see how the concept of the local was itself being redefined within these big-box spaces. Critically, this protectionist approach often had nothing to do with global markets and everything to do with global bodies. Far from a postmodern globalized collapse of the "local," what some have termed "deterritorialized" or "placelessness," the presence of Mexican residents in Lafayette proved that "space [was] socially constructed, and contested, in practice" (Rodman 1992: 647). The threat of globalization and migratory peoples seemed to create a marked increase in protecting the local from the global.

The research recognized how space encompassed more than merely the backdrop of cultural reality.[11] Space may describe the physical set-

ting in which life in this community is located, but space is not simply the banal environment in which people live. Beyond this notion
of physical geography, space should also be recognized for its value as
"place" or when spatial elements are infused with meaning. For an analysis of immigration, place becomes meaningful in the way belonging
and protection rely on human socio-spatial ties. Conceptualizing the
"place" meaning provided a point of departure from which to analyze
the lived reality, physical boundaries, and appropriated environment
created by this moment in immigrant anxiety. According to Irwin Altman and Setha Low, "place refers to space that has been given meaning through personal, group, or cultural processes" (1992: 5). Moreover,
Margaret C. Rodman noted that "places bespeak people's practices, their
history, their conflicts, their accomplishments" (1992: 649). For instance,
the actual geopolitical border space between Mexico in the United
States *means* something to people on both sides of the divide. Though
the Mexico/United States border is nothing more than an arbitrary line
separating communities whose connectedness goes back centuries, the
resulting borderlands elicit considerable power as meaningful places of
separation. Thus, the borderlands are places of very real jurisdictions
that unfortunately determine life-and-death scenarios for those willing to challenge the boundaries. Moreover, in the politics of immigration this arbitrary line has tangible implications in the minds of those
guarding or protecting the border from supposed interlopers. Thus, I
posit a difference between "the border" as a particular geopolitical line
of national difference and the resulting borderlands as the places where
conceptualizations attributed to the border influence the way people live
and interact with one another. In this regard, the borderlands could and
do expand beyond the space directly adjacent to a national border.

This very real and very dangerous concept of the border then becomes actualized in places that maintain bordering environments even
thousands of miles away from national geopolitical demarcations. As
Nicholas De Genova explains, "The policing of public areas . . . serves to
discipline Mexican/migrant workers by surveilling their 'illegality,' and
exacerbating their ever-present sense of vulnerability" (2006: 81). Thus,
individuals map notions of belonging, community, and citizenship according to the way national borders are conceived. A struggle to control
the meaning of belonging in space led to contested places for Latinos

who, regardless of immigration status, felt vulnerable to the spoken and felt distances throughout Greater Lafayette. Mirroring actual encounters at physical border zones where state powers police who is imagined as belonging, local borderland mindsets dictated the way Latinos could be perceived.[12] Emerging mental borders in the corn belt of the Midwest broaden the reach of border theory to the interior United States.[13]

In Lafayette, the prevalence of spoken and written anti-immigrant narratives framed suspicion against Latino residents. This in turn led to fears and anxieties by Latino themselves, who associated some places with possible personal threats. In particular, undocumented residents navigated Lafayette with caution and fear. Guille, a Venezuelan community advocate in the school district, mentioned various occasions when undocumented immigrants were harassed and added, "Alguien me dijo [Someone told me] that Wal-Mart was empty on Sunday. And at Aldis [a grocery store], she said there was no one. They're [undocumented immigrants] very afraid of going out now. They're worried." Indeed, while undocumented immigrants continually live under a fear of deportation, the environment of heightened national and local vigilance during the 2006 immigration debate led to more immediate anguish every time someone stepped out of his or her home. As one established resident mentioned, "la gente tiene miedo . . . había un tiempo donde no quisieron ni salir" [the people are scared . . . there was a time when no one wanted even to leave their home]. Latinos, regardless of citizenship status, expressed concerns that the national debate created an ominous environment in Lafayette. The fear of deportation left many households paralyzed. Reports of large-scale Immigration and Customs Enforcement (ICE) raids in places like Iowa were common in Spanish-language newspapers and satellite news broadcasts. These reports scared local residents who felt terrified that their families could be torn apart from one day to another. Guille's exposure as a community advocate gave her contact with parents who feared grocery stores as well as school buildings. Guille recalled home visits to inquire about attendance when,

· They came to my car and approached me with 'Ay señora, es que muchos no quieren ir ni asta el Wal-Mart. Por que a oído que allí los están agarrando . . . Y el chisme por allí es que si nos agarran a los niños los van a meter todos a un orfanato.

Oh ma'am, it is just that many don't want to go even to Wal-Mart. I've heard that they have taken people from there. . . . The talk around town is also that if they take us, they will put our children in orphanages.

Though Guille attempted to diffuse the hysteria, she admitted that regardless of her explanations, many parents still feared sending their children even to school.

The immigration debates created a heightened sense of discomfort and anxiety for all Latinos, who felt targeted and unwelcome in particular public spaces. For example, though in Lafayette for only six months at the time of our interview, Mago and her family had already experienced a fair share of negative encounters with the White community. Mago's husband, Pepe, was a citizen of the United States, and so were their two eldest daughters. Still, as in many mixed-status families, Mago and her two youngest were undocumented. During the late 1980s, the recession in California caused Mago and her two daughters to return to Mexico while Pepe searched for better employment in the United States. Though he lived primarily in California in the 1990s, Pepe joined his sister in Lafayette in 2003 and secured a full-time job. By 2006, the family reunited in central Indiana and lived in a small two-bedroom house while they searched for a larger home. Knowing very little English and still trying to acquaint herself with living in Lafayette, Mago and the children walked to the grocery store or to run small errands. It was during these strolls to the store that Mago encountered some disturbing reactions. When I asked Mago if she recalled moments or places in Lafayette where she might have felt uncomfortable, she noted, "Sí, en la calle cuando caminamos de aquí a la Target nos encontramos Americanos, ay unos que nos saludan y nos sonríen y ay otros que nos hacen gestos y no nos pueden ni ver" [Yes, on the street. When we walk to Target, we run into [White] Americans, and there are some who wave to us and smile at us and then there are those that make faces and can't even turn to look at us]. Like Brandon at Wal-Mart, the evasion of touch or gaze did not go unnoticed by those who felt belittled by these microaggressions. Mago perceived this aversion as rude and an intentional denial of human consideration. Similar to the "spirit murder" Patricia Williams (1991) speaks of, the avoidance to recognize someone's presence was read by

Mago as an act of dismissing her right to be seen as an equal or even her right to exist at all. Indeed, looking to the role of microaggressions in perceived racial discrimination, Robert M. Sellers and J. Nicole Shelton's research found that instead of overt attacks, "The most frequently reported racial hassles seem to involve strangers who did not have much contact with our participants (e.g., being ignored, overlooked, not given service; treated rudely or disrespectfully; others reacting to you as if they were afraid or intimidated)" (2003: 1087). Aware of their extralegal presence in society, undocumented immigrants were very keen at picking up on the way people responded to them. Constant fear created a heightened awareness of one's surroundings. Survival in towns where Latino residents were either "new" or not a numerical majority required that they have a double consciousness: always aware of how they see themselves and how others see them.[14] Indeed, Mago continued by expressing other moments of *rechazo*, or rejection, that occurred once inside commercial centers: "En las tiendas cuando va uno. Incluso en la mal, en L. S. Ayers, allí las cajeras como te ven raro o ni buenas tardes, ni gracias, ni nada. Y cuando voy a mi medicina se quedan mirando" [In the stores, in fact in L. S. Ayers [now Macy's] the cashiers give you a look and they don't say good afternoon, nor thank you, or anything. And when I go pick up my medicines, people just stare]. This kind of display of bad customer service was mentioned by other residents. Yumey, a college-educated U.S.-born Mexican American female, recalled being rudely told an item was "too expensive" by a sales clerk who presumed a particular price range based on ethnicity. Her mother, Chela, referenced this identical moment during a separate interview. Chela recalled feeling uncomfortable by the sales clerk's presumption that her family could not afford a particular item at the store. Moreover, Chela's youngest daughter, a teenager at the time of the interview, interrupted her mother to tell me how this exchange reminded her of the scene in *Pretty Woman* (1990) in which Julia Roberts was denied service at an upscale store. For a young girl to note the parallels between her mother and a fictional prostitute based not on dress but on the way her body was racialized was disturbing on a multitude of levels. Chela and her daughters were all U.S. citizens and felt anger toward, but not fear of, this clerk. These exchanges were particularly troubling for undocumented residents who navigated Lafayette with trepidation. For Mago, the contempt transmitted in stares or evasive behavior kept her in constant fear and discomfort. She was already apprehensive about her immigration status and felt even further shunned by the subtle negativity present in the public spaces of Lafayette.

Embodied Differences and Gendered Interpretations

Confrontations on the street, in commercial centers, or at work sometimes manifested into gender-specific microaggressions that revealed how Mexican men and women experienced their lives in central Indiana differently. Female encounters with prejudice were encapsulated by the contemporary moment and rhetoric against immigration. They voiced concerns regarding the national debate and how it had fueled a kind of outward hostility not theretofore experienced. Men, on the other hand, understood the contemporary moment through comparable experiences. As illustrated by Maggie's aversion at Wal-Mart, Latino men encompassed a particularly gendered, racialized, and classed position in national anxieties about immigration. Notably, both men and women faced their own battles with racial and gendered antipathy, but men were the "primary targets" of discrimination. According to Jim Sidanius and Rosemary C. Veniegas (2000), "whereas discrimination against both dominant and subordinate women is not primarily driven by the desire to harm, destroy or debilitate, arbitrary-set (i.e., male-on-male) discrimination has a distinctly more ferocious edge" (63). In other words, men often faced the brunt of hate-based attacks in ways different from women. Traditionally associated as those all too willing to "take our jobs" and feared as innately violent or criminal, Latino males often become read through a prism of threatening behavior that drew non-Latino responses with a "more ferocious edge."

Like other men of color, Latino men have experienced a particular racialized process that includes punitive control, subordination, and emasculation.[15] As a result, Latino men, and immigrant Latino men in particular, described a social environment that was always hazardous for them. That is, far from the threatening figures imagined by Maggie or even Jane in the previous chapter, Latino men revealed that they felt consistently physically and verbally harassed throughout their existence in the town. From the 1960s well into the 2000s, Latino men lamented their being exposed to attacks from non-Latino, mostly White, Hoosiers who consistently racialized them as an undesirable presence. Indeed, Latino men contended that the current instances of racism were more subtle and less overtly mean-spirited and were not as prevalent as they once had been. The consensus among most Latino men interviewed for the research was that there had been an optimistic change for the better. Of the twenty-two total Latino males interviewed, sixteen noted that they had faced some form of racism in Lafayette. Out of these sixteen men, twelve also noted an improvement from the more outward manifestations of racism they'd experienced. When I asked Luciano, an entrepreneur who'd recently left a manufacturing job to open his own grocery store, why he felt racism was decreasing around town, he explained that racism was not absent; it was just less outwardly displayed. As he explained, "At work people are more afraid of getting fired if they call you something like that, but on the street you're more of a target." Therefore, fear of being called racist and the disciplinary consequences of using that label in the workplace or in society may have curtailed some manifestations of intolerance. Still, there were other public spaces where one could be targeted for his or her very presence as a brown-bodied individual in a White-majority town.

Even if bigoted behavior continued to exist throughout Lafayette, many men voiced an appreciation for an increasingly better environment than was there upon their arrival. This was particularly important for men who had sons and feared that their U.S.-born or -raised male heirs would inherit this racialized experience. Though there was concern for their daughters, it was in experiencing the United States as a man that gave them personal exposure for what it could be like for their sons. Adolfo originally lived in Lafayette during the mid-1970s, but the size of the town and the negative reaction of the townspeople encouraged him and his wife to seek a better experience in California. Years later, the recession of the 1990s devastated California's economy. The loss of employment availability enticed Adolfo and his family to return to central Indiana in search of more stable employment opportunities. With a social network still in the area, he and his family returned in 1994 and noticed how much the town had changed in just those two decades. According to Adolfo: "Por primera vez cuando vine aquí, la gente se le quedaba uno como mirando como algo raro que nunca habían visto.

Lo miraban a uno de arriba y bajo. Se les asía raro. Ahora no, ya que ay mas gente" [When I came here for the first time, the people would stare at you, as if you were something weird that they had never seen. They would look you up and down. It was rare for them then, but not now, now that there are more [Latino] people]. Adolfo and others believed that the marked increase in Latinos to the area altered the way towns-people treated the growing Spanish-speaking community. Adolfo still hesitated to call Lafayette home, but he realized that twenty years later he felt safer walking around town. At the time of our interview, his eldest son was on his way to receiving a master's degree and his other two sons had not, to his knowledge, encountered any negativity in the area for being Latino. Thus, Adolfo concluded that Lafayette had grown into a good place where his sons would be accepted and could prosper.

Prior to the employment boom of the mid-1990s, manufacturing and industry positions were limited to men in Lafayette. Thus, traditional gender roles were followed as men ventured out to find employment in the industrial sector of town while women raised children and main-tained the home. A rise in demand for employees in the late 1990s meant that women were encouraged to apply for and began work alongside the men in multiple assembly lines and shifts in the area. The growth of women in the workforce leading up to the national immigration debate in the early 2000s correlates with their reports of increased exposure to negative attitudes; prior to the previous decade women often had little interactions around town. Upon first arriving, women felt confined to a limited number of spaces in Lafayette that left many depressed and iso-lated. Men, on the other hand, had long traversed the streets and work-places of the area only to encounter outwardly negative reactions. Like Adolfo, Eudoxio recognized a marked improvement in the way non-Latino locals responded to a Latino presence:

> EUDOXIO: Ahorita, yo creo que ya están acostumbrados a vernos tantos aquí. Pero antes, cuando yo llegue, seguido le decían a uno cosas. Cómo 'para que se vinieron para ca', 'que se regresen a donde vinieron. [Now, I think that they are becoming accustomed to see-ing so many of us here. But before, when I arrived, we were always harassed. Things like "Why did you come" and "Go back to where you came from."]

SUJEY: Y ahora ya no tanto, ya no lo siente igual? [And now not so
much, you don't feel the [racism] as much?]

EUDOXIO: No, ya no tanto. Yo creo que por eso ya se están haciendo la
idea que aquí estamos, que vamos a venir mas, y no nos vamos a ir.
Pero si ay muchos lugares aquí donde ay mucho racismo. Si usted va
y se arrima allí, les van a decir cosas. [No, not so much anymore. I
think it is because they [have] begun to realize that we are here, there
will be more of us and we are not going anywhere. But there still
are a lot of places where one can find racism. Places where if you go
there you will be harassed.]

SUJEY: Como que lugares dirá, por donde, o que sitios? [Like what
places, whereabouts, in what areas?]

EUDOXIO: Lugares como bares y luego también en una licorería también tuve unas experiencias de esas. En la calle un par de veces le
han dicho a uno cosas. Pero eso era antes . . . . Avía muchos bares en
particular, donde allí frecuentaban mucho lo que les dicen aquí los
rednecks . . . Como que viven mas en las rodillas, como aislados. Y
como aquí era mas o menos así antes, todavía queda gente. [Places
like bars or in a liquor store where I also had encountered that kind
of reception. Sometimes on the street they would say something. But
that was then. . . . There were a lot of bars where what they refer to
as the rednecks would frequent. They live on the outskirts of town,
isolated. And since that is what it was like here before, well you still
have some of those people.]

Eudoxio spoke critically of these outward manifestations of bigotry. He
believed that a general lack of exposure to Latinos fueled ignorance that
agitated those identified as "rednecks." Furthermore, Eudoxio believed
that the racial climate in the area was shifting toward further understanding. Similar to Adolfo's observations, Eudoxio held out hope that
the sheer numbers of Latinos in the area would help create awareness
that favored their acceptance in the community.

Though men never directly positioned these experiences as strictly
male-gendered racialized attacks, it was only men who referenced these
earlier confrontations and only men who felt that the social environment was improving. For these men, interactions were better inasmuch
as they were no longer insulted, literally spat upon, or physically as-

saulted on a routine basis. However, just as the economic and Latino makeup of the town was progressing, a national debate on immigration was on the horizon.

Even as employment opportunities increased and widened to include Latinas, Spanish-speaking residents were still commonly employed in less desirable positions and shifts, leaving them at a disadvantage in the hierarchy of labor. For example, a local ice cream manufacturer held an unstated rule that Latinos would be employed in the "boiler" section of the plant because, as Sergio noted, "They thought Mexicans could handle the heat better." An employee at an automotive manufacturing plant explained that his shift boss often placed Latinos on the third shift, because it was assumed that non-Latinos would not be willing to volunteer for those hours. Thus, Latinos literally entered the workforce on a lower hierarchal status than non-Latinos.

This deprecation of a Latino workforce would come into play during the 2006 immigration debate as once more non-Latino employees felt free to dismiss and verbally insult their Latino co-workers. As Luciano explained earlier, outright racist behavior would not be tolerated in the twenty-first century. Thus, openly race-based vilification was not as common as it once was. Now, in the twenty-first century, complaints of language use or lack of cultural assimilation veiled the antipathy held toward Latino co-workers. Samuel began working in Lafayette washing cars at a car dealership. He enjoyed the steady employment and appreciated that even without English skills he could still showcase his initiative. Samuel recognized that this was not a glamorous job, but he did it well and continually impressed his boss. Still, he remembered co-workers' ridiculing him: "Cuando yo llegue a trabajar todos, todos me miraban bien feo. Empecé hablarles lo poquito que sabia. Y los que no me querían los iban despidiendo" [When I first got the job, everyone, I mean everyone, gave me a sneer. I spoke to them with what little [English] I could. And the ones that didn't like me were eventually fired]. I asked him to elaborate on those who would tease him and why they were fired. Samuel, being a devoutly religious man, felt he had an angel watching over him because his boss, a White male, would not tolerate the racism of his co-workers, especially if they did not do their job as well as Samuel did his. Appreciative for his boss's acceptance, Samuel understood rather quickly that language was a way to win over his co-workers or at least strip them of the power they held over him. For others, the inequity continued no matter what one did or how hard one worked. Exequiel, an undocumented worker, was conscious of the disproportionate amount of work he endured because of his status: "Para quedar bien hacemos mas. Para que no nos llamen flojos hacemos mas para el manager, pero el Americano le levanta el dedo y le dice una grosería como 'do it yourself'" [To make a good impression, we do more. So they won't call us lazy, we do more work for the manager while the American sticks up his middle finger and says "do it yourself"]. Exequiel's wife, Adela, was in the room during our interview. It was Adela who had to explain that the *dedo* Exequiel was referencing was the middle finger. She worked in the same factory, but on a different shift. Though Exequiel was a church-going man, someone whom all their friends went to for advice, and had recently saved enough money to purchase a home, it was this exchange at work that created a visual twitch in Adela's face. Exhibiting something between a grimace of disgust and an expression of embarrassment, Adela seemed to know all too well the disrespect her husband faced on a daily basis at work. Exequiel further explained that his co-workers did not have to fear the loss of their lives and livelihoods if they were caught being rude. He, on the other hand, had to work that much harder in order not to receive negative attention. Adela interrupted by noting her own experiences that embodied this imbalance: "A veces necesita ir uno al baño 20 minutos antes del break pero sigues trabajando aunque otros Americanos van" [Sometimes you have to go to the bathroom twenty minutes before break, but you keep working while the Americans just go]. The implicit privilege of their co-workers weighed on Exequiel and Adela as they expressed how their bodies literally bore the marks of exhaustion as a result of their willingness to exert themselves in the name of making a good impression. Their non-Latino co-workers, on the other hand, could risk being rude and insubordinate without blinking an eye.

The workplace became a space rife with tensions as Latino employees felt dismissed, verbally insulted, or exploited by non-Latino co-workers. Octavio was a citizen and had a seamless command of both English and Spanish. Still, he too related stories of frictions he encountered with non-Latino co-workers. Notably, Octavio did not have the same fears as Exequiel or Adela, but he was aware of how his body, or rather his actions, was read by other employees. At work Octavio spoke Spanish with his Mexican friends and relatives, but when an English-dominant co-worker came around, "si procuramos de no hacerlos sentir mal y empezamos a hablar en ingles para que sepan de lo que se trata" [We sincerely attempt not to make them feel bad, and we begin to speak English so that they know what is going on]. Even though Octavio made an effort at bilingual switching at work, he noted that he still felt slighted by people he worked alongside for years. Brought to Lafayette as a young child in the 1960s, Octavio worked hard to "live *sin fronteras*" (Anzaldúa 1987: 195). Attempts to be the crossroads between Latinos and non-Latinos meant that he frequently code-switched and was cognizant of how co-workers interpreted the use of Spanish as a means of self-segregation. Octavio worked to dissuade non-Latinos of this anxiety. When someone was willing to listen, he would explain how Spanish was a "go to" language because it is what some Latinos were most comfortable speaking. It was their first language, and they could communicate better in their native tongue. In other words, Octavio tried to decenter non-Latino co-workers so they would realize that the lives of Latinos did not revolve around insulting or leaving *Americanos* out of the conversation. Still, he lamented that regardless of the language one spoke, some direct and indirect resentment bubbled to the surface as a result of the immigration debate.

Leading up to and following the May Day labor boycott, Octavio recognized a rise in the level of hostility surrounding immigration. Non-Latino co-workers criticized the actions of the boycott and "Luego luego empezaron con por que no te vas a México" [Right away they began with "Why don't you return to Mexico"]. Never mind that Octavio had attended elementary school, junior high, and high school in the area; his legitimacy as a local member of community was immediately called into question. Earlier in the year, Octavio overheard a White worker complain that a Mexican worker was given vacation time and joked that the former was probably an "illegal" and was sent out of the country. Octavio was frustrated with this exchange and noted "va seguir así, mientras que existe la problema van a seguir punteando el dedo" [it will continue like that. While the problem exists, they will continue pointing the finger]. The problem, according to Octavio, was not the presence of undocumented immigrants; instead, the trouble was the systematic way in which *Americanos*—or White Americans—scapegoated his fellow countrymen.

Regardless of gender, Latinos expressed that they were often the target of jokes and had to endure verbal ridicule at work. This disrespect was tolerated by bosses who simply ignored the animosity or by companies that, perhaps unwittingly, fueled such behavior. By positioning Latino workers in the "grunt" work or in unpopular shifts, they fostered and sustained a culture of superiority. In addition, multiple Latino interviewees revealed how the break room of a popular manufacturing employer had the television always tuned to the Fox News channel. Throughout the day, as the news coverage shifted to the immigration debate, non-Latino employees would direct accusatory commentary to Mexican co-workers, lamenting the presence of Mexicans they assumed to be undocumented. As Sandra recalled, during one segment on Fox News that referred to a recent immigration raid in another state she overheard a non-Latino co-worker state: "'si ya los corrieron por que no se van'" [if they were fired, why are they still here]. Simplifying the debate to job availability, Sandra's co-worker further elaborated that what was needed was raids everywhere to rid the country of "illegals." Sandra was a permanent resident, had been in this country for more than two decades, but she remembered what it was like as an undocumented immigrant and why she chose to struggle here as opposed to unemployment in Mexico. Sandra punctuated this story with an uncomfortable laugh, relating the naïveté of believing that raids would be the magic answer, "no nomas somos nosotros, también son ellos en búsqueda de nosotros" [it is not just us [in search for jobs], it is also them [companies, bosses] in search of us]. In other words, Sandra understood the reality of an immigrant-dependent economy even if Fox News was clearly not communicating this complexity to its base.

Sandra and other women were stunned at the brazen verbal insults and enacted distances in the workplace. Though negative exchanges with or sneers from non-Latinos were not unheard of, the frequency with which Latino workers encountered it at work during the national immigration debate was disheartening. Sharing these negative experiences brought Latinas and Latinos together and enhanced solidarity between them. Yesica recalled the rumors she endured within the Latino community in the 1990s for speaking "too much" with other male co-workers. Gossip soon reached her husband (now ex-husband), whom she then had to convince of her fidelity. On the weekends, in social occasions, and at church Latinos were used to a certain amount of gendered segregation, but while employed in the manufacturing industry Latinas and Latinos often worked together. They were always aware of how their interactions with the opposite sex could be viewed or interpreted even within the workplace, but by 2006 gender conventions shifted as Spanish-speaking men and women united under an atmosphere of inhospitality. This solidarity can best be described through intersectionality. Looking to the role of intersectionality in the borderlands of the Midwest means recognizing the interlocking nature of oppressions that both women and men face as they lived at "the Crossroads of America."[16] Latinas and Latinos held distinct social locations along different structures of domination. Thus, their bodies were gendered, classed, and racialized along a different, yet related, axis of inequality. Men faced racialized, classed, and gendered assaults that positioned them as a violent, threatening menace all too eager to "take your jobs." Women, for their part, also encountered racialized, classed, gendered allegations that viewed them as irresponsible, oversexed, or part of an insidious plan to birth "anchor babies" and undermine U.S. immigration policies. Thus, notions of an immigrant Other are not simply racialized but are also incredibly gendered. These intersections were part and parcel of the immigration debate and certainly united Latinos, regardless of gender, to contest these assaults.

Feeling the sting of being both racialized and gendered, Caridad felt she was suspected of being undocumented because of her dark complexion. Caridad related feeling particularly targeted after workers at her factory were let go because of "no-match" letters:

> Como empezaron a despedir a la gente que no tenían papeles, pues yo me sentía mal por que todo el mundo al verme morenita decia 'no esta no tienen nada tampoco.' Y hasta me decían los compañeros y a mi cuando, y a mi cuando.

> Since they were starting to let go of all the people that didn't have the proper papers, I would feel bad because due to my dark complexion they would say this woman doesn't have [proper papers] either. And in fact, my co-workers would even tell me "When is it your turn, when is it your turn."

Being racially targeted and suspected of being undocumented became commonplace for Caridad. She dismissed the personal attacks because she didn't have anything to fear from the accusations. Still, a certain sense of vulnerability came with being a woman in a male-dominated factory. Confident in her legitimate residency and right to work in this country, she revealed feeling intimidated by non-Latino workers who seemed to want an excuse to fire her or anyone else who looked like her. Perhaps this is why she was so disturbed by a situation with a male Latino co-worker that gave her "*mucha tristeza*" [much sadness]. Caridad spoke of a Latino co-worker who was employed with the company for seven years when he was let go as a result of the discovery that the Social Security number he was using was "no-match" to his name. On his last day, this co-worker went to say good-bye to his team when Caridad noticed, "le dio la mano a un Americano y el dice 'bueno nos vemos.' Y en cuanto se dio la vuelta el Americano dijo 'uno menos'" [he went to shake hands with a [White] American and said to him, "Well, I'll see you later." And as soon as he turned around the [White] American said, "One less"]. Caridad was deeply offended by the White worker's dismissive tone. She felt that the White co-worker had been very disrespectful and racist in his remarks. Moreover, the employee who was leaving had been an incredible asset to the team. Caridad's *tristeza* came in knowing how that one gesture stripped her Latino co-worker of any contributions he had made to the company. Ironically, according to Caridad the last laugh was on this White worker. After this one employee left, four more Latinos were hired and brought in to work with him as temporary workers; as Caridad noted, "Por uno menos llegaron cuatro mas" [for one less came four more].[17]

Though Caridad felt that her White co-worker eventually paid for his comments, she was most offended by this type of passive-aggressive behavior, seen time and again at work. When I asked her if she felt that racism existed in Lafayette, Caridad responded with: "Sí, allí en el trabajo ay racistas. Como cuatro con quien trabajo que no te ven bien. Les dices oye necesito esto y no, te ignoran" [Yes, at work there are racists. Like four of them I work with look at you funny. When you ask for something they just ignore you]. As Luciano mentioned, non-Latino employees may have felt weary of being called racist or resented being fired for their prejudice. As a result, being ignored or ridiculed seemed common in the narratives of Latino co-workers. Women especially reported that these subtle yet pervasive dismissals affected their daily workplaces. Unlike the men, who could point to instances in the past or present when they felt directly confronted by those who rejected them, women expressed how these softer forms of racism affected their encounters with non-Latinos. The *rechazo* did not manifest itself in blatantly cruel assaults, but as Consuelo referenced earlier, "*se siente*" [you can just feel it]. Latino employees were not oblivious to the nonverbal attacks and physical avoidance. For instance, unlike Samuel, who was encouraged to learn English, Chela recalled a situation at her job when her attempts to speak English were often received with mocking humiliation. In one such exchange, Chela asked a White female co-worker for some clarification on an instruction. Humbly asking "Em, excuse me, but . . ." Chela was quickly interrupted. Hearing Chela's accented "excuse me," the co-worker responded gruffly that Chela should learn English, and how could she expect to work with someone who did not speak English. Chela simply needed clarification. With four years of studying English, she understood perfectly her White co-worker's scornful comments. Moreover, female employees were still in the minority in this particular position. Chela felt a deeper sting knowing that this female co-worker chose to insult Chela's accented English rather than work together on a task: "fue muy grosera" [she was very cruel]. Unwilling to bond on their shared gendered position in the workplace or give Chela a second to finish her query, this co-worker drew a clear line between herself and those she deemed unworthy of consideration. Notably, though communication lines were severed between these two women, this moment did convey deeper metanarrative messages of degradation.

The rhetoric surrounding immigration at the time seemed to encourage anxiety, resentment, or fear of Latinos that spilled over into tense exchanges or microaggressions in the workplace. Latino respondents noted that in the months following the national pro-immigration rallies they overheard co-workers, customers, and friends making snide comments about Mexicans and undocumented immigrants. For Yumey, working two jobs in the service sector of town, these encounters were often problematic and disturbing. As a hair stylist in a posh upper-middle-class salon, she encountered customers who brought up the topic of immigration while receiving a style or cut from her. Though Yumey would purposefully avoid these conversations for fear of where they could go, some customers and co-workers did not employ the same discretion. Non-Latinos approached her to talk about "the illegals" or "Mexicans" and would make statements that surprised Yumey. She never expected such closed-minded assertions from some of these individuals. This became particularly awkward between her and her customers. Caught in this unique power play, often Yumey felt muted and uncomfortable as to what she could and should say in order to keep the customer happy as well as be true to herself. With co-workers, she was more willing to express herself and serve as a vehicle of education to inform and disrupt negative rhetoric. Some welcomed her perspective and others gave incredulous stares. With customers, she hoped her own uncomfortable silence would be enough. Thus, silence became a tool used by all residents to navigate incredibly tense and awkward situations.

Denied Belonging in the Next Generation

First-generation Latino immigrants faced denied acceptance in multiple spaces, but their children, U.S.-born or -raised Latinos, were also targeted as probable interlopers. Moreover, confrontations in this generation seemed to occur with generational peers. No longer just the "rednecks" whom Eudoxio mentioned or the working-class employees who presumed illegality on the part of all Spanish-speaking co-workers, even college-educated students in upper-middle-class areas enacted power against Latino residents. Strategic positioning against Latinos continued among the youth, who were far from a postracial generation. In fact, Sergio recalled that even a decade earlier, during the last major debate on immigration and California's infamous Proposition 187, the negative attention to Latinos on the West Coast filtered onto Purdue's university campus. One of Sergio's friends, a young undergraduate, attended Purdue University. Though Sergio himself was a student at a different university in Indiana, he was in West Lafayette visiting his friends when "we were walking home and some guys from a [fraternity] house yelled something out about wetbacks or something like that. A huge fight ensued. We were still young, in our twenties, and still hotheads from East Chicago." Sergio explained that he was most shocked at the level of racism enduring on a college campus. Raised in

East Chicago, Sergio always had trepidations about the rest of Indiana. Affiliated more with the Chicago area, Sergio never wanted to see the rest of Indiana because he feared the "rednecks" who lived outside of the northwestern part of the state. Eventually, Sergio did venture to central Indiana, where he encountered biases against Latinos. On a scholarship to a small liberal arts school, Sergio remembered a housemother from his dorm who kept making him spaghetti for dinner. The spaghetti, according to the housemother, was to make Sergio feel at home because as she said, "You're Eye-talian, aren't you." Sergio repeated her Hoosier accent in pronouncing "Italian" and then explained that after he clarified that he was actually Mexican the housemother responded with "Oh. Oh well, they're clean people." Sergio was flabbergasted and responded with "Uh, yeah *we* are." Later, after graduation, Sergio worked at a local ice cream factory, where his status as a U.S.-born Latino granted him the luxury of working on the freezer side of the production, as opposed to the heat-intensive boiler room where first-generation Latinos worked. Sergio remembered that the boiler room had an 80 to 90 percent Mexican workforce, with the freezer side equally segregated with a majority White workforce. Sergio remembered a particular tension-filled weekend when overtime was canceled because a majority of the workers in the boiler room asked off to celebrate the wedding of one of their co-workers: "These white guys were all, 'Damn Mexicans are all related' and all this other crap. And I was like, 'Dude, I'm right here.'" Sergio was viewed as different from first-generation workers because he was completely fluent in English and had grown up in the United States. However, the insults and negativity still bothered Sergio. Read against his East Chicago experience, the scenarios taught Sergio that the rest of Indiana lacked exposure to people of color, and in 2006 this unfamiliarity created further schisms in society.

The next generation confronted moments of hostility and, sometimes for the first time, faced what their parents had faced in being read as outcasts. Raised in a supposed postracial environment that shielded obvious signs of segregation and racist proclamations, the members of the next generation took longer to identify the challenges they faced for being Latino and/or Spanish-speaking. Yumey's first experiences in central Indiana exemplified this denial. Born in California, Yumey moved to Lafayette with her family when she was an adolescent. Even though she was in California as a child during the events surrounding Proposition 187, it was in Indiana where she felt direct opposition to her presence. The eldest of four, Yumey interpreted the bullying she and her siblings received as attacks on Californians or as her own lack of experience with a rural midwestern mindset. As she recalled, "My world drastically changed. Here no one spoke Spanish, people wore Wranglers instead of Levi's, everyone openly talked about religion, and there was no diversity. A complete opposite from California." Yumey wanted to believe that classmates were cold toward her because she was not a native Hoosier and convinced herself that this shunning and lack of friendships were not the result of discrimination. There had to be another reason people were being rude to her. As she noted, "I really didn't have Caucasian friends in California . . . so maybe it was me not knowing how to handle them." Internalizing her marginalization, Yumey did not think much of these earlier encounters. Later it became increasingly difficult to ignore the signs of intolerance. After graduation, Yumey went on to study at Purdue University. There she joined a Latina sorority, graduated, and found employment in Lafayette all while still living with her parents. In her mid-twenties by the time of the interview, Yumey enjoyed spending time with her younger siblings and exposing them to events and opportunities on the west side of town, where Purdue often held events otherwise not available in Lafayette.[18] It was one of these trips to the west side that shattered Yumey's image of *tranquilidad* [calmness] in this community.

As in other areas of the Midwest, winters often last well into April in central Indiana. As the temperature warmed in the spring of 2006, the town awakened. The slightest signs of the earth thawing and flowers blooming enticed people outdoors to celebrate the end of another dreary, cold winter. The streets flooded with children playing, as adults welcomed the pleasant climate. Salt stains were washed off cars, and windows opened to take in the spring breezes. Regardless of ethnicity, these routines came to define spring for many of the area's residents. Always wanting to expose her younger siblings to university life, Yumey was on her way to Purdue with her youngest sister on one of these warm days. With the car windows fully lowered, both enjoyed the Spanish vocals of crossover artist Shakira. Suddenly, Yumey realized she was in the wrong lane for a right turn. As she crossed two lanes of traffic she inadvertently cut off a truck full of male Purdue students. What followed next was recounted by Yumey:

> I guess the guy got frustrated with me, so he started yelling out stuff. I was like yeah I know I'm at fault, but then I heard he said something. Something, something "you spic." I turned around and I was like who are you talking to—oh you're talking to me. It was a bunch of college kids, Anglo Sajones, y era un chino atrás [Anglo Saxons and some Chinese guy in the back] and they were all laughing. It just made me really mad. That was the first time I really felt like tense and not scared but it kind of shook me. Like, oh my gosh I'm being attacked verbally by someone. . . . When they were driving off he said something, something, something "go back home." Oh my gosh, I was so furious because you know what, I'm an alumni, I have a degree, I've accomplished more than you have, I'm driving a better car than you are and *this is my home.*

Yumey's frustration with this exchange was multi-layered. She was surprised that someone would go out of his way to yell racial epithets at her and her sister. The fact that these were college kids, like herself, was even more shocking, especially as she was trying to encourage her younger sister to excel in school and attend college. Last, the idea that someone who was Asian, or *chino* as she referenced, would participate in these exclusionary assaults was beyond her comprehension. Yumey attempted to understand these various issues within the immigration debate:

> I think it was because of all the stuff that had been happening, so I thought I'm going to try to let it go, but it definitely took me a couple of days to get over it. I had plenty to say back, but I thought I'm going to be a better person and I'm not going to say anything because of the whole thing in the rally was we're going to be *peaceful about it.* The only thing I did was that I left my music the way it was. I didn't roll up my windows—I wasn't going to give him the benefit. What I wanted to do was really make *good eye contact* when he was driving away, but *he didn't,* he didn't even look back at me. And I was thinking, you know, if you don't have the face to look back at me after you've said something like that . . . . Just to let him know "You know what, I'm not intimidated by you. And we're on the same level, buddy." (Emphasis added)

Yumey's interview was conducted in July, and she recalled the incident's occurring shortly after the immigrant rallies and boycotts in April and May. As she noted, it was at these rallies that she learned how to respond to these mean-spirited comments. Rather than shout back, cause an accident, or provoke them into thinking worse of her, Yumey calmly countered by simply and unabashedly existing. Like the larger message immigrants rights groups were promoting, the very act of being and demanding the right to exist would be their ammunition. Evoking the principles of Martin Luther King Jr. and Mahatma Gandhi, Yumey reacted by being "a better person" and instead chose another avenue of active resistance. Rather than lower herself to her antagonist's level, she proudly continued to sing Shakira and refused to let him intimidate her. This seemingly banal act of leaving the radio at full blast demonstrated her refusal to acquiesce to the will of men who seemed to think they were in power. Yumey asserted a right to belong in *her home* and critically modeled an embodied sense of confidence for her younger sister. Moreover, by summoning the driver to look her in the eye, to recognize her as a person, Yumey refused to be ignored. Unwilling to accept the dismissive tones of his words and actions, Yumey fought to be acknowledged as a viable, accomplished member of her community. Ultimately, this was the struggle so many Latino residents battled on the streets, in workplaces, and in commercial centers around town.

Although Yumey felt vindicated by her handling of this incident, her satisfaction was incomplete because she never did make eye contact with the driver. In other words, she lacked a sense of closure from knowing that those in the car would go on without realizing the wounds that their actions had inflicted. Weeks after this moment, Yumey continued to be visibly upset when narrating it to me. She recognized that the other driver had a legitimate traffic grievance, but she was very disturbed at his attempt to bring immigration into the exchange. She cited her accomplishments, her education, her belongingness that all defied the ignorance exhibited by the driver and his friends. However, her distress was not solely aimed at his racialized assertions that she was an immigrant. What really bothered Yumey was the wrath and ugliness directed at all Latinos regardless of their actual immigration status. Like her parents, she claimed ownership and belonging to Lafayette—"This is my home"—and to have that taken away from her so easily was incredibly upsetting. Moreover, the presence of an Asian passenger seemed to irritate her even more. Instead of solidarity from someone whose belonging could just as easily go denied, she was insulted by his traitorous laughter. Ironically, even as Latinos argued against racialized assumptions that marked all Spanish-speakers as undocumented or positioned all undocumented immigrants as criminals, Yumey's use of the word *chino* [Chinese] is itself a colloquial racialized label for all Asians regardless of actual national affiliation. As with Maggie earlier in the chapter, here again we see evidence of the logic of Orientalism that pits people against one another in unwitting acts of maintaining heteropatriarchal White supremacy. Yumey, the Asian passenger, and the other men in the truck operated under particular logics that shielded the interrelated roles they all played in maintaining the inequities in society. Notably, Yumey was not denying the Asian passenger a right to exist in the United States; she just felt disappointed that he was all to willing to use the logics of Orientalism against her and her sister.

Overcoming the *Rechazos*

The act of being dismissed, being ignored, being made invisible was present in the daily navigations between Latinos and non-Latinos in Greater Lafayette. The snubs or vocal jabs effectively deprived individuals of the courtesy of being thought of as peers, neighbors, or simply contributors to a community. Notably, the microaggressions felt by Latinos throughout central Indiana were not specific to this region. Instead, they followed the larger practice of stripping people of human consideration through labels such as "illegal" that branded individuals always as already criminals. Presumed dishonest, dangerous, or too fertile, Latinos worked that much harder to prove their merit through job performance or willingness to struggle with English. It was more complex for the next generation, whose worth was a supposed given, but whose belonging in 2006 was called into question. Unlike their parents, the members of this generation had been raised and steeped in American exceptionalism. The rhetoric and dismissive actions heightened in 2006 caused an uncomfortable recognition that intolerance was still very much present in the twenty-first century and that bigotry was not limited to the mindset of "rednecks."

Regardless of actual citizenship status, immigrants and U.S.-born Latinos alike faced troubling moments informed by prejudice. The narratives of the area's Latinos spoke to the steady stings that accompanied microaggressions. Though the oppressive environment did not manifest itself in outright physical attacks, subtle painful actions communicated disdain and dehumanizing indifference. Indeed, seemingly innocuous acts, like avoiding someone in a parking lot, did hurt people. Latinos internalized both the evasions and direct mean-spirited comments as signs of their precarious status in the area. Looking to these microaggressions can help us understand how fear and prejudice seeps into the daily imaginary of those who would otherwise see themselves as accepting. Perhaps unaware of how their actions transmitted the negative political climate at the time, non-Latinos did demonstrate a kind of *rechazo* painfully felt by Latinos throughout 2006. Thus, the immigration debate became embodied into the experience of those living, working, and struggling daily in central Indiana. Icy stares and snubs felt by Latino residents communicated their abject position in the community and illustrated the contemporary "Crossroads of America."

Gendered, classed, and racialized harassment spoke to the larger cultural milieu that marked certain individuals as unfit of national belonging or even human consideration. Indicative of the enduring power of racism, the narratives collected in 2006 showcased how divisive politics penetrated the way people thought and acted toward one another. For men, the contentious environment in 2006 was difficult, but still not as bad as some of the direct harassment they had faced earlier. Scripted within notions of racialized fear and violence, men of color were read on a different spectrum from that of women. White women, like Maggie and Jane in an earlier chapter, felt threatened by what they perceived to be menacing Latino men. Whether in a parking lot, listening to music outside their apartment, working on a manufacturing line, or walking on the street, Latinos were positioned in racialized and gendered scripts that dismissed them as dangerous or unworthy of even a handshake. Their place in the logics of Othering positioned Latino men as threats to employment, livelihood, and safety. Viewed through the prism of machismo and low-wage labor, Latino men confronted direct and indirect attacks that predated the 2006 immigration debate. This unfortunate familiarity with animosity provided a comparative lens for interpreting the environment that accompanied the 2006 immigration debate.

On the other hand, women were troubled by these outward manifestations of animosity. Women had felt a certain distance from their non-Latino neighbors. However, they assumed that linguistic and cultural differences were the reasons for the isolation between the communities. As the media and political rhetoric ramped up in 2006, Latinas confronted other, more dubious, sources for the coldness they experienced from non-Latino residents. Whereas before it seemed that the town was ambivalent about their presence, women now noticed scornful looks and commentary that had not been as obvious even a year earlier. By 2006, Latinas had already been working alongside men and non-Latinos for more than a decade without much trouble. Prior to the national immigration debate, miscommunication occurred and some resentment was felt, but those scenarios were limited to particularly ignorant individuals. The difference in 2006 came with how quickly non-Latino co-workers turned from ambivalent to outright hostile. No longer limited to a select number of ill-mannered "rednecks," tensions in the workplaces, at Wal-Mart, and in public boiled over to an uncomfortable temperature. Still, women did not always encounter the direct insults or threats that men endured. Instead, they found that indirect microaggressions communicated equally problematic messages of *rechazo*. Women picked up on sneers, facial expressions, or seemingly hushed commentary throughout Lafayette that revealed obvious distaste for the Spanish-speaking population. At times targeted for merely being Latina and presumed undocumented, other times chastised for having "too many" children or being too simple-minded to know the language, Latinas faced particular forms of rejection related to their gendered positions in the anti-immigrant rhetoric. Thus, twenty-first-century manifestations of animosity created solidarity between Latinas and Latino men who collectively confronted local and national adversity.

Notably, these men and women did not simply absorb the negativity present during the 2006 immigration debate. Instead, they found other ways to assert their rights and combat intolerance. Perhaps it was even defending their right to belong that created a heightened animosity. What seemed an easy target was now a vocal and active community unwilling to be the nation's scapegoat. The unwillingness of Latinos to

accept their ostracization was threatening to those who felt that undocumented immigrants, and those mistaken as such, had no rights. Read
as threatening to a limiting narrative of belonging, Latinos across the
nation showcased a level of activism that asserted their rightful "place"
squarely in the United States.

Lafayette Latinos enthusiastically participated in the Indianapolis immigration rallies and the May 1 labor protest, but, perhaps more important, they found other avenues of asserting their right to belong. Directly
and indirectly contesting the dismissal they felt, Latinos demonstrated
their claim to central Indiana as home through seemingly apolitical moments in their daily lives. Like the microaggressions presented in this
chapter, contesting these snubs also took place in otherwise overlooked
scenarios that subtly declared Latino claims to the local. Comparable to
the national pro-immigration rallies, local public religious rituals demonstrated a right of Latinos to exist publicly unashamed of their ethnic presence. Perhaps not as directly political or confrontational, when
practiced amidst these otherwise cruel experiences with antagonistic
non-Latinos, public religious rituals can illustrate how Latinos were
unwilling to succumb to the negativity. Rather than simply chronicle a
dismal scenario, the voices throughout this book illustrate how to confront and recover from an otherwise caustic environment. The following
chapter recognizes how people endured and triumphed over political or
social impediments to community.

5

"United We Are Stronger"

Clarifying Everyday Encounters with Belonging

Civic engagement includes both formal political activities and more everyday or vernacular forms of cultural and social citizenship.
—Caroline B. Brettell and Deborah Reed-Danahay

Reading the letters to the editor, hearing about work harassment, and sitting across from participants who held such negative feelings toward undocumented immigrants was at times infuriating. As a child of once-undocumented immigrants myself, I felt the sting of ignorance personally. After some interviews, I was enveloped by the foulness that lingered from engaging with the realities of contemporary intolerance. As a researcher I needed to collect these narratives; as an individual I absorbed the negativity like a sponge and felt deeply wounded every time I heard of, read of, or witnessed the hostility in Lafayette. This pain and disappointment were so penetrating that I had to mentally compartmentalize it throughout the fieldwork. Otherwise, I risked overlooking incredible coalitions between Latinos and non-Latinos in the area. The December procession of the Virgin of Guadalupe provided one such moment of kindness and community that helped assuage feelings of despair.

Prior to the evening procession, I spent much of the day fielding "excused absence" requests at one of the local high schools. Hired as a part-time community liaison, I worked at the high school to help with communicating to Spanish-dominant parents and mentoring the school's growing population of Latino students. For students, I acted as their contact person for discussing college aspirations, familiarizing them with financial aid options, and helping them resolve tensions with school administrators on issues of misconduct. Primarily, I helped translate for students when they felt a communication gap with their counselors. As an advocate, I was there to assist students and parents navigate the Indiana high school experience. I never directly disciplined students. My goal was to inform the families, students, and administrators about one another's role in creating a successful high school experience. On the morning of December 12, this meant intervening with campus security regarding reports of religious and ethnic harassment toward Latino Catholic students. Notably, the culprits were the campus security officers and not the students. Despite efforts by a previous Hispanic liaison to educate the school about the importance of December 12 as a religious holiday for local Latino Catholics, on this morning campus security profiled Latino Catholics as gang members because the officers incorrectly conflated Virgin de Guadalupe iconography with gang affiliations. Needless to say, I was furious. Field notes from that day express my irritation:

> Tired and sleepy from this morning's mass. Been up since 4am, but I still went to work to make sure all the students got their excused absences for the day. Was on the voicemail all day, listening [to] and recording messages from parents, when I heard Josefina's voice from around the corner. She's never in the office for truancy or mouthing off, so I thought it was weird that she was here now. I walked over and gave her a stern "Mmm hmmm, why are you here" look, [and] she responded: "No Miss, I didn't do anything. I promise." I've heard that one before, so I interrupted her counselor to quietly ask what was going on. He said he was just as surprised. Security [had] brought her in, but he had not talked to her yet. I casually walked to security's office. I was worried about what Josefina could have possibly done. Normally she's wandering the office for financial aid and college applications advice. In my head I said a little hopeful "please don't let it be anything too serious." Bob [a security officer] unlocked their door and unleashed the Suhater [explanation below] when he told me Josefina was in trouble for refusing to turn over her Virgin of Guadalupe t-shirt. He explained that the image was considered a gang affiliated item. I could feel the heat rising to my head and my heartbeat increase. I sternly told him, and the officer sitting behind him, that what they were doing was disrespecting a student's religious affiliation.

The Suhater is a nickname I developed some years back (derived from my name Sujey and the word "hater"). This *apodo* was given to me by some high school teens in Texas whom I supervised in 2000 for Upward Bound. These teens realized I expected a lot from students and did not tolerate misbehavior, or in other words I hated on their "fun." In Lafayette, the Suhater came out only when I was disappointed with adults and their offensive behavior. The officers were stopping students with Virgin of Guadalupe t-shirts, demanding they turn them inside out or wear their gym clothes instead. Josefina explained to me later that she had a math test and could not stay home, so she had come straight from morning Mass to school. She, like other Latino Catholics, wore the t-shirts to commemorate the day even if they could not stay home like many of their peers. Josefina refused to turn over her t-shirt or change, and for that she faced disciplinary action. Ultimately Josefina was released back to class and the religious screening put on pause. The security guards expressed that their training and knowledge of local gangs led them to police the image of the Virgin on student's clothes. I explained that it was a violation of religious freedom and especially today they needed to stop targeting these students. It was agreed that they would stop, at least on December 12, and that they would review their policy.

On this day, I was tired from the dawn Mass I'd attended and irritated with the disrespectful actions of campus security. I carried these feelings with me as I tried to switch into fieldwork mode to march in the evening Virgin of Guadalupe procession. After the procession began, we found ourselves on a rather busy street with drivers visibly frustrated by our presence. Though police had been hired to accompany the procession, cars still dangerously swerved close to us or illegally maneuvered their way around us to get to their destinations. It was just after a car came dangerously close to a stroller that a girl around eight years old pointed out the presence of a White woman standing outside her front porch holding a white statue of the Virgin Mary above her head. The little girl's mother nodded to the woman on her porch, and she in turn reciprocated the acknowledgment. Just moments before, I was helping this mother with her stroller and chatting with her in between songs and prayers. After witnessing this exchange with the woman on the porch,

I asked the mother if she knew the woman with the Mary statue. She plainly replied "No, pero las dos somos Católicas" [no, but we are both Catholic women].

Given the earlier encounters with campus security and the distress felt at the hands of hazardous drivers, my own initial response to the woman on the porch was pessimistic. I wondered if she was comparing the ethno-Catholic procession with her own image of Mary. Was she asserting that her white-plaster Mary statue was nobler? Admittedly, I read the situation through cynical eyes. What I learned from that mother was a lesson in recognizing critical allies amidst otherwise tense interactions. The friendly nod and response of Catholic solidarity along the route taught me that sometimes alliances and solidarity could help offset unpleasant experiences elsewhere. Political and media attention to immigration in 2006 heightened the climate of anxiety against Latino ethnicity and speaking Spanish. Talk of assimilation once again dominated critiques of Latino incorporation. But on this dreary December evening, the nods between these women related a different kind of social environment, one that included not just tolerance but acceptance for ethnic difference and recognition of religious solidarity. The woman on the porch signaled a display of mutuality and support that was appreciated by the mother on the route. Together, they taught me the meaning of community and the importance of those moments of overlap. Like an actual Venn diagram, this moment along the route spoke to the differences and similarities between residents of this small midwestern city. Yes, they were both Catholic, but these women practiced their Catholicism in slightly different ways. Still, the differences did not offset their communal belief system. This experience made me wonder: What would a community look like under this model? How could otherwise disparate residents respect their differences and unite under overlapping similarities? And, how did Latino residents assert their right to maintain differences, to live out their ethnic Latino selves, without compromising their belonging to a shared American midwestern experience?

Beginning with popular, if problematic, assertions by White residents about their Latino neighbors, the chapter accounts for the power of misconceptions to build boundaries against Spanish-speaking or phenotypically Latino residents of the town. Here it is important to note that these non-Latino responses were not like Jane's in chapter 3 or Maggie's in chapter 4. They did not write letters or participate in political campaigns, nor did they actively rally against undocumented immigrants. Instead, these were typical non-Latino respondents who were surrounded by the discourse on immigration. Often vacillating with their positions on immigration, these White respondents seemed unsure what to believe or whose facts to go on. They were hungry for information. Unfortunately, they still relied on popular tropes to reinforce their fears against monolingual lawbreakers. The words of an overt bigot sounding off in the newspaper could be easily identified as wrong, but at issue was the majority population's lack of critique toward popular tropes and half-truths that the very same zealots from whom they distanced themselves actually relied upon. The individuals in these narratives held the potential for being like the woman on the porch, reaching out toward solidarity, but their preconceived notions hastened the possibility for mutuality.

For their part, Latinos carried on with their unique ethnic sense of belonging that joined their transnational ties with their localized Hoosier experiences. In the past, political debates on immigration pitted U.S. Latinos and immigrant populations against one another. Under expectation of total assimilation, some Latinos distanced themselves from the immigrant experience to highlight their own American citizenship. In contrast, the twenty-first-century debate on immigration resulted in a critical rise in co-ethnic solidarity. Directly and indirectly associated with the immigration process, the experience of undocumented immigrants folded into the contemporary Latino consciousness. Mixed-status families, congregations, and neighborhoods potentially provided Latinos with knowledge of the bureaucratic problems with the immigration system. Thus, when nativists pushed a political agenda that criminalized individuals and ignored the larger inequities of the immigration process, many post-millennial Latinos responded by taking to the streets with ethnic solidarity and vocal opposition.

As a critical moment of asserted belonging, the political activism displayed during the spring 2006 immigration rallies attracted popular and scholarly attention. Media outlets broadcast Latinos and their allies in the millions asserting comprehensive, not just punitive, immigration reform. Scholars identified organic grassroots mobilization efforts and chronicled this new moment in Latino political identity. Searching for

A Day of the Dead altar in honor of immigrants' dying en route to the United States. Photo by author.

what Bloemraad and Trost (2008) noted as the "sites of information, political experience, and mobilization," the literature recognized preexisting social networks and the role of community organizations, ethnic media, churches, family, organic intellectuals, and youth in coordinating these events. Notably, these public protests did not just magically appear. This chapter highlights more personal and impromptu examples of asserting ethnic solidarity to confront the limitations of belonging in the politics of immigration. Layers upon layers of lived ethnic consciousness built solidarity, social networks, and the committed enthusiasm to march for social justice. Therefore, to understand the contemporary machinations of Latino political protests, one must begin by exploring other, more subtle "instruments of survival" that may not be as obviously apparent or overtly political. Indeed, attention to the protests themselves could overlook other, more banal, assertions of complex belonging that are just as critical to the underlying consciousness necessary for public protest and civic activism.

Latino lived experience involves a transnational identity that on the one hand maintains ethnic bonds elsewhere and on the other hand asserts legitimacy and belonging to the U.S. national imaginary. The coming together of those two hands releases a force I call *ethnic belonging*. Like the rhythmic claps that kept the beat of "¡Si se puede!" along the routes of public marches, ethnic belonging creates a melody from experiences that blend ties to the United States with transnational beats. This lived harmony between transnational ethnicity and national belonging was enacted at public protests but also informed daily Latino navigations. Ethnic belonging takes inspiration from Renato Rosaldo's notion of cultural citizenship as "the right to be different and to belong in a participatory democratic sense" (1994: 402). However, instead of cultural identity enacted through civic and political citizenship, ethnic belonging accounts for those daily acts that construct ethnic identity and weave an ethnic sense of belonging necessary for cultural citizenship efforts. Thus, ethnic belonging represents organic moments of creating ethnic solidarity that precede participatory citizenship in community organizations or public protests traditionally explored in the literature on cultural citizenship. Though not as visible as civic activism, ethnic belonging points to those beginning steps necessary for claiming the "right to be different and belong." Exploring the subtlety of lived ethnic consciousness can shed a light on what occurs on the days leading up to and following public protest. What happens once homemade signs come down and protesters go home? Can personal moments of ethnic belonging still create powerful societal change? Can praying on streets of Lafayette mean more to the cause of immigrant reform by connecting the heartstrings of two Catholic women from seemingly discrete cultures? This analysis expands notions of cultural citizenship and civic activism by locating those more intimate instances that affirm one's ethnic right to belong. Moreover, by including non-Latinos in the conversation, this chapter accounts for the need to build bridges of understanding and expand the role of allies in the struggle for belonging.

Every/Day Matters

Looking beyond public protests to less celebratory displays of community belonging required a need to understand how everyday encounters mattered in their potential to create or limit community. Strangers' sharing a moment of religious solidarity or a security guard's targeting of religious youth marked how community was felt, contested, and expanded to the area's growing Latino population. These possibly overlooked examples of everyday lives revealed patterns that illustrated what Latinos and non-Latinos experienced during this moment in immigration politics. Most non-Latinos in Lafayette did not directly write in to the newspaper or actively participate in programs that welcomed Spanish-speaking residents. Most Latinos were also not constantly involved in one way or another with political protests or community organizations. With the exception of a few committed individuals from all points of the political spectrum, most Lafayette residents lived their ordinary lives without much thought to engaging the politics of immigration. As such, the ordinary encounters collected in this chapter called on me, the ethnographer, to pay attention and listen to the way both Latinos and non-Latinos spoke about their everyday, as if begging to be heard.[1] Similar to Caroline Brettell and Deborah Reed-Danahay's work with Vietnamese immigrants, I looked to the everyday vernacular forms of belonging addressed in both Latino and non-Latino approaches to community. Non-Latinos may not have much to say about immigration, but what they did have to say or the way they understood the immigration

7

debate revealed how the rhetoric trickled down to the masses. I begin this chapter with a range of non-Latino responses to interview questions about immigrants to illustrate how the national rhetoric against immigration entered local imaginings of who belonged and how acceptance to community was conditional upon certain expectations.

Newspaper letters to the editor and my own exposure to intolerance were a painful reality; thus, I was relieved when I met non-Latinos who seemed more accepting of Latinos than some of the more vocally hostile individuals. Still, though people appeared more willing to engage in a complicated discussion about immigration, residents continued to rely on problematic assumptions regarding Latinos. In total, roughly one-third of the seventy-nine individuals I spoke to were non-Latino. Four out of the twenty-five were actively searching for ways to advocate on behalf of Latino residents; their narratives will be highlighted later in the chapter. The other twenty-one were either willfully unaware of the Latino experience or, in the case of a few participants, outright hostile. Out of twenty-five non-Latino interviewees, thirteen immediately responded that either they or people around them had concerns that immigrants should speak English and be legal. Nine out of these thirteen were White participants who acknowledged not having personal contact or familiarity with the Latino community. As a result, linguistic and legal assumptions were not due to direct contact but rather came from indirect hearsay.

Some non-Latino residents were more critical of the caustic environment resulting from the immigration debate, but they too held their own problematic assertions. Primarily, they comforted themselves by investing in the notion that letters to the editor and xenophobia were no more than marginal "hold-outs" or a "vocal minority." As Chloe, a White female, suggested in her interview, "I do see holdouts, things that I think say, 'We don't want you. Go away.' Like the driver's license issue. The letters to the editor. Again, it's the vocal minority. I think that makes it look like everybody in Lafayette is against the Mexican influx, which is not true." Chloe was concerned that the letters were giving Lafayette a bad name and providing only a slanted view of the possibilities of working together. Chloe once lived in Latin America and knew what it was like to reside in a different country. She acknowledged that discrimination existed in Indiana, but she wanted to promote an idea that mutual co-existence was possible. For other White respondents, like Betty, Indiana residents were simply unaware of or unconcerned with immigration and therefore had no opinion. I asked Betty to tell me what other non-Latinos in Lafayette thought about immigration. "They would have no opinion. It doesn't involve them, and they don't have any opinions about it. I think that's the attitude." Ann, another White female participant, validated Betty's perceptions. I asked Ann what she thought of the immigration issue, if she had seen it discussed on the news or in the paper. She responded by stating, "I pay no attention to what is being said in the newspaper. It does not affect me."

Ann may not have frequented the editorial section or taken part directly in these disparaging conversations, but the public discourse promoted a monolithic image of immigrants as dangerous criminals that, if not contested, condemned all undocumented immigrants and those suspected as such. Ann's inexperience with the immigration debate would seem to relay a general apathy toward this political moment. Indeed, Betty and Chloe convinced themselves that antagonism toward immigrants was marginal. If any negative opinion did exist, people only needed further information to release them from their ignorance. As Chloe suggested, "I think those who don't—or who express opinions that are so negative, or who say if they just learn English—don't know anybody who has gone through that experience." Jane Hill's (2008) folk theory of racism illustrates how enticing it is to believe that racism is merely the lack of information, that racist aberrant individuals are "ignorant, vicious, and remote from the mainstream. Their ignorance can be cured by education" (6). This investment in racists as fleeting holdouts relies on idealistic hopes that "racism should soon disappear entirely, except as a sign of mental derangement or disability" and does not account for deeper structural issues with racism (Hill 2008: 6). Though Chloe and Betty wanted to believe that non-Latino Hoosiers did not care or were not knowledgeable about immigrant lives, the narratives described by Latinos themselves demonstrated how distrust, ignorance, and racism resulted in overt and covert dismissals against a population perceived as criminal. Though individuals like Ann might claim that they paid no attention to the national debate on immigration, the micro-aggressions described earlier revealed how the rhetoric of exclusion did in fact seep into the local imaginary and shaped the way even otherwise amiable individuals altered their opinion toward Latino neighbors.

In otherwise pleasant conversations with White research participants, when the conversation turned to immigration it was as if the "illegal" switch had been activated and the mode of communication shifted dramatically. For instance, I interviewed Beth Ann and Ted over lunch one warm afternoon. We ate and chatted about their courtship on Purdue's campus, their memories of raising their grown son in town, and the changes they had seen in the past thirty-five years. Ted and Beth Ann met as undergraduates in West Lafayette in the late 1960s. They graduated, married, and were both later employed by Purdue University. West Lafayette became their home, the town where they would raise their son, Michael. Beth Ann remembered their search for a home in the county schools where Michael could be educated with a "more diverse population, where you didn't have only kids from affluent households." Beth Ann was invested in exposing her son to an environment where he came to know multiple experiences and was not sheltered by upper-class elite academics. The interview included laughter and amusing tales of living in Lafayette. However, the cordiality of the conversation seemed abruptly changed by the topic of immigration.

Beth Ann referenced her knowledge of local immigration through contact with students from China, India, Poland, and Russia, but when the conversation included non-academic immigrants the mood of the interview shifted.[2] This jarring turn came as I moved on to the topic of Latino immigration to Lafayette. I asked, "What about the latest trend in immigration? Have you noticed any increase in Lafayette's Hispanic population?" Beth Ann responded, "They have to come here legally, period. And they have to learn English after a transition period. If we went to their country, they would expect us to learn their language." The climate promptly shifted from a jovial discussion about Lafayette to a stern criminalization of undocumented immigrants and a frustration with their lack of English proficiency. Beth Ann's body shifted, her forehead became more stern, her response now less conversational and much more accusatory. Now, instead of our having a convivial exchange, her voice shifted toward more short, abrupt statements that seemed to come out of left field. Eduardo Bonilla-Silva calls this kind of verbal situation "rhetorical incoherence" or moments when racism enters a conversation and a speaker resorts to repetition, lengthy pauses, or grammatical shifts that signal an overall discomfort with discussions of race. In multiple exchanges with non-Latino participants, the word "Hispanic" became interchangeable with anxieties over undocumented immigration and a linguistic takeover. Beth Ann's answer appeared almost naturally as if the metaphor "immigrant-as-a-threat" was always and already obvious. Critically, Beth Ann's opinions about immigrants did not exist in a historical vacuum. Rather, they were informed by a public rhetoric about immigration that affected the way she, and others interviewed, positioned the Latino community in the area. It was also telling that Beth Ann, not Ted, was at the forefront of voicing this opinion. Indeed, Ted just sat quietly watching his wife. With both Jane and Beth Ann, there appeared an added attempt to deeply vocalize their right to have these opinions. In a bizarre kind of feminist assertion, these women felt they had to speak up and let their positions be heard. Instead of yielding their political position to men, these women vocally expressed their views and made sure I heard their positions. Regrettably, the process of affirming their rights as political actors meant suppressing the merits of their Latino neighbors.

Participants like Beth Ann were conflicted with their positions. On the one hand they wanted to be welcoming and not labeled as racist, yet they were inundated with media and politicians that railed against the presence of undocumented individuals who were challenging the legal authority of the nation.[3] As Liz, a White female, confessed: "Yeah. I'm not against tightening up the border somehow 'cause I understand that there's economic reasons and whatever legitimate reasons for not just letting people walk in." Liz struggled with how to approach the "legal" debate and the border issue. She did not feel that a wall was the answer, but she'd also heard a lot about dangerous elements such as drugs and gangs coming through the border. Liz also cited economics and thus reflected the fears of immigrants' "taking jobs" or draining the welfare system. The topic of what to do about immigration has never been simple, but too often simplistic answers dilute the complexity and revert to familiar protectionist arguments. Betty related having Latino neighbors who "fixed up their sidewalk" and "did lots of work" to improve the curb appeal of their home. Still, Betty remembered how, "right after we moved in, our very well-meaning, caution-oriented neighbor came and told us, basically, that we needed to watch out for them because he could swear that he smelled pot walking past that house." Even though both

Liz and Betty vehemently opposed the negative rhetoric surrounding immigrants, they equally justified some of the popular anxiety or, in the case of Betty, excused it as "well-meaning, caution-oriented."

Rescuing debates about "tightening up the border" or pardoning outright racists as "well-meaning" took away from directly critiquing these assumptions head on. Why we needed to tighten up one border and not another, for instance, relied on larger demarcations of how we Othered immigrants from the South. This Othering materialized in presuming a particular house smelled like "pot" even as the family only visibly attempted to improve their neighborhood. Again, both Betty and Liz were more open than most in their willingness to welcome Latinos to the area even if they also inadvertently accepted the discourses of exclusion they were against. It is critical to recognize that solidarity is complicated and people do not exist on fixed planes of social justice. Like these participants, people may chastise popular denunciations of undocumented immigrants but were equally conflicted by other aspects of the debate.

Interview participants continued to reference "legal" immigration and the need to prioritize English. Upon further discussion, respondents admitted to not knowing the complexity of the immigration system, nor could they confirm whether Latino immigrants did in fact speak English. Like the letters to the editor, it was a foregone conclusion that Latino immigrants had no interest in either speaking English or becoming legal residents. The interviews I conducted resembled the opinions in the newspaper, with nine out of twenty-five non-Latino participants also lamenting disrespect for U.S. laws by undocumented immigrants and doubted if laws would be followed in the future. Additionally, oversimplifications of the immigration process in interview responses resembled those from the letters to the editor. One participant even said, "There's rules, could you just follow 'em. . . . I know the church has outlets to help them try to get this stuff and I'm sure we probably need more of that. . . . There may be plenty of avenues for help but I don't think they're very well publicized." While this respondent noted that undocumented immigrants should be offered a chance to adjust their status, her belief that the avenues for documentation were plenty or that the church had the means to help those seeking assistance reinforced her lack of knowledge of the actual process.

Probing their positions deeper, I asked respondents if they knew how one could enter the country "legally." All twenty-five respondents were oblivious to the immigration process and did not know if Lafayette's Latinos were citizens or permanent residents of the United States. One respondent, Lacy, even suggested, "If they're gonna come over here, then they need to be a U.S. citizen, number one." Lacy, along with 25 percent of the non-Latino interviewees, conflated being a permanent resident of the United States with being a citizen. Indeed, this misperception was also seen in the letters to the editor and in casual conversations with people around town. When someone approached me at a coffee shop or while getting a haircut to ask about my research, I often responded by referring to the local Latino population. Non-Latino strangers would almost immediately respond with some variants about having or acquiring citizenship. Clearly, the process toward a permanent visa and the five-year waiting period between residency and applying for citizenship were unknown to the majority of non-Latinos I encountered. When individuals were willing to hear me explain the process, I often heard in response what my hairdresser, Chris, said: "Oh, I had no idea."

A clear gap existed between the rhetoric and the reality of undocumented immigrants. Very few respondents admitted even knowing or having talked to Latino residents of Lafayette. When individuals like Lacy proclaimed, "My personal opinion on this is if they're going to come over here, then they should learn to speak our language," they relied on popular inferences that immigrants were not willing to learn English and that Latinos in general were always and already Spanish speakers. Whenever the topic of language arose, I followed up by asking the interviewees if they knew of English classes or ways immigrants could learn English. Though participants acknowledged that some Latinos could be learning, most non-Latino participants struggled with what they knew and what they heard in the media. For example, Lauren stated, "I wish they all could speak English. Um . . . 'cause I would feel the same way if I went to wherever and I didn't know the language. I mean if I was just visiting for a while it would be different, but if I was gonna live there, I'd be like, 'Okay I gotta learn this or I'm out.' So that's the way I feel about it, but I think they're doing a pretty good job of *trying* to learn it." Lauren acknowledged that people were trying to learn English, but she couched her appreciation within an accusatory framework that presented Latinos as unwilling to assimilate into their new surroundings. Only five non-Latino participants praised Latinos for learning English without faulting them for not knowing or learning it fast enough. Indeed, a dominant microaggression listed by U.S.-born Latino participants was the prevalence of White residents' sincerely expressing shock at their English proficiency. No matter if someone had been born or raised his or her entire life in Lafayette, it was assumed that all Latinos were Spanish monolinguals.

A majority of non-Latino participants, twenty-two out of twenty-five, revealed an internal struggle with asserting open-mindedness toward immigration and reifying some of the negative associations in the debate. In reality, no clear, sharp lines delineated a welcoming or xenophobic environment. The spectrum of opinions shifted depending on the topic, with an individual often taking stances on some issues and not others. Primarily, non-Latino interviewees expressed concerns with undocumented arrival, criminal behavior, learning English, welfare abuse, economic competition, and other related stereotypes affiliated with the Latino population. Initially, participants projected a kind of liberal open-mindedness expected of a college-town environment. As Marci, a White woman who'd grown up in northwestern Indiana and had been exposed to Latinos her entire life, expressed, "I think Purdue pushes for people to at least act like, on the surface, that they're more progressive than they are. People get worried about saying things that aren't P.C. [politically correct], because we're supposed to be so progressive." Indeed, several participants attributed negative assumptions about Latinos to their in-laws or unnamed friends who provided enough distance from implicating themselves within disturbing frameworks. In her twenties at the time of the interview, Jenny was one of the youngest White residents I spoke to. Her perspective was interesting because unlike those in their forties or fifties, Jenny spoke from a younger, seemingly more open-minded perspective. Still, Jenny admitted that she "heard people talk about it, yeah. Um . . . calling names and everything. But I don't really associate with that, because I don't care. I mean they can say what they want to say but . . . I don't have a problem with them, in general." Like Jenny, nineteen other non-Latinos also relating hearing "names" or negative associations with Latinos and expressed that they did not themselves accept those stereotypes. As Marci herself recognized, "I still hear some pretty vehement comments being made." Marci, Jenny, and others ignored these moments of racism, viewing them as beyond their responsibility. They heard these comments, recognized they were wrong, but did nothing to challenge them. Very few individuals actively confronted those who espoused such troubling opinions, excusing the speakers as an older generation or as just plain ignorant. As Jenny spoke about her mother-in-law it was clear she lacked the tools to confront these messages and to some extent justified the racialization: "My mother-in-law's a little concerned about it [the rise in Latino population], because when she moved there, there weren't a whole lot of Hispanics that lived in the area. They're pretty much 'the area' now. I mean she'll still go outside. She's not afraid for her life or anything like that. Don't get me wrong, but I mean, she does just think well [trails off]. And a lot of them listen to different styles of music. Loud and almost like circus music, like polka." Jenny was uncomfortable with her mother-in-law's negative opinion of her Hispanic neighbors, but rather than contest the negative stereotypes Jenny simply searched for a way to validate (the loud "polka" music) why her mother-in-law had a reason to feel concerned. My encounters with the majority of non-Latinos in Lafayette was this kind of imbalance between projecting open-mindedness toward Latino arrivals and justifying the rhetoric that critiqued them. For instance, Bernice, in her forties, shifted constantly in her answers regarding Latinos, and specifically Mexican, arrivals:

> I don't know if this is even true. This is something that you hear. I would want people that come to this country to really be citizens of this country and be American. Not have an agenda that has to do with Mexico and the Mexican economy. Which you hear that sometimes there's just gonna be this voting bloc. I also have a concern about the drugs. The influx of— again it's not even so much the people and the citizenry; it's just the more open that we get with the Mexican border . . . . We already don't have any controls. I mean let's be honest.

Later in the interview Bernice advocated for some kind of immigration reform because "people aren't paying taxes that could be. People are maybe not having more stress and more domestic violence and more things like that because they can't be who they are." Bernice was inconsistent in her fears of a "Mexican agenda" or drugs on the one hand and empathy with the psychological impact of being undocumented on the other. This complexity revealed exactly what so many non-Latinos grappled with when navigating what they heard in the popular debate and what was lived experience for Latino neighbors.

Non-Latinos Actively Engage Latino Belonging

Non-Latino allies who did challenge the negative popular discourse gravitated toward one another and actively participated in opportunities to interact with the Latino community. Ironically, one of the events that brought Latinos and non-Latinos together happened in the religious spaces once fiercely denied to Latino worship. Primarily organized by the *Grupo de Jóvenes* [Hispanic Youth Group], the Good Friday performance of the Viacrucis drew Catholics of all backgrounds. The Viacrucis performance and procession included youth participants who portrayed Jesus, Pontius Pilate, Roman soldiers, Symone of Cyrene, the Virgin Mary, Veronica, and countless other period spectators. This lived enactment of faith was an Easter tradition among Latino parishioners. The popularity of director Mel Gibson's *The Passion of the Christ*

The annual Lafayette Viacrucis. Photo by author.

in 2004 brought more and more non-Latino Catholics out to attend the performance. Though English-dominant Catholics enjoyed the event alongside their Spanish-speaking brethren, in 2006 the *Grupo de Jóvenes* invited participants from the English-dominant youth group to actually join them in the re-enactment.

During the height of the immigration debate in April, Latino and non-Latino youth came together for the first time to worship in this manner. Later that December, an increase of non-Latino families also attended the Virgin of Guadalupe novenas, knelt along side Mexican parishioners, and together worshiped the Mother of the Americas. Indeed, two older White women also joined the *Matachine* dancers in the December 12 events.[4] For both the Stations of the Cross and the Virgin of Guadalupe celebrations, St. Boniface's Hispanic Council voted to include bilingual services to make an effort toward inclusivity for monolingual English speakers. Latino parishioners hoped that sharing these festivities would strengthen the church and spur mutual understanding between the area's White and Latino Catholics.

The church, and faith in general, provided the starting point toward mending the scars that the immigration debate was leaving behind. Influenced by a history of struggle and advocacy in his own Baptist faith, Pastor Walker promoted collaboration rather than competition in his Baptist congregation. Even without Latino parishioners among them, Pastor Walker preached a message of acceptance and cooperation to predominantly Black worshipers. He deeply felt the area needed more collaboration between these communities of color. He felt that the particularities of living in central Indiana provided significant overlaps between Black and Latino experiences and worked to make those connections for his parish. As Pastor Walker asserted, "I never did like the analogy that historians and sociologists used to use when they talked about America being the melting pot. That means that everyone has to be the same way. I sort of think of America as vegetable soup. We're all in this together, but each one's got our flavors. There's nothing wrong with having a good bowl of vegetable soup. So we've got to stop trying to be a melting pot and be more like a vegetable soup and enjoy the different flavors that make this soup great." Pastor Walker disagreed with the inclination to flatten rich cultural differences in an attempt to promote artificial cohesion through assimilation. Instead, he felt truly uplifted by the power and strength of diversity that was possible in the community. In the local NAACP chapter and the Mayor's Commission on African Affairs, Pastor Walker made sure to extend his attention to all communities of color in the area and encouraged members of his church to have an open mind and an open heart toward their Spanish-speaking neighbors. He grew tired of the way immigration was being used as a wedge issue, spreading falsities and oversimplifications in thirty-second sound bites. He was particularly upset about the English-only rhetoric infiltrating even his own parish: "We're the only country in the world arrogant enough to say that you have to speak English. In every other country I've been to people learn multiple languages. [Being] bilingual is a requirement . . . and so why can't we be like the rest of the world? If we know we have a strong population that is Spanish-speaking, then we ought to at least make sure that Spanish is being taught in the schools." In personal communications and in sermons, he spoke on behalf of immigrants and the importance of bilingual skills. He pleaded with members of his church to use biblical scripture or even recognize their own marginal experiences as a means toward critically engaging the contentious rhetoric. Pastor Walker lamented that after church service he sometimes overheard remarks which mirrored the politics of immigration prevalent on television screens and newspapers. His frustrations were not limited to the local. With a doctorate in U.S. history, Pastor Walker was even further disappointed by the lack of historical reflection in the nation. Specifically, he referenced talk about building a new border wall in the Southwest as "building the Berlin wall" and added, "Why do we have history if we don't go back and look at the failure of the past and learn from it and not repeat it?" Pastor Walker felt that the past provided important parallels to the present. He felt people had more in common than they were willing to admit.

During a particular conversation with Pastor Walker, we spoke about the overlaps possible between the Black and Latino communities, especially when educating the rest of the town on how to understand the particularities of their experience. For instance, he felt that the schools were ill equipped to address racial or cultural differences. Pastor Walker lamented that he had had to intervene one winter when the local high school attempted to restrict Black youth from wearing 'do-rags because they were perceived as associated with gangs. As a member of the NAACP, Pastor Walker felt called to educate local school officials that the 'do-rag was not merely a stylish headpiece, but it did indeed function as a head covering during cold winter days. He had to explain to the school that knit caps or other winter headgear were simply not appropriate to Black youth because of friction and hair texture. In the end, he succeeded in convincing the school that the ban was simply bad policy. I mentioned that I too had experienced a similar example of "postracial" or seemingly "race-neutral" discrimination practices during the Virgin of Guadalupe festivities at the high school. Pastor Walker expressed disappointment that the schools still targeted youth of color and then wondered why they did not succeed. As Pastor Walker noted, "When you talk about 400 years of oppression, some things are systemic and built into the system, and people just do things because that's the way it's always been done, not knowing the impact it's having on the ability of the people to successfully make it." Thus, he felt that a lack of success among youth of color in the high school could be directly tied to the way the school normalized these students as always and already delinquents. For this reason, Pastor Walker actively tried to build connections between the Black and Latino communities, which, he felt, had significant battles in common.

Other non-Latinos may not have had shared experiences of marginality with Latino residents, but they too struggled to reframe the social environment through convivial opportunities that accepted their Latino neighbors as assets rather than threats. Some White residents worked toward inclusive policies that respected the contributions of Latino residents regardless of immigration status. For example, among the members of the Mayor's Commission on Hispanic Affairs were dedicated White residents who sought ways to understand the Latino community and promote this awareness to other non-Latinos. Active in multiple Latino organizations and a member of some of their executive boards, Matt was a bilingual case manager for the county court system. Matt was a global citizen himself; his father was a tropical medicine specialist and often took his family on sabbatical to live outside of the United States. Thus, Matt lived in China as a child, where his first language was Mandarin and not English. In the 1940s he was in Lebanon and by the 1950s he had spent some time in Kenya. By later in life, Matt had worked in, lived in, and visited "every Latin American country except Cuba."

After he had worked for several years in Latin America, Matt's bilingual skills were much welcomed in the court system of Tippecanoe County. As a case manager and substance-abuse counselor, Matt assisted Spanish speakers with court-ordered arrangements and acted as a cultural translator to many who were unaware of the laws that resulted in their infractions. As he noted, "These guys aren't criminals; they just don't know the rules here. Our job should be to explain, not to arrest. They are good people, good hardworking people who don't deserve what they are being called in public." Indeed, Matt was visibly disgusted by the assumptions people made about Latino criminal behavior, as he noted: "Latino crime convictions [are] still far below [those] of other communities and yet they are called 'illegal' or 'criminals'; we should be ashamed." The "we" in Matt's account could have been White Americans or a general public willing to adopt the rhetoric against otherwise "good hardworking" people. Either way, he was troubled by the level of ignorance infiltrating local and national debates. To make a positive impact on this disturbing phenomenon, Matt actively participated in many of the area's Latino advocacy groups and nonprofit organizations. In an effort to educate and inform White residents about their new Latino neighbors, he often spoke at events or to individuals about the need to look beyond politics and understand the precarious experience of Mexican residents. He knew first-hand what it was like to live in a new country and worked tirelessly to create an atmosphere of acceptance and exchange between the area's Latino and non-Latino residents.

In addition to Matt, the commission included other White residents with various levels of familiarity with the Latino community. Some participants were asked to join by their employers, who felt it would benefit them to assign someone to do this kind of community outreach. Liz was assigned to the commission by her employer and only knew that there had been a substantial population growth in the area and at her place of employment. Willing to learn more, she accepted her employer's insistence that she join. As a result of her participation in the commission, Liz developed a blog, "Hola Lafayette," that attempted to prompt dialogue about common misconceptions and false assumptions aimed against the Hispanic population. As Liz noted in the first entry of the blog, "I am a resident of Lafayette who simply refuses to believe that the growing Hispanic and Latino population is a 'problem' that needs to be 'dealt with.' I think FUD—fear, uncertainty, and doubt—drives a lot of the backlash, and I'm here to try and counter it, in whatever small and unassuming ways I can." While the commission discussed concerns and local needs, Liz felt awkward having to ask for clarification on some issues like the immigration process or complaints of discrimination throughout the town. Other commission members always made her feel that her questions were worthy and they wished more non-Latinos were willing to ask. As a result, Liz ended the meetings with much more knowledge and perhaps more questions than she came in with. She felt a call to explain these issues to the majority population, who she felt was also unaware of the details. More specifically, Liz was disappointed by the vitriol represented in the newspaper editorial pages and online commentary. She was upset that non-Latinos were exposed to only these extremist perspectives without any access to the other side of immigration. Liz was hungry for particulars about immigration that she was unclear about. Eerily anticipating the DREAMER conversations that would lead to the Deferred Action for Childhood Arrivals (DACA) policy in 2012, Liz noted: "See, that's what I need to know more about. Kick people out is the craziest idea in the world to me. Are you kidding me? Then, there's—I've been reading again, which—it's all fascinating stuff to me. The kids in high school that were born here, but it turns out they're not natural-born citizens or whatever because I don't know why. I thought, if you were born here, you were a citizen. Apparently, maybe not." Looking back at the transcription of the interviews I had with Liz (three formal interviews in 2006, 2009, and 2012), I found it interesting that each time, my queries to Liz prompted queries from her. In the transcriptions it is difficult at times to discern who was the interviewer and who was the interviewee. Liz asked just as many questions as I did, and I tried to explain the DREAMER experience or the topic of visa requirements so as to clarify some points. She always absorbed this information with gratitude and of course more questions. Like Pastor Walker, she eagerly wanted to share this clarity with others. Her blog was created to promote healthy, informative discussion as an alternative to rash accusatory language.[5]

Other non-Latinos on the commission, like Tami, expressed hearing negative exchanges in public and wanted "to be able to be part of something that maybe was looking at addressing increased understanding, increased tolerance, and also addressing some of the issues that Latinos face." Issues like translation services, access to community resources, and general positive exchanges between Latino and non-Latino residents were the topics Tami hoped to cover. Because the commission acted mainly in the form of an advisory council to the mayor, primarily its goals were identifying needs and suggesting resolutions to the mayor. In order to act on, or "address," the issues directly, some members of the commission joined other Latino and non-Latino community members to form the Community Activity Committee (CAC). Formed in 2006 to bring Latino and non-Latino residents to plan a Tippecanoe Latino Festival, the CAC conceived of holding an event each year that would serve as a space for distributing information about bilingual services and bring Latinos and non-Latinos together to celebrate the local cultural and culinary contributions of Latino Hoosiers. Various local organizations had already sponsored annual *Día de la Mujer* [International Women's Day], *Día del Niño* [Children's Day], and *Día de los Muertos* [Day of the Dead] festivals, but the CAC identified the need to coordinate one massive event that was fun but could also bring different Latino-serving organizations together and provide a clearinghouse for Latinos to actually see and get information on the multitude of services available to them. Sponsored mainly by the community college and local businesses in town, the festival took place in April 2007 to celebrate and create "a forum for Latino/Hispanic groups to celebrate their ideas, origin and culture."[6]

Ethnic Belonging to Define Their Own Sense of Community

The non-Latino response to the politics of immigration ranged between antagonism and active collaboration, and for Latinos this meant it was difficult to gauge which way the wind blew people's opinion on their presence. Latino residents encountered a variety of reactions, from friendly smiles or apathetic indifference to sneers and discomfort heightened by the immigration debate. Speaking Spanish in public or one's mere presence could trigger anxieties fueled by irrational negative associations. Thus, Latinos could not rely on external validation when building their own sense of community. Instead, they asserted an ethnic belonging that blended their particular ways of living (speaking Spanish, cultural celebrations, transnational commitments, and ethno-religious traditions) within the midwestern social landscape. Ethnic belonging, like Rosaldo's cultural citizenship, reconciles national belonging with a commitment to ethnic solidarity, cultural practices, and transnational interests. However, "ethnic belonging" refers to those moments when individuals and families live out their ethnically different ways of belonging that may or may not have anything to do with civic duty, cultural organizing, or communal activism. This ethnic belonging precedes community organizing in that it means simply the way people live out their daily lives. I suggest that it is this ethnic belonging, or those common moments of daily cultural and ethnic practices, that get invoked to assert a camaraderie for cultural citizenship. Latinos in Lafayette did exhibit cultural citizenship inasmuch as they created the Tippecanoe Latino Festival, marched in Indianapolis for immigration reform, or found community organizations in the area. Their ethnic belonging, however, has more to do with those ordinary activities that illustrated ethnic difference without apology.

These daily ordinary moments of ethnic belonging acted as a kind of coping mechanism that redrew belonging and membership in community to include their particular ways of living. Nira Yuval-Davis asserts that "the politics of belonging involves not only the maintenance and reproduction of the boundaries of the community of belonging by the hegemonic political powers but also their contestation and challenge by other political agents" (2006: 205). Thus, Latinos in Lafayette demonstrated their agency in refusing to give up their ethnic ways of being. Everyday practices of ethnicity are not always obviously political or directly oppositional, but they build upon one another to assert a right to exist ethnically in a community.[7] As anthropologist Frederich Barth (1969) recognized, ethnic identity is not merely optional, but in some cases significantly *operational* in asserting cultural difference. Contesting popular pressures on immigrant arrivals, ethnic belonging accounts for the ways these families built "difference into the fabric of their daily lives, and at the same time creat[ed] distinct identities that undermine[d] notions of assimilation as an unifying set of similarities" (Lamphere 2007: 1150). Ethnic confrontations to assimilation rarely arise from carefully crafted agendas or politically motivated acts. Instead, ethnic belonging was enacted in the daily lives of Latino Hoosiers who lived, worked, and went to school without having to think about their ethnic opposition to the mainstream. Their ethnic difference was created in their daily experience even if it was not always obviously embodied in political activism or massive social movements.

Here we may adopt and adapt the feminist adage that the "personal is political" by exploring the politics of everyday life. Personal interaction in the workplace, educational strategies in the classroom, and, yes, even attendance at sporting events can provide significant opportunities for asserting an ethnic right to belong. Thus, this analysis looks to the everyday enactment of ethnic identity as it was transmitted through otherwise ordinary experiences. The informal qualities of ethnic belonging become even more important when one considers that not everyone can "speak truth to power" in very public ways. There are, after all, real material fears tied to overt protest. Many of the participants in the rallies were citizens themselves, or at least did not have to worry about their own deportation. There were also those undocumented marchers who risked everything to protest. And then there were those who wanted to attend but felt paralyzed by the fear of what could happen. Open-air rallies could present potential danger to those already anxious about their status. Though tens of thousands attended large-scale protests in 2006, it is important to remember that for every marcher present there were several more who may have feared the potential media coverage and police presence. For instance, an Indianapolis immigrant advocacy group reported that eight people lost their job as a result of joining the 20,000 other marchers who gathered in 2006.[8] In Lafayette, some undocumented immigrants stayed home from jobs and recreational activities because it was rumored that immigration raids were occurring simultaneously with the Indianapolis rally.

In my own personal participation at multiple immigration rallies, I have observed police officers snapping pictures of attendees and the steady presence of counter-protestors angrily shouting at Latino marchers to "go back home." The intimidating presence of police officers and angry nativists could certainly dissuade immigrants vulnerable to deportation. These Hoosier experiences attest to the lived practices of ethnic belonging that differ from politically charged and potentially risky public displays of protest in the politics of belonging. In 2006, Lafayette residents participated in the immigration rallies and Latino businesses closed on May Day as an economic boycott against divisive legislative actions. Additionally, Latinos also displayed an ethnic sense of belonging in other, more routine articulations of ethnic belonging. Even if not intended as modes of protest, attending sporting events, bilingual church services, family birthdays or *quinceañeras* provided the ethnic scaffolding that later manifested into politicized protests for the right to enact this ethnicity in U.S. national spaces. Multiple layers of enacted ethnic belonging surfaced in Latino-based community organizations, public performances, and sporting events where Latinos asserted their right to be different from non-Latino co-workers, classmates, friends, and strangers. Through these various examples of ethnic belonging, Latinos demonstrated a resolve to educate others on their particular ethnic experience that strengthened, rather than weakened, in the face of public animosity about their legitimate presence in community.

Traditional Moments in Cultural Citizenship

Whether through church or other local organizations, Mexican residents were increasingly involved in efforts that recognized their contributions to community. For instance, the steady increase in Mexican residents during the 1990s resulted in the creation of the Lafayette Alliance For Latino Resources (LAFLR). Though disbanded by the time of the research, the community organization was the first attempt to organize local Latinos beyond the spaces of church. The group consisted of faculty and staff from Purdue University as well as local leaders in Lafayette's working-class Mexican population. Though he had passed away by 2006, I was told that one of directors was the son of the area's pioneering Mexican settlers. He worked hard to keep communication lines open between LAFLR and the community members who would benefit from their efforts. In 1998, the members succeeded in helping to form the Centro Hispano [Hispanic Center] within the already existing Community and Family Resource Center (CFRC), a center established to aid all families in Tippecanoe County as a hub for counseling, early childhood education, after-school programming, and a food pantry. Notably, though CFRC was not a Latino-based organization, staff first identified a Spanish-speaking community in 1963 when it published a description of its services in both English and Spanish.[9] The historic willingness to reach out to these "new" community members meant that CFRC's Centro Hispano was well positioned to assist Latino families get acquainted with local services and provide a staff member to help translate for Spanish speakers. By 2006, the Centro had expanded to administer a Spanish Head Start program. The success of the Centro Hispano is a testament to the hard work of LAFLR members. Unfortunately, LAFLR eventually disbanded because of a lack of cohesive goals for future projects.[10]

Even with tensions among its membership, LAFLR was incredibly important for establishing a community consciousness among Latino residents and coordinating with non-Latino service providers to address Latino-specific needs. As an offshoot of LAFLR, the Centro Hispano encouraged CFRC staff to expand their services and eventually developed a *Grupo de Apoyo para Mujeres* [Women's Support Group]. Although the women's group was inactive in 2006, CFRC staff described how participation had lapsed and they were actively recruiting women to start it again. I later learned that prior to this CFRC group another community-based support group formed of Spanish-speaking mothers. Indeed, it was this group that initially formed La Coalición Latina [The Latino Coalition], a community organization that according to some accounts predated LAFLR and represented more of the working-class immigrant population of town. Rocío, a local leader in the community, arrived in Lafayette directly from Mexico in 1992. She was dependent on a controlling husband, and her abusive relationship was compounded by the lack of social networks in the area. She recalled feeling lonely, depressed, empty in her relationship: "de nada sirve si estás vacía y no tienes nada" [[the relationship] is worthless if you feel empty and there is nothing [between the two of you]]. With two small children at home in the early 1990s, Rocío found solace in the local Head Start program and their affiliated *grupo de padres* [parents group]. Open to all parents, the group was made up of mothers who provided one another with what Rocío tearfully remembered as "un soporte que igual hablábamos y empezábamos a hacer más amistades, yo no conocía a nadie . . . estaba sola" [a support where we talked and provided each other with friendship. I didn't know anyone. . . . I was alone]. Like the networks established at church, the group of mothers "*me abrió la puerta*," or opened the door to fruitful possibilities.

Eventually, some women began to meet outside of Head Start activities. They gathered for coffee or to have a bite to eat with one another. Rocío remembered someone's saying in one of these meetings, "falta un centro hispano. Tenemos que hacer algo. Sí se puede. Y así organizamos clases" [we lack a Hispanic Center here. We need to do something. We can do it. And that's how we organized ourselves for classes]. The Latino Coalition found a space in Lafayette's Lincoln Center, the site of Lafayette's segregated school in the 1920s.[11] La Coalición offered after-school tutoring programs for children, prenatal care classes, clinics on cancer education and tobacco and alcohol prevention, GED courses in Spanish, ESL classes, and sponsored holiday events to celebrate Mexican cultural traditions. Rocío explained that La Coalición provided critical programming: "había programas que venía gente que hablaba de cosas emocionales, problemas emocionales, relaciones de pareja, relación con los hijos. Venían consejeros bilingüe, en aquel tiempo había uno o dos bilingüe que eran un milagro porque ni ahorita los encontramos" [There were programs where people would come to discuss emotional topics, emotional problems, couples issues, issues with children. We had bilingual counselors; in those days there were two bilingual counselors which was a miracle because you cannot find those even now]. Without financial support from larger organizations like the CFRC, the Latino Coalition struggled, relocated, and underwent moments of reorganization. Renamed as the Latino Center for Wellness and Education, the organization remains in Greater Lafayette and maintained its original goal to "improve the quality of life in the Latino community."[12]

In addition to community organizations, individual advocacy went a long way toward improving the quality of life for Latinos and building bridges of understanding for non-Latinos. Like Chloe and Betty earlier, other Latinos also desperately hoped that more information on the immigrant experience would lessen the racism still prevalent throughout central Indiana. Though Puerto Rican, Carlos felt an ethnic solidarity with the area's Mexican Latino majority. After graduating from Purdue University in the 1990s, Carlos settled and started a family in Greater Lafayette. Though I spoke to him in 2004, two years prior to the national immigration debate, he was already actively advocating on behalf of the Latino experience. As Carlos related, "We want a better life, but not [to] give up where we came from. Our history is very important to us. Germans wanted a new start, to forget the old country. It's not the same for Mexicans; some are very sad to leave their country."[13] According to Carlos, this complexity was difficult for the White community to grasp. Daily he struggled to explain it them to and to "be the bridge" between different people and organizations. He felt it was his duty to expose non-Latinos to Latino people, foods, and culture. By doing so, he felt he was encouraging a kind of experiential understanding that combated ignorance. As "bridge" builder, Carlos identified an opportunity to clarify some issues affecting both Mexican and non-Latino community building. On the matter of racism, he noted: "Everybody thinks there is no discrimination, and I say there is, I've felt it. Nothing blatant, nobody's come to me and said hey you spic get out of here. But I know, you can tell, you could see it on their face." Carlos noted the differences he felt when entering businesses in town wearing cut-offs and a t-shirt as opposed to when he wore suits. Treatment of working-class Latinos different from that of the upper middle class irritated Carlos. As he asserted, "It shouldn't matter what I wear." A shared Latino identity encouraged Carlos to interject on the attacks he consistently heard made against Mexican Hoosiers. Though not Mexican, he tried to lessen the ire that was growing against Mexican residents and disprove the assumptions already undermining community relationships even prior to 2006.

Latino residents felt committed to defending and explaining the complexity of immigration to those who were misinformed. Gloria arrived in Lafayette in 1999 from Aguascalientes, Mexico. With an uncle in the area, she came with hopes of educational opportunities at the local university. Regrettably, the linguistic and financial barriers proved too difficult to overcome, and she never attended Purdue. Even without a college degree, Gloria found good work in an office. It was at her job where the immigration debate continually came up. Working as the liaison with Spanish-speaking customers, Gloria brought in a significant amount of business for her company. This success was why it was surprising for her to hear co-workers make disparaging comments about Mexicans in her presence. As Gloria explained, "I believe that right now, with all the changes, the population wants to be rooted. Like me, they already feel part of Lafayette. I mean, I say why don't they want me here if I'm from here and I'm not going anywhere. But unfortunately, if you are illegal they think you're breaking the law on purpose. We need to make the Anglos understand how very difficult it is. . . . The people do not want to drive without driver's licenses, but they have no option. They are being blamed for something they don't have a choice in." In noting how the community settled in and embedded themselves into the local social landscape, Gloria tried to explain that undocumented immigrants belonged even if they were not, as she stated, given a choice to reside in the United States legally.[14] The commitment that Gloria exemplified to making the "Anglos understand" was apparent throughout multiple conversations with U.S.-born and naturalized Latino residents. Arguing to be accepted, Latino residents recognized their own rights and privileges as naturalized and/or native-born citizens. These individuals used their juridical privilege to argue on behalf of those being denied a voice and a place as legitimate members of community.

Ethnic Belonging in Unexpected Places

Often unclear about or oblivious to the laws that were supposedly violated, non-Latinos experienced fears of an undocumented population slipped into protectionist arguments that used extralegal entry as a political bogey-man to camouflage angst of a general Latino takeover. Panic over Spanish proliferation, political activism, or "circus music" had more to do with anxieties regarding cultural change than whether someone bypassed a notoriously broken bureaucratic system. To some, the existence of a Latino community signaled a challenge to a homogenized White imagined national community. Latinos were not part of a "Mexican agenda" to take over, or reclaim, Aztlán, but they did actively redraw how they fit into the imaginary.[15] Assimilation expectations, like those present during the German immigrant experience, continue to dominate the way immigrants are often judged for their perceived unwillingness to adopt. This push toward a kind of ethnic amnesia relies on false notions of purity and an image of the United States as devoid of ethnic influences. In practice, ethnic populations have always infused the United States with their particular difference. For instance, the seal of the United States reads "E Pluribus Unum" in order to recognize that from the beginning the country was uniquely united because of its different residents, not in spite of them. In 2006, the popular rhetoric surrounding immigration communicated an expectation that immigrants should immediately sever ties from other nations, cultures, languages, and experiences. This unidirectional absorption theory prevalent in receiving nations ignores how "mutual transformation" has always occurred and how immigrant families have successfully altered the new spaces they inhabit (Nelson and Hiemstra 2008).

By enacting their ethnic difference, Latino residents challenged the assimilationist rhetoric undergirding the immigration debate and asserted their own unique form of ethnic belonging.[16] Ethnic belonging was evinced in the ethno-religious spectacles of the Viacrucis and Virgin of Guadalupe celebrations in Lafayette, but it was also present in other public demonstrations of ethnicity. Affirming their right to enact an ethnic identity that did not undermine their belonging in the United States, Latinos displayed the linguistic freedom to speak Spanish amidst public debates that conflated English-only assertions with patriotism. Referring to the impact of otherwise precarious populations like undocumented immigrants, Judith Butler (2009) described how speaking Spanish exposed the limits of a U.S. national imaginary. Butler writes, "The singing in Spanish on the street gives voice and visibility to those populations that are regularly disavowed as part of the nation, and in this way, the singing exposes the modes of disavowal through which the nation constitutes itself. In other words, the singing exposes and opposes those modes of exclusion through which the nation imagines and enforces its own unity."

The Spanish anthem, or *Nuestro Himno*, was released in 2006 by Spanish popular music stars to assert a right of Latinos to exist and speak Spanish in the United States at a political moment in the nation that denied them both. Hitting the airways in late April 2006, *Nuestro Himno* garnered significant negative response from those who were offended that Spanish-speaking presumed foreigners had appropriated such a quintessential American symbol. *Nuestro Himno* was released in coordination with the massive public mobilization of immigrant supporters, mostly Latinos, who marched in defense of undocumented immigrants. The song and the image of Latino bodies overtaking major American cities was entirely too much for those already troubled by the foreboding future of a twenty-first-century Latino majority predicted by demography experts.

By summer some of the *Nuestro Himno* controversy had subsided. However, with the World Cup in June and the local Colt World Series (a baseball tournament for fifteen- to sixteen-year-old boys) to follow in August, I was curiuos to see how competing nationalisms would be handled locally. The *Mundial*, or Soccer's World Cup, was often viewed in local Mexican restauraunts or in people's homes. The Colt World Series, however, happened publicly and drew a multitude of Lafayette residents. The addition of a team from Juárez, Chihuahua, tested how nationalism and transnationalism co-existed on a diamond field in the Indiana summer. This annual event brought local and global aficionados together for a week of international baseball. The games kicked off with a moment of silence to honor the memory of a young baseball player whose life was cut short earlier that year by a tragic traffic accident, described in chapter 3. With his family in attendance, the hundreds who showed up for the opening events bowed their heads and paid their respects. Of those in attendance, roughly one-third of those filling the bleachers were Mexican fans. Their sizeable presence was due in large part to the last-minute qualification of a team from Mexico. According to the Colt World Series and Colt League National Championship records, the last time a team from Mexico played in Lafayette was in 1978, but an eleventh-hour win by players in Juárez ensured their spot in the 2006 tournament. Accompanied by a few parents and coaches, the players loaded up two vans and left Juárez, Mexico, for Lafayette, Indiana. To help defray the travel costs, Colt World Series organizers always asked locals to host players and their families. With little notice, a call from organizers went out to a Mexican community leader to help recruit host homes. The word spread quickly as families and co-ethnics lined up to support *paisas* [fellow countrymen] from Juárez. Even though locally no one had direct ties to Juárez as most of Lafayette's Mexican residents came from Central Mexico, families ecstatically supported the Mexican team.

International teams were invited to the World Series every year, but the Lafayette team always had a home field advantage in the stands. This time fans for Mexico came out in force and wore their red, white, and green soccer jerseys in solidarity with the Juárez team. Notably, this small, seemingly innocuous wardrobe choice flew in the face of national debates that positioned Mexicans as too ethnic, unassimilable, and a threat to local cultural standards. Host families and fans in the stands created a visual statement of ethnic belonging. Moreover, that some of these host families were White and still willing to wear Mexican colors added to the collective

Baseball fans demonstrating their transnational ties at Colt World Series. Photo by author.

fashion statement on transnational ties. Uninhibited by the debates occurring just weeks prior, fans continued to wear their Mexican pride literally
on their sleeves.

This added fan base made a unique presence when the national
anthem of Mexico echoed throughout the ballpark. Traditionally, an-
thems from the countries of teams represented such as England, South
Korea, and Slovakia usually played with respectful seated silence from
the bleachers. However, in 2006 the recording of a Mexican military
band echoed across a central Indiana summer's day and inspired brown-
bodies throughout the stadium to stand. Methodically, the men, women,
and children stood in honor of the familiar sounds of a Mexican homeland and displayed their transnational ethnic belonging. Local White
Lafayette fans politely watched as Mexican fans placed their right hands
palm-down across their hearts. With elbows proudly raised, these Latino Hoosiers belted out "*Mexicanos al grito de Guerra*" [Mexicans to the
battle cry]. The resonating sounds of adults loudly singing the national
anthem of their youth overpowered the stadium's sound system. Even

Signs of support for Mexico's Colt's Baseball Team. Photo by author.

the families of the players from Juárez turned with tearful appreciation. Though most of the fans held permanent residency status or were already U.S. citizens, their juridical standing and midwestern locality did not alter their public display of transnational co-ethnicity.

Fans took pride in their support for a Mexican team and did not hesitate to showcase their ethnic transnational admiration. Even with the emotions surrounding the grieving family or the national debate on immigration, the Mexico fans did not look ashamed or apprehensive to display their ethnic belonging. These individuals did not restrain themselves from demonstrating their "right to be different and belong." Instead, they exerted an unabashed display of ethnic solidarity that directly and indirectly responded to the present climate of exclusion. In a setting perhaps not as politically motivated as the immigration rallies or boycotts, these fans still declared their right to exist in these spaces while maintaining their ethnic cultural difference.

Certainly, attendance at sporting events or singing the Mexican national anthem at the top of one's lungs did not immediately produce social or political change. However, claims to cultural citizenship are not limited to mass political mobilizations. Though many of the Mexican fans present at the baseball games also attended the Indianapolis immigration rally, the organic manifestation of ethnic belonging on the field was not strategically coordinated. Instead, the spontaneous display of Mexican ethnic belonging at this ballpark represented more instinctive expressions of asserting a bicultural, binational, and bilingual experience. These particular experiences are why Miguel Diaz-Barriga (2008) suggested we expand cultural citizenship by recognizing the ways in which "belonging is 'felt' in everyday life and the ways that its meaning is articulated and contested" (137). What makes ethnic belonging different from cultural citizenship is its very feltness and informality in daily lived experience. This banality provides individuals more freedom to enact ethnically distinct practices of difference. Felt as a sentiment of co-existing affinities, ethnic belonging accounts for the daily lived experiences of being both Mexican and American, of living transnational lives, of feeling "at home" in Indiana and in Jalisco, and, most important, not having to choose one over the other.

Among the baseball fans was Osvaldo, the coach of the local championship adult soccer team. In a separate interview prior to the Colt games, Osvaldo and I spoke about his players and their commitment to the team and one another. Though many worked up to sixty hours a week and others even the night shift, these players still attended exhausting practices, traveled across midwestern states, and brought home several championship cups. Their families also interacted as familial and personal networks grew on the field. Osvaldo hosted one of the Colt players and attended every game he could. His father, an avid *béisbol* fan since his days in Mexico, also attended the games and rose his octogenarian body at every close call to make sure an umpire's call was accurate. For Osvaldo, sports were always a family event. Once a professional soccer player from Veracruz, Osvaldo delighted in coaching both adults and children. Osvaldo was happy to lend his once-professional experience to coach the children of his players. For the first time, Mexican families joined the children's soccer trend so prevalent across parks throughout the United States. Having an ex–professional soccer player as their coach certainly lent to the Mexican team skills that other children did not have. Each consecutive weekend brought wins to this all-Mexican youth team. Their winning streak raised eyebrows, and White parents expressed their resentment. As Osvaldo suggested, "We would win too often. So they started making up rules. They didn't want the same [Latino] kids on the same team. They got mad because I coached them in Spanish. There was some foolishness where they did not want me to coach in Spanish, that it would be disrespectful to the other teams. . . . That is why we left and joined another league in Indy [Indianapolis]." Ethnic belonging for these families came in the form of asserting their right to speak and inculcate their children in Spanish. By withdrawing from the local league, parents enacted ethnic agency in searching for other avenues where they could still belong without forgoing a positive ethnic self-image for their children. Soccer matches, baseball games, and other recreational activities addressed everyday feltness by locating the otherwise mundane acts of living in a community and building ethnic belonging without formal, conscious decisions to enact oppositional cultural citizenship.[17] Osvaldo did not set out to challenge the structural inequalities of a youth soccer league, but by choosing to continue speaking Spanish elsewhere, he and the parents sent a message to the local league that they would not acquiesce to assimilationist demands. Sporting events on the weekend and daily assertions of ethnic identity did not garner as much public national attention as immigration rallies, but they did illustrate a more acurate reality of how Latino families daily asserted their ethnic right to belong.[18] Looking to these more quotidian enactments of belonging situated how poeple exhibited their ethnic belonging in seemingly banal encounters.

For the next generation of Latinos, their ethnic belonging occurred when they were around their parents or a group of co-ethnics who helped strengthen their resolve to be different. Difficult moments of ethnic belonging for youth emerged in school settings where they would have to decide how to assert their Latino identities. Children can be cruel and often read difference as detrimental on the schoolyard. Alma's school years were rife with bullies and negative experiences. She recalled first arriving to Lafayette via southern California:

> When I was first starting here, I was put in a special needs program because there was no ESL. So I remember going up to my dad and telling him there was a kid who, um, had a little moment in class. And he was

like what do you mean. He [the classmate] wouldn't stop shaking. Well, he was having a seizure, and I didn't know what that was. But that was the only classroom where they had more aides to help you, and so they would help me with my homework. . . . I was in that class for like a year until my dad finally went and talked to the principal and told him we can't have that. You can't do that.

Alma's schooling suffered while she was in the special needs program, but her negative encounters continued with bullies in mainstream classrooms. She recalled feeling bullied even by her own teachers, who refused to stick up for her and even encouraged the teasing. For Alma and so many Latino children, educators and their attitudes toward the general Latino population mattered intensely. Indeed, teachers, parents, administrators, and students all attested to the way spatial and social borders continually manifested in the schools. Teenage angst and classic bullying were taken to new politicized levels in 2006. I was rarely in the classroom when I worked in the school as the Hispanic Outreach Coordinator, but my exposure to teachers, administrators, and students revealed how the dialogue of immigration penetrated educational environments. For instance, Mago, an undocumented mother who spoke about *rechazo* in an earlier chapter, voiced her concerns as she recounted what her children told her about their school encounters, "que en las escuelas les estaban diciendo 'go back to Mexico where you belong.' Ángel me dijo que el defendió a otros niños" [that in the schools they were saying "go back to Mexico where you belong." Angel told me he defended some of the other kids]. The intensity of the immigration debate reached the schoolyard and was transmitted in the form of verbal assaults and harassment.

Not surprisingly, English as a New Language (ENL) students were particularly targeted for embodying all that was found objectionable in the immigration debate. Though these students were in school to learn English, they were belittled for not adopting English fast enough. Moreover, mainstream non-Latino students referred to the hallway that housed the two ENL classrooms as "the border." ENL teachers related that their students were being harassed in the hallway. Apparently, the mornings were particularly bad for ENL students who waited outside the classroom for their teacher to unlock the door. Spanish-speaking students, and any English-dominant Latino who was seen associating with them, faced verbal and physical attacks.

Even as ENL students stood just outside their English classroom, they were absurdly commanded to learn English and endured yells of "you need to speak English." Especially in 2006, youths felt free to spew ethnic slurs and target brown-skinned classmates as threats. As Guille, the district-wide Hispanic community liason, commented, "el racismo existe en casa, escondido. Pero son los niños que lo hablan" [racism exists hidden in the home, but it is the children who speak it [publicly]].

Felt distances and antagonism in the schools were not always so overtly stated; sometimes more subtle examples of animosity entered the classroom. Instead of direct hostility, some non-Latino students revealed a lack of empathy or relatability toward the undocumented experience. Ms. Thomas, a teacher who taught Spanish to non-native speakers and English to ENL students, revealed the marked difference in student outlook toward undocumented immigrants in 2006: "When I taught Spanish before, the kids had some sympathy for illegals, like 'they come here and they're looking for a better life for their children.' And now the whole attitude has changed, 'they need to go back to where they came from, they need to learn English, this is our country, they're taking our jobs.' . . . Even my honor kids are very nasty about it. . . . I've never had this negative of a reaction before. It worried me." Ms. Thomas was concerned about the social pendulum that swung against Latinos in the area, for although the attacks were aimed at the undocumented, the slippage between Spanish speaker and undocumented occurred often. As in years past, she had students research migrant working conditions, watch movies, and examine the historical political scapegoating of Mexican immigrants in order broaden their understanding of the undocumented experience. To Ms. Thomas's disappointment, the students returned to the issue of legality and refused to, as Ms. Thomas noted, "see the immigrants as people." As the object of this resentment, ENL students were taunted, threatened, and stalked in academic spaces. Ms. Thomas recalled Spanish-speaking students' asking her what "beaner" meant because that was what kids called them in the hallway. Additionally, another teacher at the high school also related a story about a student who was continually spat at while boarding the school bus. Ms. Ceja astutely noted, "There are things happening that adults in the school don't necessary see. Or, I hate to say this, but there were students saying that teachers were racists and said, 'You Mexican students always want to fight' . . . so there's some tension among the teachers against the [Mexican] population." Mago reiterated this concern with teachers when noting that her daughter's teacher at the same high school told his class that photographs of the Indianapolis immigration rally had been digitally enhanced. According to her daughter, the teacher doubted that so many people would march in defense of immigrants.[19] ENL students faced this denigration as well as held fears of being "picked up" or deported at school. Though not all the ENL students were undocumented, it was clearly a concern for many of the students that either they or their relatives would be deported. Facing internal anxieties and external assault, ENL students lived lives that their English-dominant non-Latino peers could not even imagine.

Teachers sympathetic to the Latino and ENL students' situations meant the world to students and their families. Mago repeatedly referred to one teacher, Mercedes, as a godsend in her children's lives. Mercedes was a schoolteacher and the granddaughter of one of the first Mexican workers who had stumbled upon Lafayette in the late 1950s. Like other Mexican children raised in central Indiana, Mercedes identified Lafayette as home and claimed belonging and "ownership" as one of the original families to settle in the area. With degrees from Purdue University, many of the second generation of Mexican Hoosiers in Lafayette could have chosen to leave Indiana as had so many White Hoosiers before them.[20] Instead, several chose to stay in Lafayette and become an integral part of the educational and personal development of the next generation. Mercedes became an ENL teacher at the same school she and her father both attended. As a second-generation Mexican Hoosier, she vowed to create a different atmosphere from the one she had once faced. Mercedes insisted that her students have a positive self-image: "I want them to embrace and love their culture and be proud. Educate themselves . . . . They're not going to be embarrassed the way I was."

Mercedes created an environment where her English Language Learners (ELL) students could flourish and recognize their contributions to local, national, and global communities.[21] Specifically, Mercedes

Bulletin board made by students to explain the realities of a broken immigration system. Photo by author.

used the dispute over immigration reform as a "teachable moment" for students throughout the campus. To combat the stereotypes and rhetoric between students and adults, she challenged her students to explain exactly what the immigration rally was protesting and supporting. Rather than simply feel angry, fearful, or disappointed by the debate, Mercedes wanted her students to think through critically what was at stake. She developed a lesson plan whereby students researched the immigration debate and devised a way of sharing their findings with the entire student body. Mercedes' ELL students worked with three other English-dominant social studies classes to post their research on immigration to large bulletin boards throughout the campus hallways. In fact, Mercedes encouraged students to attend school during the May 1 boycotts because, as she noted, "If you stay at home for the strike, you're staying at home with people who know about this, people who agree and believe with you . . . [but] if you all come here and get organized and wear a white shirt, well obviously people are going to notice that and people are going to ask. Then *pum* [*boom*], you're going to educate somebody. So what's better? And they made their choice. Everybody showed up with their white shirts." In this sense, Mercedes empowered students to take action in a manner that could become productive to the overall conversation and climate surrounding immigration. ELL as well as other English-dominant Latino students gravitated to Mercedes' classroom and assisted in making maps, flags, and signs for the bulletin boards. From April until the end of the spring semester, bulletin boards displayed signs of "Don't panic, We're only Hispanic," "We're all immigrants, you've just been here longer," "We have a dream too," and "United We Are Stronger." Short student narratives also displayed anonymous, emotionally personal thoughts on what immigration reform might do for their families. The class was featured in the local newspaper, where they proudly broadcast their case to the rest of the town.[22] Through this exercise, Mercedes encouraged her students to find strength and educate themselves and in the process provide valuable information to others. The students created a venue for conversation, a place for information, that Mercedes felt would honor the positions the students were attempting to defend. Moreover, in this exercise the students found what Mercedes noted as a "voice to be strong and be proud," a virtue she admitted not having at their age.

Living *sin Fronteras*/without Borders

Though historically written out of national and local imaginaries, Lafayette's Latino communities exemplified what it meant to ethnically belong as part of a diverse and vibrant collective. Far from denying their transnational identities or operating within soft forms of multiculturalism, these families held firm to their linguistic, cultural, or ethnic affiliations and in the process reformulated, in their minds, what it meant to be an acceptable member of society. For them, their ethnic belonging meant more than just drinking beer at a local brewery on Cinco de Mayo. They struggled and fought to assert their own rights as ethnic transnational beings and argued for the rights to do so within the United States. Living in Lafayette did not mean giving up Viacrucis celebrations, cheering on Mexican teams in public, or raising their children to be proud of their heritage. Indeed, instead of falling into the pressures of assimilation, this community enacted resistance in their subtle everyday lives. This lived ethnic belonging was a source of strength and an opportunity to share their unique experiences with the rest of the population. Rather than feel shame, they openly celebrated and defied the caustic environment produced by a politics of immigration.

Though targeted by divisive rhetoric, Latinos produced alternate modes of belonging. The result was a unique blending of ethnic belonging that situated Spanish speakers as legitimate, if culturally different, members of community. They confronted daily racialized, classed, linguistic, and ethnic borderings through their own subtle avenues of ethnic belonging. In essence, they heeded Gloria Anzaldúa's advice on living and surviving the Borderlands: "To survive the Borderlands / you must live *sin fronteras* / be a crossroads." Fittingly, Indiana's state motto is "The Crossroads of America." In this crossroads, Latino families lived *sin fronteras* [without borders] by refusing the limitations of ethno-nationalist boundaries, carving out space for Latino Hoosier identities.

Intervening in a particularly heightened contemporary moment of immigration politics, Latino residents organized protests, but they also responded to negative portrayals with personal enthusiasm to change minds and establish legitimacy in daily uncoordinated performances of ethnic belonging. Mercedes, Gloria, Carlos, and the fans at the Colt World Series demonstrated a longstanding resolve to maintain their ethnic sense of self with a simultaneous drive to improve community relationships in their town. As Mercedes' class illustrated, these daily acts of ethnic assertions could in fact create more opportunities to change minds than perhaps even public protests. Though ethnic belonging and activist protests were both necessary, these Lafayette residents included equally important spontaneous examples of ethnically claiming a right to belong. Moreover, the regional specificity of "new" destinations required Latinos to actively approach their position in the local imaginary to reshape the way they were perceived and accepted in these rural, exurban, and "new" communities. Perhaps individuals like Carlos or Gloria may never join a community organization or participate in a public protest, but their interjections of ethnic belonging were critical in asserting ethnic rights to space and disputing negative preconceptions hovering in the local imaginary.

Conclusion

The Politics of Belonging Wages On: How State-Based Legislation Affects Community in Indiana

Community is all about boundaries between us and them, boundaries that are naturalized through reference to place or race or culture or identity.
—Miranda Joseph, *Against the Romance of Community*

The narratives in this book have illustrated the impact of immigration politics on a town and how race, gender, class, and ethnicity determined one's right to community. All residents of Lafayette took part in religious, ethnic, and familial communities of their own, but there was a collective sense of belonging to this particular midwestern city. Interacting at multiple moments and in multiple spaces, the residents of Lafayette all contributed to the totality of living and surviving in this shared meaningful place. Though Latinos exhibited ethnic difference, they still belonged to this community even if they were not always accepted.

Focusing on the denied acceptance and boundary making implicit in communities, Miranda Joseph (2002) appropriately warns against romanticizing community and replicating the system of inequality embedded in its very conceptualization. Though her critique is significant, some individuals do not have the privilege of disavowing community. For immigrants, and especially undocumented immigrants, belonging to community mattered deeply. The collective "we" and the politics of determining who belonged to local and national ideas of an "us" had material consequences for those within and outside of community. Even with the incredible limitations that such concepts promote, the importance of community and belonging operated daily on Latino Hoosiers. We must absolutely think beyond the constraints that community achieves, but we cannot forget the way community operates in practice and how individuals are actually engaging in redefining community and belonging without completely rejecting them altogether.

Exploring both fluid and rigid definitions of community, this book broadened the concept of national and local community in order to allow for numerous modes of belonging. Debates surrounding immigration revolve around the notion of community: Who already belongs? Who should enter? What must outsiders do to be accepted into national, regional, and local imagined communities? These debates are not new, and as chapter 1 illustrated, palimpsests of belonging can be layered upon one another across time in the same space. To understand how community is currently defined or patrolled, one must look to these layered Otherings and acknowledge how past denials of belonging resonate in the present. The racialization of people of color, the denial of preexisting Indian rights to land, and the convenient erasures of anti-immigrant moments all played a part in the contemporary bordered experiences of Indiana. The written Othering and felt distances in chapters 3 and 4 demonstrated precisely how the borderlands extended to Indiana. Latino residents were made to feel excluded—barred from participating fully in the imagined community. Negative associations marked Latinos as interlopers who belonged elsewhere and threatened "more deserving" non-Latinos with their presence. Notably, Latino residents were not dissuaded and continued to add their own constructions of home to Hoosier history. Chapters 2 and 5 both located examples of ethnic belonging where Latinos developed ways to survive. They navigated the borderlands of the Midwest and found ways to deal with the *rechazo* they faced in Lafayette.

Regardless of the obstacles, these families stayed and established their own modalities of belonging through social networks, ethno-religious events, community organizations, sporting events, and the public schools. Their survival strategies were useful when confronting the caustic environment created by the 2006 immigration debate. Fed by a national politics of exclusion, written attacks and felt rejections occurred throughout Lafayette. The negative rhetoric permeated even otherwise "well-meaning" non-Latino residents who uncritically accepted assumptions against Latinos as criminal threats to community. Notably, some non-Latino residents did push against these misrepresentations. Their efforts showcased a possibility to resist and proved that this wave of animosity is not inevitable for other communities equally pressured to react negatively to their Latino neighbors. The importance of allies would be demonstrated years after 2006 when the state of Indiana turned toward punitive Arizona-style state-based measures against undocumented immigrants.

A Politics of Exclusion Continues

The collaborative efforts of individuals and organizations to build community and combat the divisive politics of 2006 cannot be understated. Latinos and non-Latinos faced an uphill battle to live "*sin fronteras*—without borders" at the Crossroads of America (Anzaldúa 1987). Their resolve would be tested time and again as isistent individuals continued to inject fear into the community. Unwilling to let the immigration debate die, particular politicians swung the pendulum of belonging back toward divisive techniques. Even as H.R. 4437 was eventually defeated, state legislators across the country continued to target immigrant communities. For instance, in 2007 Oklahoma passed one of the harshest anti-immigrant legislations in the country. Encouraged by this political win, Indiana state Senator Mike Delph of Carmel, an affluent suburb north of Indianapolis, introduced Senate Bill 335. S.B. 335 was aimed at cracking down on businesses that hired undocumented immigrants, holding the business accountable by revoking its license to operate in the state of Indiana. By the time S.B. 335 was introduced in January 2008, a false sense of comfort had settled within Latino communities throughout Indiana. Relieved that H.R. 4437 had been defeated but disappointed that a path to citizenship was no longer on the table, Latino Hoosiers were disturbed by Senator Delph's obvious racial attacks, as when he couched the words "gangs," "drugs," and "disease in fast-food restaurants" in his concerns against Hispanic immigrants."[1] Additionally, the bill criminalized the transportation of and aid to undocumented immigrants (including that done by churches and community organizations) and solicited funds to train local law enforcement to carry out immigration enforcement. After some public hearings, a 10-to-1 committee voted to pass the Senate bill along to the full Senate. As a result of earlier collaboration efforts, Latino and non-Latino allies traveled to Indianapolis (the state capital) to speak against the bill. Locally, community leaders in Lafayette worked together to sponsor a forum on the topic in February 2008. Personal communication with panelists revealed that the forum resulted in healthy positive discussions. Thankfully S.B. 335 was defeated, but regrettably this was not the last time Indiana residents found themselves embroiled by immigration politics.

In 2008, as the presidential election loomed, national attention once more turned to immigration reform. The political climate at both the national and state levels reinvigorated attention to this contentious topic. In response to this renewed interest, the *Journal and Courier* included a six-part month-long series on immigration in July 2008. Individual and family interviews accompanied controversial discussions on border walls, racial profiling, comprehensive immigrant reform, and even historical parallels to Irish, Italian, and Chinese immigrants in the past. Notably, ties to local German predecessors remained absent. In addition, online commentary continued the xenophobic attacks prevalent in 2006. On one occasion, the *Journal and Courier* censored a previous post by a self-identified Lafayette resident who asked for the return of the Ku Klux Klan.[2] Because Indiana was considered a swing state, Democratic candidate Barack Obama visited the state often and even made a stop in Lafayette at the very high school where I once worked. Though I was no longer in the area at the time, local contacts related an aura of activism and *hope* that invigorated progressive politics. Indeed, Tippecanoe County went blue as Barack Obama and Joe Biden narrowly won the majority of votes in the area. The euphoria, however, would not last long. The pendulum, it seemed, was still swinging. The Obama/Biden win provided the impetus for conservatives to join with Tea Party extremists and encouraged politicians like Mike Delph to rebrand his level of conservatism through this new thread in the Republican Party.

Delph's history of failure with his anti-immigrant legislation did not deter him from again introducing a bill that targeted undocumented residents. Legally, undocumented status warrants only a misdemeanor in the court systems. To change this, Delph and others across the country introduced in their states bills that required officers to ask individuals for their status and threatened undocumented immigrants with severe fines, jail time, and deportation. The successful passage of Arizona's infamous S.B. 1070 in 2010 encouraged legislators elsewhere to introduce their own "show me your papers" bills in their states. Undeterred by the bipartisan opposition of S.B. 335 and the negative backlash Arizona received as a result of S.B. 1070, Delph introduced S.B. 590 in early 2011. The bill threatened to revoke business licenses to those who knowingly employed undocumented workers, required the use of the E-verify system, and criminalized day labor practices. Last, the bill included stipulations that criminalized the transporting, aiding, or shielding of undocumented immigrants from detection, outlawed sanctuary cities, denied consular IDs as valid forms of identification, and rescinded a previously approved policy that left open the possibility for in-state tuition for undocumented youth graduating from Indiana schools and barred them from any forms of financial aid. Delph also included English-only stipulations for all state-related business. Indeed, the bill's obvious aim was to make life so incredibly difficult and unwelcoming that undocumented residents would leave the state immediately.

Community leaders once again organized trips to Indianapolis. This time, however, they focused on speaking directly to their representatives and testifying in public hearings against the bill. Latino and Non-Latino religious leaders, community members, and business representatives all expressed concern over the lived and financial impact of state-sanctioned hostility against certain members of the population. They met with politicians and held media events to showcase their collective opposition to the bill. Following the example of similar efforts of resistance in Utah against Arizona-style legislation, these Hoosiers signed the Indiana Compact, a document that contested the criminalization of immigrants and their families, opposed the separation of families, emphasized the need for a welcoming and business-friendly Indiana, and finally adopted a "spirit of inclusion" that promoted a "humane approach" toward undocumented immigrants. The signers of the Indiana Compact argued that all Hoosiers would feel the negative reverberations of businesses' divesting from the state, boycotts from potential conventions, and state funds' being used to defend the law against inevitable lawsuits. Their civic activism did result in some changes to the bill. Unfortunately, supporters of S.B. 590 persistently soldiered on until it was signed into law on May 10, 2011, by then-Governor Mitch Daniels. Legislators added safeguards throughout the text of the now-adopted State

Enrolled Act (SEA) No. 590 that explicitly noted how the law "shall be enforced without regard to race, religion, gender, ethnicity, or national origin." Possibly added to protect the bill from accusations of racial profiling, SEA 590 mirrored its predecessor in Arizona by leaving open the notion of "reasonable suspicion" to the interpretation of law enforcement officials. By itself, this caveat was not deemed unconstitutional by the U.S. Supreme Court's 2012 ruling against Arizona; however, the justices did warn against the possible manner by which such a stipulation could be enforced.

The 2008 introduction of S.B. 335 and the passage of SEA 590 were precisely why I made brief research trips back to Indiana. In search of friends and updates from respondents, I visited Indiana in 2009 and then again in 2012. Notably, some families had left for better economic opportunities elsewhere. The national recession did negatively affect local employment for all in the area, but a majority of those I initially met in 2006 remained. In 2012, I stayed with Mercedes and marveled at how much her son, a baby in early 2007, had grown to be a bright six-year-old. Additionally, I spoke to Beth Ann and Ted and was delighted to hear that their opinion of undocumented immigrants had evolved. Once adamant that "they be legal" and speak English, by 2012 Beth Ann noted very plainly and simply, "I think there should be some path to citizenship." Beth Ann had moved away from her initial unfavorable view of undocumented immigrants. As I inquired further as to what she meant by a "path to citizenship," she responded, "I'm not even sure about the whole green card thing and the way that works, but I think in our federal laws there probably is a problem in the path to citizenship. . . . I guess the actual path to citizenship now is many, many years, a dozen years or so, something like that. Which seems kind of a heavy price to pay. It seems like that should be streamlined." Beth Ann also revealed that she now knew there was a difference between the first generation and second generation with regard to language acquisition. I asked her if she remembered her stance in 2006 on learning English and she replied, "Maybe that's unrealistic to think that way, that they'll do that." Both Ted and Beth Ann referenced the DREAMERS, whom they called the "dream X" students, and the polemic rhetoric coming out of Arizona. Exposure to DREAMERS' stories and the negativity in Arizona seemed to have shifted their position. Now they favored a resolution that took into consideration the on-the-ground realities of people whose lives they now understood much better. Both Ted and Beth Ann also referenced SEA 590 and knew that Indiana legislators had passed a law "similar to Arizona's," but beyond its passing they did not know the specifics. I visited another dozen individuals on that 2012 trip for updates, and all except two knew the specifics of SEA 590. Latinos and non-Latinos either thought the law had not passed at all or had been changed so much that it no longer resembled Arizona's punitive measures.

Knowledge of SEA 590 depended largely on one's intimate interactions with the law or whether one knew someone who was caught up in the bureaucratic changes the law required. The local community college suffered immensely. Sergio, no longer a student in Indiana, found that administrative duties for the community college gave him perspective on the impact of SEA 590. Sergio lamented that the law was detrimental to so many of his students who could no longer receive in-state tuition. By late 2012 Sergio and other administrators at the local community college were busy helping students collect their documents for DACA. Still, Sergio addressed the absurdity of laws like SEA 590, which served to scare so many only for political gain: "Delph and [they] didn't even put any funds to back up their law. So you can tell people do this and do that, but without funding who's going to abide by the new rules?" Who, indeed.

Sergio and Lucas, a member of CAC, revealed that the implementation of SEA 590 was haphazard at best. Instead of streamlining the way state officials interacted with the undocumented, SEA 590 created disparate and contradictory approaches. Since the passage of the law, Latinos in Indiana have been leery of certain areas of the state that targeted brown-bodies at rates much higher than in other regions. Latino drivers, regardless of documented status, expressed that certain regions of Indiana were hostile toward the popularly referred crime of "driving while Mexican." In particular, Latino Hoosiers related stories of encounters with the law that yielded drastically different experiences depending on where one was stopped. In some jurisdictions, law enforcement simply handed out citations to drivers for their traffic violations rather than criminally charge them and report them to immigration officials.

Lucas was close friends with Efraín and Veronica, and in 2012 I inquired about their present situation. I missed them at their church service and was truly concerned about their well-being. Had they endured the backlash on their extralegal presence? Did they still own their home? How were their children? Lucas mentioned that their oldest was able to attend university but had to move out of state and attend a private university that gladly rewarded him an academic scholarship. I was happy to hear this; their son was old enough to remember the difficult border crossing he, his mother, and sister had endured. It seemed he had overcome much hardship in his youth. The family, however, was not immune to other structural challenges on their success. Lucas related the recent moment when he was called to help negotiate Efraín's release from jail. After S.B. 590 passed, Efraín was stopped for a minor traffic violation on his way to a religious service. He was charged with a Class C misdemeanor for driving without a license, jailed for a few hours, and fined.

Raquel, a victim advocate at Lafayette's domestic violence shelter, related an almost identical encounter about her friend Lorena, who was pulled over in another town, just a few miles away from where Efraín was stopped. Like Efraín, Lorena was asked for a driver's license. She responded with a Spanish accent, and the officer asked her to provide proof of residency. Because she had no proof, Lorena was deported and had to take her U.S.-born children "back" to a country they had never known. Indiana Code 9–24–18–1 stipulated that driving without a driver's license was a Class C misdemeanor unless the person had a prior offense, in which case it became a Class A misdemeanor. Lorena had no prior offense, but her status as an undocumented immigrant led her into deportation proceedings. At most, this kind of Class C misdemeanor carried a stint in jail and a fine regardless of the status of the driver. Efraín fared better than Lorena because the officer who stopped him did not feel that proof of legal residency was necessary, but these scenarios reveal how defining "reasonable suspicion" varied throughout the state. Moreover, Lorena's experience illustrated that some police officers continued to rely on ethnic markers to probe those they stopped. In Efraín's case, the town's law enforcement worked for years to develop a trustworthy relationship with the Latino community. Once S.B. 590 passed, they ensured Latino residents that their race, accented Spanish, or skin color would never be used as a marker of "reasonable suspicion." However, other jurisdictions purposefully left unsaid what would warrant an officer's further probing of someone's status, and this flexibility led to drastically different modes of carrying out the letter of the law.

Exploiting the fear and anxiety left unsettled by the 2006 national immigration debate, hyperbolic speeches and rhetoric of impending hordes of undocumented immigrants led to bills like S.B. 590. Yet, even with these very real threats on their material conditions, individuals like Efraín, Veronica, or countless others refused to "self-deport." Latino Hoosiers in Lafayette fought an upward battle to legitimate their rightful belonging in this midwestern community. To do so, they used their own cultural citizenship and formed networks of solidarity through cultural, religious, gendered, and ethnic bonds. Life for individuals like Efraín and others was made much more precarious as a result of state-based legislative actions, yet they forged on. Making the best out of a horrible situation, these residents created alternate spaces of belonging for themselves and others like them. In the process, they befriended critical non-Latino allies who also fought to make this a welcoming, considerate place to live for all.

As new immigrant populations continue to appear in nontraditional, non-urban locales, scholarship regarding these populations must recognize the need to examine these "newer" sites in dialogue with, and in contrast to, the experiences of more traditional borderlands. While comparisons can be made between central Indiana and immigrant settlements in larger midwestern cities and the U.S. Southwest, Greater Lafayette must also be recognized for its unique circumstances that mark this and other "new" locations as historically relevant and distinct to this contemporary moment in immigration. Though they faced different challenges from that of brethren in more traditional receiving communities, Latinos in central Indiana created new networks, new traditions, and new ways of coping with the realities they faced. Clearly, the battle for belonging wages forward as communities across the United States continue to struggle with their response to undocumented immigrants. In places like Arizona and other locations, state-based legislation curtails the lives of undocumented immigrants and continues to create antimosities toward anyone suspected of being undocumented. The lived experience in the pages of this book documents how a people can come together and assert their rights to live peacefully among one another without having to forfeit ethnicity, language, or humanity. Not everyone will agree on the immigration debate, but we should at least recognize the complexity of human lives embedded in the rhetoric. This book is a wake-up call. Rather than continue the litany of political half-truths, we must go about the difficult task of creating a collective community that embraces its complexity. *Por que el corazon de la nación sigue latiando*, but how we treat the souls that make up our national heartbeat remains to be seen.

NOTES

PREFACE

1. Though pseudonyms are used for individuals, I decided to maintain the name of the town. Rather than conceal the location, I hope to reveal both the beauty and struggles of this particular environment. "The Greater Lafayette area" refers to the adjoining cities of West Lafayette and Lafayette, Indiana. Together, the population in these two towns comprises the majority of residents in Tippecanoe County. Notably, West Lafayette is the home of Purdue University and houses a majority of those affiliated with this institution. Lafayette, on the other hand, is home to more blue-collar families working in the area's manufacturing positions.

2. Similarly, in his work on San Diego immigrants, Leo Chavez (1994) includes the complaints of parents not able to take their children to Disneyland. In San Diego, the restrictions were based on border inspections leading to Los Angeles.

3. Interestingly, the opposite was also true for those immigrants who had left more urban areas of Mexico and considered Lafayette too small; however, these more urban immigrants were not the majority of those who had settled in Lafayette.

4. West Lafayette was colloquially referred to as the West Side because it is west of the river.

5. Early-twentieth-century arguments used the term "the Mexican problem" to explain how Mexicans immigrants were unassmilable.

6. The term "Latino Hoosiers" is a play on the word traditionally affiliated with people from Indiana. "Hoosier" is the colloquial term used to refer to people from Indiana and traditionally is not extended to residents of color in the state. Within the state of Indiana it is used as a way of defining residency and belonging as an Indiana resident. I am also aware that in other states, Missouri for instance, it has negative connotations. The use of "Hoosier" here is meant to connote the first and not the latter meaning of the word.

7. For more on redefining citizenship beyond the "legal" label, see Oboler (2006).

8. Chavez (1994).

9. Ibid.

10. While a majority of the Latino interviewees were either first- or second-generation Mexican residents, I did interview four people from Puerto Rico, three individuals from El Salvador, and one person from Venezuela.

11. Participants were explained the focus of the study and its use in academic settings and asked to give verbal consent to use their image and/or voices in the project.

Most interviews were recorded, but some were written because of the preference of the participants or malfunctioning equipment.

12. At the time of my leaving in 2007, the university had developed programming that attempted to reach the Lafayette side, but too often these moments were few and far between.

INTRODUCTION

1. Lopez (2006).
2. These are the lyrics to a song sung along Indianapolis city streets during the 2006 immigration rallies. Translation of the lyrics in Spanish and English is taken directly from the broadsides passed out along the route. Broadsides were printed in English on one side and in Spanish on the other.
3. This immediate association with criminality and undocumented status can be traced in Robin D. Jacobson, *The New Nativsm* (2008). Also, see Daryl Williams's letter against Arizona's S.B. 1070, wherein he argues that undocumented entry is not a criminal act because it lacks *mens rea*, or the intent to injure, that is traditionally tied to criminality.
4. A good example of this type of corrective includes writing African Americans back into Hoosier history. For example: Lassiter et al. (2004).
5. For a history of northwestern Indiana's Mexican populations, see Lane and Escobar (1987), Rosales (1976), Sepulveda (1976), and Vargas (1993).
6. Chicagoland is the local name for the Chicago metropolitan area.
7. This notion of midwestern-nice is borrowed from the infamous "Iowa-nice" label given to Iowa residents, especially during national presidential election seasons.
8. For examples of border theory in anthropology, see Alvarez (1995), Berdahl (1999), Chavez (1994), De Genova (2005), Kearney (1998), Lugo (2008), Rosaldo (1989), and Velez Ibañez (1996).
9. Flores (1993), Foley (1990), Kearney (1998), Lugo (2000), Rodriguez (1996), Velez Ibañez (1996).
10. Flores (1993), Foley (1990), Kearney (1998), Lugo (2000), Oboler (1995).
11. Chavez (2008), Santa Ana (2002).
12. This was a statement made on May 5, 2005, and posted on his website (http:// sensenbrenner.house.gov) on the passing of the Real ID Act and the strengthening of border security between what he termed "'Smuggler's Gulch,' a canyon along the westernmost California–Mexico border frequently used for illegal entrance into the U.S."
13. Earlier versions of H.R. 4437 existed in California's 1994 Proposition 187 and Arizona's 2004 Proposition 200.
14. See Millard and Chapa (2004) and Smith and Furuseth (2006) for more on Latino settlement in "new" areas in the South and Midwest.
15. In his work on Iowa, Lionel Cantu (1995) noted that employers used their own Latino employees as recruiting resources. For other work on immigrant networks, see Krissman (1995), Margolis (1994), Menjívar (2000).

16. Chapter 2 provides an instance where job competition created longstanding familial strife with the workers.

17. For more work on the rise of Latino immigration in these nontraditional regions, see Coutin (2005), Fink (2003), Millard and Chapa (2004), Smith-Nonini (2003), Smith and Furuseth (2006), Villenas (2001).

18. This situation has also been cited in Cantu (1995), Grey (1999), and Smith and Furuseth (2006).

19. Anzaldúa (1987).

20. The word "Hoosierlandia" is meant purposefully to allude to the Spanish word for Disneyland, or "Disneylandia." The book's rendition of Disneyland, or Hoosierlandia, can be tied to Baudrillard's simulacrum as used to discuss the false simulation of a welcoming environment.

21. For more on the abject stutus of contemporary Mexicans, see Gonzales and Chavez (2012).

22. Abrego and Menjivar (2011).

23. Jacobson (2008).

24. Rosaldo (1994: 402).

25. For more work on Latinos and citizenship, see Castañeda (2006), Flores and Benmayor (1997), Fraga et al. (2010), Oboler (2006), and Plascencia (2012).

CHAPTER 1. *RECUERDOS DE* LAFAYETTE

1. Literally translated as "the mornings," this traditional Mexican song is often sung in honor of a birthday or holiday for an individual like Mother's Day.

2. This chant translates roughly into the English "ra ra sis boom ba" and is used at sports venues but also as a way to cheer someone on a birthday or special event. On this day, a longtime Latino Lafayette resident studying to be deacon led the crowd in this *porra*, or cheer, for the Virgin of Guadalupe. Also of note, the songs listed are both secular and religious melodies often seen in Mexican popular culture.

3. Having indigenous dance performances like this one has come to define the Virgin de Guadalupe ritual tradition both in Mexico and in the United States. Like the children's costumes, it is considered by those who practice it to be a way to pay homage to the indigenous basis of the Virgin of Guadalupe narrative. To others who have recaptured a more politically conscious indigenous identity, these performances can be seen as romantic representations that are culturally inaccurate and insensitive.

4. For more on ethno-Catholicism, see Treviño (2006) and on ethno-religious practices, Pitti (2003).

5. Ironically, supporters of the Tea Party in a post-2008 election season expressed inconsistent messages as they simultaneously advocated for immigration control and limited government.

6. Readers interested in the creation of a White identity should also see Haney-López (2006), Ngai (2004), Omi and Winant (1994), and Roediger (1999).

7. I contacted the business reporter for the *Journal and Courier* because I was told by several individuals that the *Journal and Courier* had published a picture of the sign in its newspaper. The above quote was gathered through e-mail correspondence with this reporter.

8. For more on immigrant networks, see Krissman (1995), Menjívar (2000), and Vélez-Ibañez and Sampaio (2002).

9. One of the brothers had since passed away while the other still resided in Salazares, Jalisco.

10. All names in the analysis are pseudonyms. The name of the family responsible for employing the first generation of Mexicans and the name of the restaurant will remain anonymous.

11. This concept of Greater Mexico comes from the work of Américo Paredes, who placed areas of the United States with significant Mexican populations within the larger cultural Mexican imaginary.

12. The word "*contrabando*" has been used to denote smuggling contraband into the country in popular Norteño music and is most often used with regard to drugs. But Don Osvaldo's use of the word here is meant to describe his undocumented status and his being smuggled into the country by *coyotes* (smugglers).

13. For more on the history of changing visa requirements and designations for legal entry, see De Genova (2006).

14. This feeling of uneasiness was still present in narratives of recent Mexican residents to Lafayette.

15. In the 1990s Laura's desires were finally realized. One by one, her siblings discovered the advantages of living in Lafayette and ultimately made the move themselves.

16. This is referencing Mercedes' earlier use of the word "pioneers" to describe early Mexican residents.

17. St. Boniface Roman Catholic Church, 1999 anniversary book.

18. For more on small Latino congregations, see Woodrick (2006).

19. Interestingly, surviving members of the Kickapoo tribe live in Texas and Mexico. Given the historical tie of the borderlands with a mythical Aztlán, the historical relevance of Kickapoo in Lafayette could actually cause an interesting reexamination of the reach of Aztlán well into Indiana.

20. For a more critical view of French fur trade policies in what is now the American Midwest, see R. David Edmunds and Joseph L. Peyser (1993).

21. I last accessed the website in the spring of 2008. As of 2012, the website is no longer available.

22. See Cave (2002) for an analysis of the bias constructed against the Prophet and a historiography of other scholarship that restores this individual from the attacks of the past.

23. Buss (2011), Gutierrez (1989), Mills (1997), Thrush (2007).

24. In 1838, the now more recognized Trail of Tears included the removal of the Cherokee. The Trail of Death is a lesser known but equally problematic expulsion of Native communities from the upper midwestern regions of the United States.

25. In fact, when Muncie received significant prestige across the country as the site of the infamous Middletown series in the early twentieth century, its numerous and historic Black residents were considered a "Negro population that could basically be ignored" (Lassiter et al. 2004).

26. The tension between the states was certainly palpable in this moment of growth. In fact, two years after Indiana's admission into the union Missouri applied for statehood as a slave state. A heated exchange erupted between states that feared a disruption in the balance of power and disagreed with the South's dependence on slaves. Eventually the clash was temporarily resolved with the Missouri Compromise; obviously, the division was not completely subdued and in 1860 southern states began to secede from the Union.

27. Gathered from Kevin Cullen, "The History of Greater Lafayette"—an article posted on the Community Guide of the newspaper the *Journal and Courier*: http://www.jconline.com/apps/pbcs.dll/article?AID=/99999999/COMMUNITY/50712014/1086.

28. An example of this could be seen in the book *Greater Lafayette: Indiana's Star City*, a corporate investment and relocation guidebook circulated by the city of Lafayette. This 215-page coffee table guidebook includes chapters on the history, educational institutions, economic diversity, and community attributes that could be used to entice corporate investments and relocations to the city. Notably, the text makes absolutely no mention of local cultural or racial diversity. Though it was published in 1999, the book's roughly 150 high-resolution color portraits of people in Lafayette display a total of only nine people of color. Of those nine, the majority are small insets rather than large page-size pictures.

29. "Rapid Response: Readers will miss Kriebel, Old Lafayette," *Journal and Courier*, June 19, 2011.

30. Urciuoli (1996).

31. Notes on the area's immigrant congregations were taken from a variety of sources, including the 1888 Biographical Record and Portrait Album of Tippecanoe County, The St. Boniface 100th Anniversary newsletter, Cox (1970 [1860]), Erez-Boukai (1996), as well as Kriebel's earlier text *150 Years of Lafayette Newspapers* (1981).

32. Kriebel missed the opportunity to make contemporary parallels with current immigrant dynamics in Lafayette. For example, in this article there was no mention of or tie to the popular Mexican bakery that had been in operation for some years prior to the appearance of the article.

33. St. Boniface Church 1999.

34. Kriebel (1981), Ziegler (1994).

35. To examine more of these cross-ethnic parallels between different Asian and Latino immigrant groups in the United States, see Ngai (2004).

36. For more on the anthropological perspective on acculturation, or deculturation, see Spiro (1955), Rosaldo (1988).

37. For more on the suppression of lynching in Indiana memory, see Madison (2001).

38. Southern Poverty Law Center, Knights of the Ku Klux Klan: http://www.splcenter.org/get-informed/intelligence-files/groups/knights-of-the-ku-klux-klan.

39. For more on the historical Mexican community near East Chicago and Gary, Indiana (Indiana Harbor), see Nodín Valdés (2000), Rosales (1976), Sepúlveda (1976), Vargas (1993).

40. The German Triangle is widely known by German immigrant historians as the region between the cities of Cincinnati, Milwaukee, and St. Louis.

41. It is unclear when the letter was written. Kriebel notes only that the letter was received "some years ago." Additionally, it is interesting to note that prior to speaking about the Klan's parade, Kriebel introduces this entry by describing the "cleanup" efforts of a local priest to rid this part of town of multiple brothels and the "estimated 150 women [who] worked that area of factories, mills, and packinghouses." In this context, the Irish neighborhood is set up in a negative light prior to the introduction of the "masked parade." I am not suggesting that Kriebel was purposefully malicious in his retelling of this event; however, the lackadaisical manner in which this and other information is presented serves only to reinstate some of the negative stereotypes that subtly justify the KKK's presence to continue the priest's efforts to "clean up" the neighborhood.

42. Moore (1991) provides a chart of "Klan membership among Native-born White men by county" that was obtained from the list "Local Officers of the Ku Klux Klan" and housed in archives at the Indiana Historical Society.

43. De Genova (2006).

CHAPTER 2. KNEADING HOME

1. Robert R. Treviño (2006) speaks to what he terms ethno-Catholic experiences. When the term "ethno-Catholic" appears, it is referencing Treviño's work, though I prefer the more general "ethno-religious" as a term that speaks to the role of ethnicity on all, not just Catholic, religious practices. For more on ethno-religious practices, see Pitti (2003).

2. The *Matachine* dance troupe is a tradition that comes from Mexico and serves to honor how the Virgin of Guadalupe chose to appear to honor Mexico's indigenous population. At the Basilica in Mexico City, committed *danza* troupes (groups more in tune with their indigeneity than with Catholicism) arrive days ahead of the 12th to mark their spiritual commitment to the events.

3. A few men were also present with the procession, but they were offering their assistance with securing the float's structural integrity for the children who would be riding it. My role as a female ethnographer positioned me with the women who watched after their toddlers awaiting the start of procession.

4. For more on the importance of Chicago to the 2006 immigration rallies, see Pallares and Flores-Gonzalez 2010.

5. Carlos Morales, "Piece of saint's cloak in Chicago." *Chicago Tribune*, July 26, 2003.

6. For more on the spatial significance of Mexican Chicago, see De Genova (2005).

7. For a history of Latino Catholic communities and their maintance of ethno-religious holidays, see Matovina (2005), Treviño (2006), Pitti (2003), and Woodrick (2006).

8. For more on the history of Guadalupanos—followers of the Virgin of Guadalupe—and their resistance to assimilation preasures, see Matovina (2005).

9. Richard Rodriguez in his much-debated *Hunger of Memory* (1982) speaks of this public/private dichotomy when referencing language use and positions the English language as publicly dominant over privately spoken Spanish language for assimilated Mexican Americans. For a critique of Rodriguez's public/private dichotomy, see Saenz (1997).

10. Flores and Benmayor (1997).

11. David Guss (2000).

12. For more on the racial, ethnic, classed, and gendered manifestations of space, see Arreola (2005), Bonus (2000), Davis (2000), Gupta and Ferguson (1997), LeClerc, Villa, and Dear (1999), Low (2002), Sassen (1998), Stewart (1996a) (1996b), and Valle and Torres (2000).

13. For more on the Latino focus in cultural geography, see the edited volumes *Hispanic Spaces, Latino Places: Community and Cultural Diversity in Contemporary America* (2004) and *Urban Latino Cultures: La vida latina en LA* (1999).

14. For more on border checkpoints, see Lugo 2000.

15. Lugo (2000).

16. See Odem (2004) and Treviño (2006) for the role of the church in streamlining Americanization techniques. Additionally, Cavalcanti and Schleef (2005) make the argument that maintaining religious ties hinders assimilation for recent immigrants, noting that ethnic affiliations in the church may delay assimilation and adaptation. In this section, I contest Cavalcanti and Schleef's findings by positing that church affiliation creates comfort and belonging in these new spaces and can foster that sense of belonging (not assimilation) necessary for immigrant survival and adaptation in new destinations.

17. For more on how the church helped to overcome feelings of isolation, loneliness, and rupture, see Bathum and Baumann (2007), Iber (2000), Odem (2004), Ramirez (2005), Treviño (2006), and Woodrick (2006).

18. Ramirez (2005) notes that Hispanic churches can be viewed "as critical sanctuaries where transnational identities are forged and where intergenerational and intraethnic ties are strengthened" (178).

19. Daniel Ramirez (2005) calls this type of public engagement "Church engagement."

20. For a similar look at the lack of sociocultural and economic networks in new midwestern towns, see Woodrick (2006).

21. The use of ethno-spirituality echoes the work of Treviño (2006). In Lafayette, I found that traditionally ethno-Catholic traditions, like *quinceañeras*, were being adopted by Protestants in order to maintain a sort of cultural continuity while at the same time distancing themselves from Catholicism.

22. Woodrick (2006) and Menjívar (2006) recognize the precarious position of immigrants in the United States and see the church as an alternative setting for their agency. According to Woodrick (2006), often immigrants may not feel they can publicly speak up and get involved, so "sociocultural incorporation" is found elsewhere in

other, less obvious engagement; see Menjívar (2006). As DeTemple (2005) notes, church becomes one of the spaces where the disenfranchised may gain control.

23. The use of ethno-religiousity echoes the work of Treviño (2006).

24. This resistance of White pastors to emergent Mexican parishioners can also be seen in Treviño (2006), Iber (2000), Odem (2004), and Woodrick (2006).

25. For evidence of this see also Busto (2006) on Reies López Tijerina.

CHAPTER 3. WRITTEN OTHERINGS

1. For more on this precarious history, see Balderama and Rodriguez (1995), Menchaca (1993), Ngai (2004), Perea (1997), Sánchez (1993), and Vargas (1993).

2. The website http://thomas.loc.gov/home/thomas.php is managed by the Library of Congress to provide information on legislative proceedings since 1995.

3. David Roediger (1999) wrote of similar unsubstantiated claims by residents in the Midwest during Reconstruction when legislation was passed to fend off ex-slaves who would "flood the North . . . unleash 'hordes of freedmen' to compete for white jobs" (171). Then and now, areas with minimal competition rally on the fear of Others (ex-slaves, the Chinese, Mexican immigrants) rather than on actual numbers on the ground.

4. The stagnant minimum wage and a decrease in union jobs and benefits resulted in a lower quality of life for America's working class (Ehrenreich 2002).

5. See Chavez (2008) on a rise in anxieties over "the Latino threat."

6. Considering my subject-position as a Mexican American female, I am not sure if Jane was this honest because of who I was or in spite of who I was. For more on my subject-position, see the Methods section of the Introduction.

7. In a similar vein, Roediger (1999) notes that in the nineteenth century the "Chinese were most insistently charged with being 'nonconsuming' and undermining American Standards of Living" (179).

8. This term, "anti-citizen," was borrowed from Roediger's (1999) analysis of how African Americans in post-Reconstruction America were deemed as the anti-citizen to White citizens attempting to gain power through the claiming of *legitimate* citizenry rites.

9. For more on these narratives, see Chavez (2008) and Irving (2000).

10. She further explained how the other groups of kids "the cowboys and black kids believed in the good old fashioned '50s rumbles . . . they would duke it out." In essence, Jane positioned Latino youth as somehow more violent than the White and Black youth she'd grown up with.

11. Chiang (2010).

12. For more on the racialization and criminalization of the undocumented, see Jacobson (2008).

13. Bertrand (2009), Goodwin and Goodwin (2001).

14. In other words, human undocumented immigrants were reduced to simply "illegals," and the reference to "that illegal" or "those illegals" became a demeaning act in the seemingly simple process of naming. To examine how anthropology

approaches anti-immigrant rhetoric and the use of "illegal," see De Genova (2002), New and Petronicolos (1998), Schneider (1998), Suárez-Orozco (1996), and Urciuoli (1994).

15. Chavez (1991).

16. In Davis's seminal work, "symbols of derogation" in the South operated against Black residents and included dark skin and woolly or kinky hair.

17. As contempt and intolerance shifted from the legal to the cultural, the specificity of condemning undocumented immigration developed into a general repugnance toward an entire ethnic group.

18. Lipsitz (1998) and Roediger (1999).

19. For more on sanitized discursive racist attacks, see Bonilla-Silva (2006), Santa Ana (2002).

20. For more on border policing, see Lugo (2008).

21. Benedict Anderson (1991) speaks of "horizontal comradeship" as the result of national associations and shared imagined communities. Some of Lafayette's community did believe in the camaraderie through national citizenry, but on the ground this utopian vision of nationalism is far from horizontal and can be more aptly noted as hierarchal. For more, see Chavez (1994) and Lomnitz-Adler (2001).

22. Notably, Tom Tancredo led the call against undocumented immigrants during this period. In 2008, he ran for president on a platform of sealing the border and deporting undocumented immigrants. He later withdrew from the race.

23. By 2013, this domain name had been picked up by someone else.

24. I received these mailers because my household was registered as independent. A colleague who was registered as a Democrat in the same district did not receive these mailers.

25. Familiar to southern California drivers, this sign is traditionally used by the highway patrol to warn drivers of crossing migrants.

26. "A hot button issue? More than immigration on voters' minds," *Journal and Courier*, October 26, 2006.

27. Dan Shaw, "Tragedy Strikes," *Journal and Courier*, News Section, July 13, 2006.

28. Joe Gerrety, "14 years possible for driver who killed boy," *Journal and Courier*, Crime Courts Section, May 10, 2007.

29. Joe Gerrety, "Police Account: Driver meant to hit the brake," *Journal and Courier*, Crime Courts Section, July 14, 2006.

30. A year later, even after the driver had pled guilty, opting out of a trial, comments online still called into question his legality and once again attempted to make this about immigration. A similar tactic was used in national coverage of immigration, most famously illustrated in the April 5, 2007, dispute between Bill O'Reilly and Geraldo Rivera.

31. For more on this notion of Latinos as always and already foreign, see Ngai (2004), Rocco (2006).

32. All census information was gathered from the U.S. Census Bureau, http://www.census.gov/.

33. Max Showalter, "Hispanic-owned businesses surge," *Journal and Courier*, March 29, 2006.

34. These numbers vary somewhat from those provided in chapter 1 because they include the entire countywide distribution and thus differ somewhat from the 9.1 percent Hispanic population reported in the city of Lafayette and a 3.2 percent of Hispanic residents reported in West Lafayette. Though Lafayette and West Lafayette are the two largest cities in Tippecanoe County, the other, smaller cities offset the Hispanic population percentages.

35. Alejandro Lugo (1997) provocatively describes the metaphor of the war in Gramsci's "war of position" and Foucault's politics of war to explain how these metaphors alter the ways we see culture, borders, and the nation.

36. For more on performative communicative acts, see Austin (2003 [1963]).

37. For more on constructing a gendered racialized Other, see Puar's (2007) discussion of Sikh men in a post–September 11 racism.

38. Notably, Nestor Rodríguez (1996) describes a process of "autonomous international migration" that exists outside, and in spite of, official nation-state sanctions. He explains that "because core institutions (legal, religious, local governmental, etc.) support this migratory strategy, undocumented migrants do not perceive its moral significance as deviant. Migrants may see their autonoumous migration as extralegal, but not necessarily as criminal" (1996: 29).

39. A "rally" was held on July 4, 2006, on the downtown square, but only three protesters showed up. Judging from the numbers of letters to the editors and online comments, this rally was not successful in enticing some of these authors to actively participate on their beliefs as had hundreds of local pro-immigrant advocates months earlier. Instead it seems that the rage illustrated in these letters and commentary was in fact fueled by the anonymity and distance that the Internet and letter writing provided. The popularity of hate-based rhetoric encouraged by the Internet in fact contradicted the utopic views of online global communities apparent in Arjun Appadurai's *Modernity at Large* (1996). This analysis of cyber hate-based rhetoric will be further investigated for future analysis.

40. For more on the surveillance of Spanish speakers, see Hill (1993).

41. The Lafayette Adult Reading Academy had multiple classes of English courses that always overflowed with local Latino students who attended both morning and night classes to attempt to improve their English skills. However, for the few months I volunteered in the morning English classes I found the curriculum lacking and noted that students themselves grew frustrated with the level of English training they were actually receiving.

42. Santa Ana (2002) further notes that "In 1986 Tove Skutnabb-Kangas coined the term linguicism for such practices, which are linguistic reflexes of colonialism" (216).

43. Santa Ana (2002) in speaking on linguicism refers to this kind of behavior as "the linguistic equivalent of racism" (216).

44. Additionally, as Jane Hill's (1993) provocative linguistic analysis of White Spanish suggests, the use of Spanish slang by the White community is not condemned nearly as much as the censor placed on Spanish-speaking Latinos.

45. For instance, Butler and Chakravorty Spivak (2011) describe the national reaction against a Spanish version of the national anthem in 2006 and problem with the question of "to whom does this anthem belong" (58)?

46. Chavez (1991).

47. As an interesting side note, in 2006 the Indiana Bureau of Motor Vehicles (BMV) was having trouble with a new computer system. For weeks while the computers were being updated, lines at the BMV were horrendous. During this time patrons wrote in to the *Journal and Courier* and complained about the bureaucracy of contacting the Indianapolis bureau and having to wait in lines "from desk to entrance" and the wait "taking a day of their lives" (July 30, 2006). Clearly, the bureaucracy of the U.S. immigration process is far beyond the comprehension of many.

48. Notably, queries about the process occurred only seven times throughout the entirety of interactions with non-Latinos in the research. Only four out of the seven moments occurred during individual interviews; the other queries came when I was asked to attend community organizations whose members freely recognized a lack of knowledge about the process and welcomed some clarification from someone more familiar with the topic.

49. For more on dual notions of home, see Glick Schiller (2009), Gutierrez (1999), Levitt (2001), Olwig and Hastrup (1997), and Ong (1996).

50. To examine how immigrants in general, and Latinos in particular, have been positioned outside the moniker of local, American, and legitimate, see Ngai (2004), Oboler (1995), Rocco (2006).

51. As Faye Harrison has noted, "In social contexts in which overt racism is no longer publicly acceptable, more subtly raced language appears to be more socially appropriate and morally defensible. This apparent legitimacy makes this form of racialized discourse all the more powerful" (1998: 619).

52. Chiang (2010).

CHAPTER 4. CLASHES AT THE CROSSROADS

1. As part of its customer commitment, Wal-Mart has set up extensive measures to make them the "retailer of choice" as promised on its website: http://walmart-stores.com/GlobalWMStoresWeb/navigate.do?catg=521&contId=5894.

2. In *Made in America* (1993), Sam Walton briefly speaks to his hunger to promote competition on domestic and international fronts and his aims to expand the "Wal-Mart family" by relying on familiarity and "repeating what worked, stamping out stores cookie-cutter style" (1992: 111).

3. In this case a family, but the response wouldn't be justified even if it had been all Latino men.

4. Maggie's avoidance is not unlike Jim Crow–era prohibitions against African Americans, but rather than make Latinos move away from her, Maggie chooses to distance herself from the presence of those she racially perceives as dangerous men.

5. Taken from personal communication with this case manager and from a presentation he gave at a local venue aimed to inform the Lafayette community about Latino issues.

6. For more on the rise of hate crimes against Latinos in the twenty-first century, see the Research Briefing: Understanding Trends in Hate Crimes Against Immigrants and Hispanic-Americans, NCJ 234632, May 2011, by National Institute of Justice.

7. Purdue University is continually ranked in the top five public universities with the largest international student population. In 2012, Purdue came in second, behind the University of Illinois Urbana-Champaign, in the number of international students (Amy Patterson Neubert, "Purdue's international student population ranks 2nd for public schools." *Purdue News*, November 12, 2012). The impact of these international students on small college towns is a project worthy of pursuit, especially given the rise in Latino residents in these towns too.

8. Carmela was born and raised in California and self-identified as Chicana as a means of differentiating between being raised in the United States and the difficulty faced by some friends and family who had only recently arrived in the country.

9. For more on this kind of gendered racialization, see Gutiérrez (2008).

10. This scenario is made ever more disturbing if, as these women believed, the mother may not have understood English but perhaps her children could. As is the case in some Latino households, often the children are the initial translators for the family. English learned from school allows these children to help their parents maneuver an English-dominant environment. Had that been the case, the shame of hearing your mother insulted behind her back may have caused irreparable damage for these young children.

11. Basso (1996), Stewart (1996a, 1996b).

12. Lugo (2008) underscores how border inspections of particular bodies can have immense psychological impact for those being targeted as always and already not worthy of belonging.

13. This concept of mental borders was inspired by Daphne Berdahl's (1999) analysis of the "wall in our heads" that explored the mental distances between East and West Germans.

14. Du Bois (1903).

15. For more on the Latino male experience in the United States, see Noguera, Hurtado, and Fergus (2011).

16. This is a specific reference to Indiana's state motto, "The Crossroads of America," but is certainly not limited to Indiana.

17. The use of temporary workers was actually a common practice for this operation, for it often hired a large group of temporary workers through an agency and would therefore relieve itself of further scrutiny regarding valid Social Security numbers.
18. Most of Greater Lafayette, including a majority of Latinos, lived on the east side of the river, where housing was more affordable and a majority of the manufacturing industry was located.

CHAPTER 5. "UNITED WE ARE STRONGER"

1. Kathleen Stewart (2007) notes, "The ordinary is a shifting assemblage of practices and practical knowledges, a scene of both liveness and exhaustion, a dream of escape or of the simple life" (1).
2. As referenced in chapter 4, 60 percent of non-Latino respondents associated Latinos only with the word "immigrant." It was refreshing to see that Beth Ann could recognize university-affiliated students and faculty as part of the global presence in Greater Lafayette.
3. Pearson, Dovidio, and Gaertner (2009) would call this aversive racism, or when people "genuinely regard themselves as non-prejudiced, but at the same time possess conflicting, often non-conscious, negative feelings" toward people of color (2009: 3).
4. I attempted to speak with these women in order to understand their participation and perhaps set up future interviews with them. Unfortunately, my attempts to speak to these women were unsuccessful. Later that night, at the reception in the church gymnasium, these women stood mainly with one another or with the parish priest and did not make conversation with the other families in the vicinity.
5. The last entry on the blog was made in June 2007 and mentions the hopes that an immigrant reform bill would pass in the Senate. The lack of said passage may have discouraged further discussion on the topic for the blogger.
6. From the Tippecanoe Latino Festival promotion flyer.
7. Carpio et al. (2011).
8. Reported on the Indy Channel 6 News. April 13, 2006. "8 Fired Because They Attended Immigration Rally."
9. From CFRC's history webpage: http://www.cfrc.org/index.php/about-us/agency-history.
10. I spoke to four original members of LAFLR and they all expressed anguish over the disintegration of the organization and the discord between strong personalities in the group.
11. Currently the Lincoln Center remains open as a site for transitional housing.
12. These goals are stated on the Latino Center for Wellness Facebook page.
13. It should be noted that this image of historic assimilation is inaccurate, but clearly even Latino immigrants believed this popularized notion of German assimilation.

14. Gloria tried to redraft citizenship in such a way that juridical standing would not be required to prove civic belonging. For more on this evaluation of citizenship, see Oboler (2006).

15. For more on this erroneous claim of Mexican and Chicano populations reclaiming Aztlán, see Bebout (2012).

16. For an example of popular rhetoric against ethnicity, see Buchanan, *State of Emergency*; Huntington, *The Class of Civilizations*; and Tancredo, *In Mortal Danger*.

17. Price and Whitworth (2004).

18. Notably, David Gutierrez (1999) recognizes that even soccer games can be read through differing notions of nationalism. For instance, Gutierrez wrote about negative letters to the editor that revealed frustration with the display of Mexican allegiance at a U.S.-vs.-Mexico soccer game in Los Angeles.

19. My experience at the high school garnered exposure to students, educators, security officers, and administrators of the school. Particularly disturbing was a marked tendency of the security staff and one particular administrator to identify and discipline Mexican students over and above White and African American students.

20. Governor Mitch Daniels was devising financial initiatives to stem the brain-drain in the state with what he called the "Hoosier Hopes Scholarship" that would fund undergraduates in the state as long as they made a commitment to remain in the state after graduation. Interestingly, the Sagamore Institute for Policy Research, based out of Indianapolis, was conducting a study of the state's dependence on foreign-born workers at the same time that Governor Daniels was garnering support for his "Hoosier Hopes Scholarship." As Governor Daniels attempted to encourage Hoosiers (read: White Hoosiers) in the state, the Sagamore Institute maintained that "Indiana is more dependent on immigration for total population growth than is most of the country" (Sagamore Institute 2007: 7). In other words, the state's dependence on immigrant population increased as its White population was steadily decreasing.

21. English as a New Language (ENL) was the state's designation for courses to help English Language Learners (ELL) students, the national term for those with limited English proficiency.

22. Erin Smith, "Tecumseh students worried about immigration proposals," *Journal and Courier*, April 11, 2006.

CONCLUSION

1. Dan McFeely, "Senator: Immigration Bill Misperceived as Race Issue." *Indianapolis Star*, January 17, 2008.

2. On Sunday, July 20, 2008, an online posting calling for the return of the KKK was read to me by my husband. A further search on the following Monday for this post revealed that the newspaper had "scrubbed" the comment from its online comment forum.

BIBLIOGRAPHY

Abrego, Leisy, and Cecilia Menjívar. "Immigrant Latina Mothers as Targets of Legal Violence." *International Journal of Sociology of the Family* 37 (1) 2011: 9–26.

Abu-Lughod, Lila. "The Romance of Resistance: Tracing Transformations of Power Through Bedouiwomen." *American Ethnologist* 17 (1) 1990: 41–55.

Alba, Richard, and Victor Nee. *Remaking the American Mainstream: Assimilation and Contemporary Immigration.* Cambridge, Mass.: Harvard University Press, 2003.

Alvarez, Robert R. "The Mexican–US Border: The Making of an Anthropology of Borderlands." *Annual Review of Anthropology* 24 (1995): 447–70.

Anderson, Benedict. *Imagined Communities: Reflections on the Origin and Spread of Nationalism.* London: Verso, 1991.

Anderson, Kay J. "The Idea of Chinatown: The Power of Place and Institutional Practice in the Making of a Racial Category." *Annals of the Association of American Geographers* 77 (4) 1987: 580–98.

Anzaldúa, Gloria. *Borderlands/La Frontera: The New Mestiza.* San Francisco: Aunt Lute Books, 1987.

———. "Now Let Us Shift . . . the Path of Conocimiento . . . Inner Work, Public Acts." In *This Bridge We Call Home: Radical Visions for Transformation*, ed. Gloria E. Anzaldúa, Gloria E. and AnaLouise Keating, 540–78. New York: Routledge, 2002.

Appadurai, Arjun. *Modernity at Large: Cultural Dimensions of Globalization.* Minneapolis: University of Minnesota Press, 1996.

Arias, Arturo. *Taking Their Word: Literature and the Signs of Central America.* Minneapolis: University of Minnesota Press, 2007.

Arreola, David (ed.). *Hispanic Spaces, Latino Places: Community and Cultural Diversity in Contemporize America.* Austin: University of Texas Press, 2005.

Bada, Xotchil, Jonathan Fox, and A. Andrew Selee (eds.). *Invisible No More: Mexican Migrant Civic Participation in the United States.* Washington: Woodrow Wilson Center, 2006.

Baker-Cristales, Beth. "Mediated Resistance: The Construction of Neoliberal Citizenship in the Immigrant Rights Movement." *Latino Studies* 7 (1) 2009: 60–82.

Balderrama, Francisco E., and Raymond Rodriguez. *Decade of Betrayal: Mexican Repatriation in the 1930s.* Albuquerque: University of New Mexico Press, 1995.

Barreto, Matt, Sylvia Manzano, Ricardo Ramírez, and Kathy Rim. "Mobilization, Participation, and Solidaridad: Latino Participation in the 2006 Immigration Protest Rallies." *Urban Affairs Review* 44 (5) 2009: 736–64.

Barth, Frederick. "Introduction." In *Ethnic Groups and Boundaries: The Social Organization of Culture Difference*, ed. Frederick Barth, 9–38. Boston: Little, Brown, 1969.

Basch, Lina, Nina Glick Schiller, and Cristina Szanton Blanc. *Nations Unbound: Transnational Projects, Postcolonial Predicaments, and Deterriorialized Nation-States.* New York: Routledge, 1994.

Basso, Keith H. *Wisdom Sits in Places: Landscape and Language Among the Western Apache.* Albuquerque: University of New Mexico Press, 1996.

Bathum, M. E., and L. C. Baumann. "A Sense of Community Among Immigrant Latinas." *Family & Community Health* 30 (3) 2007: 167–77.

Bebout, Lee. "The Nativist Aztlán: Fantasies and Anxieties of Whiteness on the Border." *Latino Studies* 10 (2012): 290–313.

Behar, Ruth. "Expanding the Boundaries of Anthropology: The Cultural Criticism of Gloria Anzaldúa and Morgan Riggs." *Visual Anthropology Review* 9 (2) 1993: 83–91.

———. *The Vulnerable Observer: Anthropology That Breaks Your Heart.* Boston: Beacon Press, 1997.

Berdahl, Daphne. *Where the World Ended: Re-Unification and Identity in the German Borderland.* Berkeley: University of California Press, 1999.

Bertrand, Melanie. "The Importance of Considering Multiple Semiotic Resources in the Study of Race." *Texas Linguistic Forum* 53 (2009): 50–61.

Bloemraad, I., and C. Trost. "It's a Family Affair: Inter-generational Mobilization in the Spring 2006 Protests." *American Behavioral Scientist* 52 (4) 2008: 507–32.

Bonilla-Silva, Eduardo. *Racism Without Racists: Color-blind Racism and the Persistence of Racial Inequality in the United States.* Lanham, Md.: Rowman & Littlefield, 2006.

Bonus, Rick. *Locating Filipino Americans: Ethnicity and the Cultural Politics of Space.* Philadelphia: Temple University Press, 2000.

Bourdieu, Pierre. "The Social Space and the Genesis of Groups." *Theory and Society* 14 (6) 1985: 723–44.

Brettell, Caroline. "Urban History, Urban Anthropology, and the Study of Migrants in Cities." *City & Society* 12 (2) 2000: 129–38.

Brettel, Caroline B., and Deborah Reed-Danahay. *Civic Engagements: The Citizenship Practices of Asian Indian and Vietnamese Immigrants in Texas.* Stanford, Calif.: Stanford University Press, 2011.

Buss, James. *Winning the West with Words: Language and Conquest in the Lower Great Lakes.* Norman: University of Oklahoma Press, 2011.

Busto, Rudy V. *King Tiger: The Religious Vision of Reies López Tijerina.* Albuquerque: University of New Mexico Press, 2006.

Butler, Judith. "Performativity, Precarity, and Sexual Politics." *Revista de Antropología Iberoamericana* 4 (3) 2009: i–xiii.

Butler, Judith, and Gayatri Chakravorty Spivak. *Who Sings the Nation-State? Language, Politics, Belonging.* Calcutta: Seagull Books, 2011.

Caldeira, Teresa P.R., "Fortified Enclaves: The New Urban Segregation." In *Theorizing the City: The New Urban Anthropology Reader*, ed. Setha Low, 83–17. New Brunswick, N.J.: Rutgers University Press, 2002.

Campa, Arthur. "Immigrant Latinos and Resident Mexican Americans in Garden City, Kansas: Ethnicity and Ethnic Relations." *Urban Anthropology* 19 (4) 1990: 345–60.

Cantu, Lionel. "The Peripheralization of Rural America: A Case Study of Latino Migrants in America's Heartland." *Sociological Perspectives* 38 (3) 1995: 399–414.

Carpio, Genevieve, Clara Irazábal, and Laura Pulido. "The Right to the Suburb: Immigration Policies in Southern California." *Journal of Urban Affairs* 33 (2) 2011: 185–208.

Castañeda, Alejandra. *The Politics of Citizenship of Mexican Migrants.* El Paso, Tex.: LFB Scholarly Publishing LLC., 2006.

——. "Roads to Citizenship: Mexican Migrants in the United States." In *Latinos and Citizenship: The Dilemma of Belonging,* ed. Suzanne Oboler, 143–66. New York: Palgrave Macmillan, 2006.

Cavalcanti, H. B., and Debra Schleef. "The Case for Secular Assimilation? The Latino Experience in Richmond, Virginia." *Journal for the Scientific Study of Religion* 44 (4) 2005: 473–83.

Cave, Alfred A. "The Shawnee Prophet, Tecumseh, and Tippecanoe: A Case Study of Historical Myth-Making." *Journal of the Early Republic* 22 (4) 2002: 637–73.

Chavez, Leo R. "Outside the Imagined Community: Undocumented Settlers and Experiences of Incorporation." *American Ethnologist* 18 (1991): 257–78.

——. "The Power of Imagined Community—The Settlement of Undocumented Mexicans and Central Americans in the United States." *American Anthropologists* 96 (1) 1994: 52–73.

——. "Immigration Reform and Nativism: The Nationalist Response to the Transnationalist Challenge." In *Immigrants Out! The New Nativism and the Anti-Immigrant Impulse in the United States,* ed. Juan Perea, 61–77. New York: New York University Press, 1996.

——. *Covering Immigration: Popular Images and the Politics of the Nation.* Berkeley: University of California Press, 2001.

——. *The Latino Threat: Constructing Immigrants, Citizens, and the Nation.* Stanford, Calif.: Stanford University Press, 2008.

Chiang, Shiao-Yun. "'Well, I'm a lot of things, but I'm sure not a bigot': Positive Self-representation in Confrontational Discourse on Racism." *Discourse Society* 21 (3) 2010: 273–94.

Contreras, Joseph. "Unpaid Teens Bag Groceries for Wal-Mart." *Newsweek* July 31: 2007.

Coutin, Susan Bibler. "Being en Route." *American Anthropologist* 107 (2) 2005: 195–206.

Cox, Sandford. *Old Settlers: Recollections of the Early Settlement of the Wabash Valley.* Lafayette, Ind.: Hoosier Heritage Press, 1860.

——. *Recollections of the Early Settlement of the Wabash Valley.* Freeport, N.Y.: Books for Libraries Press, 1970 [1860].

Crenshaw, Kimberlé. "Demarginalizing the Intersection of Race and Sex: A Black Feminist Critique of Antidiscrimination Doctrine, Feminist Theory and Antiracist Politics." *University of Chicago Legal Forum* 1989: 139–67.

Cuba, Lee, and David M. Hummon. "A Place to Call Home: Identification with Dwelling, Community, and Region." *The Sociological Quarterly* 34 (1) 1993: 111–31.

Davis, Allison, with Burleigh B. Gardner and Mary R. Gardner. *Deep South: A Social Anthropological Study of Caste and Class.* Chicago: University of Chicago Press, 1965.

Davis, Mike. *Magical Urbanism: Latinos Reinvent the US City.* New York: Verso, 2000.

Davis, Peggy. "Law as Microaggression." *Yale Law Journal* 98 (1989): 1559–77.

de Certeau, Michel. *The Practice of Everyday Life.* Berkeley: University of California Press, 1984.

———. "Walking in the City." In *The Cultural Studies Reader*, ed. Simon During. London: Routledge, 1993.

De Genova, Nicholas. "Race, Space, and the Recreation of Latin America in Mexican Chicago." *Latin American Perspectives* 25 (5) 1998: 87–116.

———. "Migrant 'Illegality' and Deportability in Everyday Life." *Annual Review of Anthropology* 31 (2002): 419–47.

———. *Latino Crossings: Mexicans, Puerto Ricans, and the Politics of Race and Citizenship.* Chicago: University of Chicago Press, 2003.

———. *Working the Boundaries: Race, Space, and "Illegality" in Mexican Chicago.* Durham, N.C.: Duke University Press, 2005.

———. "The Legal Production of Mexican/Migrant 'Illegality.'" In *Latinos and Citizenship: The Dilemma of Belonging*, ed. Suzanne Oboler, 61–90. New York: Palgrave Macmillan, 2006.

———. "The Stakes of an Anthropology of the United States." *CR: The New Centennial Review* 7 (2) 2007: 231–77.

De Genova, Nicholas, and Nathalie Peutz. *The Deportation Regime: Sovereignty, Space, and the Freedom of Movement.* Durham, N.C.: Duke University Press, 2010.

Delanty, Gerard, Paul Jones, and Ruth Wodak. *Identity, Belonging, and Migration.* Liverpool: Liverpool University Press, 2008.

Delgado, Richard, and Jean Stefancic. *Critical Race Theory: An Introduction.* New York: New York University Press, 2001.

DeTemple, Jill. "Chains of Liberation: Poverty and Social Action in the Universal Church of the Kingdom of God." In *Latino Religious and Civic Activism in the United States*, ed. Gastón Espinosa with Virgilio Elizondo and Jesse Miranda, 219–32. Oxford: Oxford University Press, 2005.

Diaz-Barriga, Miguel. "Distracción: Notes on Cultural Citizenship, Visual Ethnography, and Mexican Migration to Pennsylvania." *Visual Anthropology* 24 (2) 2008: 122–47.

Dominguez, Virginia. "Asserting (Trans)Nationalism and the Social Conditions of Its Possibility." *Communal/Plural* 6 (2) 1998: 139–56.

Doty, Roxanne Lynn. *The Law into Their Own Hands: Immigration and the Politics of Exceptionalism.* Tucson: University of Arizona Press, 2009.

Douglas, Mary. *Purity and Danger: An Analysis of the Concepts of Pollution and Taboo.* New York: Routledge, 1966.

Du Bois, W. E. B. *The Souls of Black Folk*. New York: Penguin, 1903.

Durand, Jorge, Douglas S. Massey, and Fernando Charvet. "The Changing Geography of Mexican Immigration to the United States: 1910–1996." *Social Science Quarterly* (81) 2000: 1–15.

Edmunds, R. David, and Joseph L. Peyser. *The Fox Wars: The Mesquakie Challenge to New France*. Norman: University of Oklahoma Press, 1993.

Ehrenreich, Barbara. *Nickel and Dimed: On (Not) Getting by in America*. New York: Metropolitan Books/Henry Holt & Company, 2002.

Ehrkamp, Patricia. "Placing Identities: Transnational Practices and Local Attachments of Turkish Immigrants in Germany." *Journal of Ethnic and Migration Studies* 31 (2) 2005: 345–64.

Erez-Boukai, Irit. *On the Banks of the Wabash: Jewish Life in Greater Lafayette, Indiana*. *Indiana Jewish History*, 31. Indianapolis: The Indiana Jewish Historical Society, 1996.

Escobar, Arturo. "Culture Sits in Places: Reflections on Globalism and Subaltern Strategies of Localization." *Political Geography* 20 (2001): 139–74.

Espinosa, Gastón, with Virgilio Elizondo and Jesse Miranda, eds. *Latino Religious and Civic Activism in the United States*. Oxford: Oxford University Press, 2005.

Fink, Leon. *The Maya of Morgantown: Work and Community in the Nuevo New South*. Chapel Hill: University of North Carolina Press, 2003.

Flores, Juan. *Divided Borders. Essays on Puerto Rican Identity*. Houston: Arte Publico Press, 1993.

Flores, Richard. *Los Pastores: History and Performance in the Mexican Shepherd's Play of South Texas*. Washington: Smithsonian Institution Press, 1995.

Flores, William V. "Citizens vs. Citizenry: Undocumented Immigrants and Latino Cultural Citizenship." In *Latino Cultural Citizenship: Claiming Identity, Space, and Rights*, ed. William V. Flores and Rina Benmayor, 255–78. Boston: Beacon Press, 1997.

Flores, William V., and Rina Benmayor. *Latino Cultural Citizenship: Claiming Identity, Space, and Rights*. Boston: Beacon Press, 1997.

Foley, Douglas E. *Learning Capitalist Culture: Deep in the Heart of Tejas*. Philadelphia: University of Pennsylvania Press, 1990.

Foner, Nancy. "How Exceptional Is New York? Migration and Multiculturalism in the Empire City." *Ethnic and Racial Studies* 30 (6) 2007: 999–1023.

Fox, Jonathan. "Reframing Mexican Migration as a Multi-Ethnic Process." *Latino Studies* 4 (1) 2006: 39–61.

Frankenburg, Ruth. *White Women, Race Matters: The Social Construction of Whiteness*. Minneapolis: University of Minnesota Press, 1993.

Fraga, Luis R., John A. Garcia, Rodney E. Hero, Michael Jones-Correa, Valerie Martinez-Ebers, and Gary M. Segura. *Latino Lives in America: Making It Home*. Philadelphia: Temple University Press, 2010.

Friedman, Jonathan. "Global Crises, the Struggle for Cultural Identity and Intellectual Porkbarrelling: Cosmopolitans versus Locals, Ethnics and Nationals in an Era of De-hegemonisation." In *Debating Cultural Hybridity. Multi-Cultural Identities and the Politics of Anti-Racism*, ed. Pnina Werbner and Tariq Modood Tariq. London: Zed Books, 1997.

Glick, Leonard B. "Types Distinct from Our Own: Franz Boas on Jewish Identity and Assimilation." *American Anthropologists* 84 (3) 1982: 545–65.

Glick Schiller, Nina. "A Global Perspective on Migration and Development." *Social Analysis* 53 (3) Winter 2009: 14–37.

Glick Schiller, Nina Ayse Çağlar. "Towards a Comparative Theory of Locality in Migration Studies: Migrant Incorporation and City Scale." *Journal of Ethnic and Migration Studies* 35 (2) 2009: 177–202.

Gómez-Peña, Guillermo. "The Multicultural Paradigm: An Open Letter to the National Arts Community." *High Performance* Fall 1989: 20.

———. *Warrior for Gringostroika: Essays, Performance Texts, and Poetry*. Minneapolis: Graywolf Press, 1993.

Gonzales, Alfonso. "The 2006 Mega Marchas in Greater Los Angeles: Counterhegemonic Moment and the Future of El Migrante Struggle." *Latino Studies* 7 (1) 2009: 30–59.

Gonzales, Roberto G., and Leo R. Chavez. "Awakening to a Nightmare: Abjectivity and Illegality in the Lives of Undocumented 1.5 Generation Latino Immigrants in the United States." *Current Anthropology* 53 (3) 2012: 255–81.

Goodwin, M. H., and C. Goodwin. "Emotion Within Situated Activity." In *Linguistic Anthropology: A Reader*, ed. A. Duranti. Malden, Mass.: Blackwell, 2001.

Gramsci, Antonio. *Selections from the Prison Notebooks of Antonio Gramsci*. London: Lawrence & Wishart, 1971.

Grey, Mark. "Immigrants, Migration, and Worker Turnover at the Hog Pride Pork Packing Plant." *Human Organization* 58 (1) 1999: 16–27.

Grey, Mark, and Anne C. Woodrick. "Latinos Have Revitalized Our Community": Mexican Migration and Anglo Responses in Marshalltown, Iowa. In *New Destinations: Mexican Immigration in the United States*, ed. V. Zuniga and R. Hernandez-Leon, 133–54. New York: Russell Sage, 2005.

Guarnizo, Luis, Alejandro Portes, and William Haller. "Assimilation and Transnationalism: Determinants of Transnational Political Action Among Contemporary Migrants." *American Journal of Sociology* 108 (2003): 1211–48.

Gupta, Akhil, and James Ferguson. "Beyond 'Culture': Space, Identity, and the Politics of Difference." In *Culture, Power, Place: Explorations in Critical Anthropology*, ed. Akhil Gupta and James Ferguson. Durham, N.C.: Duke University Press, 1997.

Guss, David. *The Festive State: Race, Ethnicity, and Nationalism as Cultural Performance*. Berkeley: University of California Press, 2000.

Gutierrez, David G. "Migration, Emergent Ethnicity, and the 'Third Space': The Shifting Politics of Nationalism in Greater Mexico." *Journal of American History* 86 (2) 1999: 481–517.

Gutiérrez, Elena R. *Fertile Matters: The Politics of Mexican-Origin Women's Reproduction*. Austin: University of Texas Press, 2008.

Gutierrez, Ramon A. "Aztlán, Montezuma, and New Mexico: The Political Uses of American Indiana Mythology." In *Aztlan: Essays on Chicano Homeland*, ed. Rudolfo A. Anaya and Francisco Lomelí. Albuquerque: University of New Mexico Press, 1989.

Hage, Ghassan. "A Not So Multi-sited Ethnography of a Not So Imagined Community." *Anthropological Theory* 5 (4) 2005: 463–75.

Halbwachs, Maurice. *On Collective Memory*. Chicago: University of Chicago Press, 1992.

Haney-López, Iahn. *White by Law: The Legal Construction of Race*. New York: New York University Press, 2006.

Harris, Craig. "Illegal Worker Arrested for ID Theft: Arrest Part of Sheriff's Illegal-hires Crackdown." *The Arizona Republic*, April 18, 2008.

Harrison, Faye H. "Introduction: Expanding the Discourse on 'Race.'" *American Anthropologist* 100 (3) 1998: 609–31.

Hartigan, John Jr., "Establishing the Fact of Whiteness." *American Anthropologist* 99 (3) 1997: 495–505.

Harvey, David. *The Condition of Postmodernity*. Malden, Mass.: Blackwell, 1990.

Hasager, Ulla. "Localizing the American Dream: Constructing Hawaiian Homelands." In *Siting Culture: The Shifting Anthropological Object*, ed. Karen Fog Olwig and Kirsten Hastrup. London: Routledge, 1997.

Hedetoft, Ulf, and Hjort Mette. *The Postnational Self: Belonging and Identity*. Minneapolis: University of Minnesota Press, 2002.

Herzfeld, Michael. *Cultural Intimacy: Social Poetics in the Nation-State*. New York: Routledge, 1997.

Hill, Jane. "Hasta La Vista, Baby: Anglo Spanish in the American Southwest." *Critique of Anthropology* 13 (2) 1993: 145–76.

———. *The Everyday Language of White Racism*. Oxford: Blackwell, 2008.

hooks, bell. *Teaching Community: A Pedagogy of Hope*. New York: Routledge, 2003.

Horton, James Oliver. "Presenting Slavery: The Perils of Telling America's Racial Story." *The Public Historian* 21 (4) 1999: 19–38.

Iber, Jorge. *Hispanics in the Mormon Zion, 1912–1999*. College Station: Texas A&M University Press, 2000.

Irving, Katrina. *Immigrant Mothers: Narratives of Race and Maternity, 1890–1925*. Champaign: University of Illinois Press, 2000.

Jacobson, Robin Dale. *The New Nativism: Proposition 187 and the Debate over Immigration*. Minneapolis: University of Minnesota Press, 2008.

Jiménez, Tomás. *Replenished Ethnicity: Mexican Americans, Immigration, and Identity*. Berkeley: University of California Press, 2010.

Joppke, Christian, and Ewa Morawska. *Toward Assimilation and Citizenship: Immigrants in Liberal Nations*. Basingstoke, UK: Palgrave Macmillan, 2002.

Joseph, Miranda. *Against the Romance of Community*. Minneapolis: University of Minnesota Press, 2002.

Kandel, William, and Emilio A. Parrado. "Hispanics in the American South and the Transformation of the Poultry Industry." In *Hispanic Spaces, Latino Places: A Geog-*

raphy of Regional and Cultural Diversity, ed. Dan Arreola, 255–76. Austin: University of Texas Press, 2004.

Kearney, Michael. "Transnationalism in California and Mexico at the End of Empire." In *Border Identities:Nation and State at International Frontiers*, ed. Thomas M. Wilson and Hastings Donnan. Cambridge: Cambridge University Press, 1998.

Knowles, John. *A Separate Peace*. New York: Bantam Books, 1959.

Kojève, Alexandre. *Introduction to the Readings of Hegel*. New York: Basic Books, 1969.

Kriebel, Robert C. *150 Years of Lafayette Newspapers*. Lafayette, Ind.: Tippecanoe County Historical Association, 1981.

———. *Old Lafayette, 1811–1853: Based upon Historical Columns from the Pages of the Journal and Courier*. Lafayette, Ind.: Tippecanoe County Historical Association, 1988.

———. *Old Lafayette Volume II, 1854–1876*. Lafayette, Ind.: Tippecanoe County Historical Association, 1990.

———. "Commercial Bakeries Had German Roots." *Journal and Courier*, December 18, 2002.

———. "Neighborhood Prevails Despite Klan, Fires." *Journal and Courier*, May 13, 2007: 5B.

Kriebel, Robert C., with Fern Honeywell Martin, Ernest A. Wilkinson, and Paula Alexander Woods. *Tippecanoe at 2000: A Hoosier County Recalls Its Past*. Lafayette, Ind.: Lafayette Printing Company, 2000.

Krissman, Fred. "The Use of Bi-National Networks to Supply New Immigrant Farm Workers to California Agribusiness." *Culture & Agriculture*, 53 (1995): 3–8.

Lamphere, Louise. "Migration, Assimilation and the Cultural Construction of Identity: Navajo Perspectives." *Ethnic and Racial Studies* 30 (6) 2007: 1132–51.

Lane, James B., and Edward J. Escobar. *Forging a Community: The Latino Experience in Northwest Indiana, 1919–1975*. Bloomington: Indiana University Press, 1987.

Lassiter, Luke E., Hurley Goodall, Elizabeth Campbell, and Michelle N. Johnson. *The Other Side of Middletown: Exploring Muncie's African American Community*. Lanham, Md.: Altamira Press, 2004.

Lawrence, Denise L. "The Built Environment and Spatial Form." *Annual Review of Anthropology* 19 (1990): 453–505.

LeClerc, Gustavo, with Raúl Villa and Michael J. Dear. *Urban Latino Cultures: La Vida Latina en L.A.* Thousand Oaks, Calif.: Russell Sage, 1999.

Leslie, William R. "The Constitutional Significance of Indiana's Statute of 1824 on Fugitives from Labor." *Journal of Southern History* 13 (1947): 338–53.

Levinson, Bradley A.U., Judson Everitt, and Linda C. Johnson. "Integrating Indiana's Latino Newcomers: A Study of State and Community Responses to the New Immigration." Center for Education & Society Working Paper Series: Working Paper #1. 2007.

Levitt, Peggy. *The Transnational Villagers*. Berkeley: University of California Press, 2001.

————. 2004. "Redefining the Boundaries of Belonging: The Institutional Character of Transnational Religious Life." *Sociology of Religion* 65 (1) Spring 2004: 1–18.

Levitt, Peggy, and Nina Glick Schiller. "Conceptualizing Simultaneity: A Transnational Social Field Perspective on Society." *International Migration Review* 38 (145) 2004: 595–629.

Limon, Jose E. *American Encounters: Greater Mexico, the United States, and the Erotics of Culture.* Boston: Beacon Press, 1998.

Lipsitz, George. *The Possessive Investment in Whiteness: How White People Profit from Identity Politics.* Philadelphia: Temple University Press, 1998.

Lomnitz-Adler, Claudio. *Deep Mexico, Silent Mexico: An Anthropology of Nationalism.* Minneapolis: University of Minnesota Press, 2001.

Lopez, Tania E. "20,000 Protest: In Unexpected Strength, Marchers Rally against Immigration Restrictions." Indystar.com. April 11, 2006.

Lovell, Nadia. *Locality and Belonging.* New York: Routledge, 1998.

Low, Setha M. "Spatializing Culture: The Social Production and Social Construction of Public Space in Costa Rica." In *Theorizing the City: The New Urban Anthropology Reader,* ed. Setha Low. New Brunswick, N.J.: Rutgers University Press, 2002.

Low, Setha M., and Irwin Altman. *Place Attachment.* New York: Plenum, 1992.

Lugo, Alejandro. "Cultural Production and Reproduction in Ciudad Juárez, Mexico: Tropes at Play among Maquiladora Workers." *Cultural Anthropology* 5 (2) 1990: 173–96.

————. "Reflections on Border Theory, Culture, and the Nation." In *Border Theory: The Limits of Cultural Politics,* ed. Scott Michaelsen and David Johnson. Minneapolis: University of Minnesota Press, 1997.

————. "Theorizing Border Inspections." *Cultural Dynamics* 12 (3) 2000: 353–73.

————. *Fragmented Lives, Assembled Parts: Culture, Capitalism, and Conquest at the U.S.–Mexico Border.* Austin: University of Texas Press, 2008.

Lutholtz, M. William. *Grand Dragon: D.C. Stephenson and the Ku Klux Klan in Indiana.* West Lafayette, Ind.: Purdue University Press, 1991.

Madison, James H. *A Lynching in the Heartland: Race and Memory in America.* Palgrave Macmillan, 2001.

Malinowski, Bronisław. *Argonauts of the Western Pacific.* New York: Dutton, 1922.

Malkki, Liisa H. *Purity and Exile: Violence, Memory, and National Cosmology among Hutu Refugees in Tanzania.* Chicago: University of Chicago Press, 1995.

Manalansan, Martin. *Global Divas: Filipino Gay Men in the Diaspora.* Durham, N.C.: Duke University Press, 2003.

Margolis, Maxine L. *Little Brazil: An Ethnography of Brazilian Immigrants in New York City.* Princeton, N.J.: Princeton University Press, 1994.

Marrow, Helen B. "New Destinations and Immigrant Incorporation." *Perspectives on Politics* 3 (4) 2005: 781–99.

Martin, Fern Honeywell, and Paula Alexander Woods. *The American Photograph Series: The Best of Lafayette.* St. Louis: G. Bradley Publishing, 2000.

Martinez, Lisa M. "Yes We Can: Latino Participation in Unconventional Politics." *Social Forces* 84 (1) 2005: 135–55.

Massey, Doreen. *Space, Place and Gender*. Minneapolis: University of Minnesota Press, 1994.

Matovina, Timothy. *Guadalupe and Her Faithful: Latino Catholics in San Antonio, from Colonial Origins to the Present*. Baltimore: Johns Hopkins University Press, 2005.

Mayer, Kathy, with Jan Mathew and Lynn Holland. *Greater Lafayette: Indiana's Star City*. Montgomery, Ala.: Community Communications, 1999.

McClure, Erica, and Mir Montserrat. "Spanish–English Codeswitching in the Mexican and Spanish Press." *Journal of Linguistic Anthropology* 5 (1) 1995: 33–50.

McConnell, Eileen Diaz. "Latinos in the Rural Midwest: The Twentieth-Century Historical Context Leading to Contemporary Challenges." In *Apple Pie and Enchiladas*, ed. Ann V. Millard and Jorge Chapa, 26–41. Austin: University of Texas Press, 2004.

McKinney, Karyn D. *On Being White: Stories of Race and Racism*. New York: Routledge, 2005.

Menchaca, Martha. "Chicano Indianism: A Historical Account of Racial Repression in the United States." *American Ethnologist* 20 (3) 1993: 583–603.

———. *The Mexican Outsiders: A Community History of Marginalization and Discrimination in California*. Austin: University of Texas Press, 1995.

———. *Naturalizing Mexican Immigrants: A Texas History*. Austin: University of Texas Press, 2011.

Mendoza, Moises. "7,000 Show Solidarity in Immigration Rally." May 2, 2010. http://www.chron.com/disp/story.mpl/metropolitan/6985382.html (accessed May 2, 2010).

Menéndez Alarcón, Antonio V., and Katherine B. Novak. "Latin American Immigrants in Indianapolis: Perceptions of Prejudice and Discrimination." *Latino Studies* 8 (2010): 93–120.

Menjívar, Cecilia. *Fragmented Ties: Salvadoran Immigrant Networks in America*. Berkeley: University of California Press, 2000.

———. "Introduction: Public Religion and Immigration Across National Borders." *American Behavioral Scientist* 49 (11) 2006: 1447–54.

Michaelsen, Scott, and David Johnson, eds. *Border Theory: The Limits of Cultural Politics*. Minneapolis: University of Minnesota Press, 1997.

Millard, Ann V., and Jorge Chapa, eds. *Apple Pie and Enchiladas: Latino Newcomers in the Rural Midwest*. Austin: University of Texas Press, 2004.

Mills, Charles. *The Racial Contract*. Ithaca, N.Y.: Cornell University Press, 1997.

Miyares, Inés M. "Changing Latinization of New York City." In *Hispanic Spaces, Latino Places: A Geography of Regional and Cultural Diversity*, ed. Dan Arreola, 145–66. Austin: University of Texas Press, 2004.

Mock, Brentin. "Hate Crimes Against Latinos Rising Nationwide." Southern Poverty Law Center *Intelligence Report* (128): 2007.

Moore, Leonard J. *Citizen Klansmen: The Ku Klux Klan in Indiana, 1921–1928*. Chapel Hill: University of North Carolina Press, 1991.

Nelson, Lise K., and Nancy A. Hiemstra. "Latino Immigrants and the Renegotiation of Place and Belonging in Small Town America." *Social and Cultural Geography* 9 (3) 2008: 319–42.

Neville, Susan, and Tyagan Miller. *Twilight in Arcadia: Tobacco Farming in Indiana.* Indianapolis: Indiana Historical Society, 2000.

New, William, and Loucas Petronicolos. "Proposition 187, Public Education and the National Imagination." *Political and Legal Anthropology Review* 21 (2) 1998: 83–95.

Ngai, Mae M. *Impossible Subjects: Illegal Aliens and the Making of Modern America.* Princeton, N.J.: Princeton University Press, 2004.

Nodín Valdés, Dionicio. *Barrios Norteños: St. Paul and Midwestern Mexican Communities in the Twentieth Century.* Austin: University of Texas Press, 2000.

Noguera, Pedro, Aída Hurtado, and Edward Fergus. *Invisible No More: Understanding the Disenfranchisement of Latino Men and Boys.* New York: Routledge, 2011.

Oboler, Suzanne. *Ethnic Labels, Latino Lives: Identity and the Politics of (Re)Presentation in the United States.* Minneapolis: University of Minnesota Press, 1995.

———. *Latinos and Citizenship: The Dilemma of Belonging.* New York: Palgrave Macmillan, 2006.

Odem, Mary E. "Our Lady of Guadalupe in the New South: Latin American Immigrants and the Politics of Integration in the Catholic Church." *Journal of American Ethnic History* 23 (Fall 2004): 29–60.

Olwig, Karen Fog. "Cultural Sites: Sustaining a Home in a Deterritorialized World." In *Siting Culture: The Shifting Anthropological Object*, ed. Karen Fog Olwig and Kirsten Hastrup. London: Routledge, 1997.

Omi, Michael, and Howard Winant. *Racial Formation in the United States: From the 1960s to the 1990s.* New York: Routledge, 1994.

Ong, Aihwa. "Cultural Citizenship as Subject-Making: Immigrants Negotiate Racial and Cultural Boundaries in the United States." *Current Anthropology* 37 (5) 1996: 737–62.

Pantoja, Adrian D., Cecilia Menjívar, and Lisa Magaña. "The Spring Marches of 2006: Latinos, Immigration, and Political Mobilization in the 21st Century." *American Behavioral Scientist* 52 (2008): 499–506.

Paral, Rob. "Playing Politics on Immigration: Congress Favors Image over Substance in Passing H.R. 4437." Immigration Policy Brief. The American Law Foundation. 2006. http://robparal.com/downloads/policybrief_2006_playingpolitics.htm.

Paredes, Americo. *With His Pistol in His Hand: A Border Ballad and Its Hero.* Austin: University of Texas Press, 1958.

———. *Folklore and Culture on the Texas-Mexican Border*, ed. Richard Bauman. Austin: University of Texas Press, 1993.

Papademetriou, Demetrios et al. "Migration and Immigrants Two Years after the Financial Collapse: Where Do We Stand?" Report for the BBC World Service. Washington: Migration Policy Institute, 2010.

Pearson, Adam R., John F. Dovidio, and Samuel L. Gaertner. "The Nature of Contemporary Prejudice: Insights from Aversive Racism." *Social and Personality Psychology Compass* (3) 2009: 1–25.

Perea, Juan. *Immigrants Out! The New Nativism and the Anti-Immigrant Impulse in the United States.* New York: New York University Press, 1997.

Pérez Huber, L., C. Benavides Lopez, M. Malagon, V. Velez, and D. Solorzano. "Getting Beyond the 'symptom,' Acknowledging the 'Disease': Theorizing Racist Nativism." *Contemporary Justice Review* 11 (1) 2008: 39–51.

Pierce, Chester M. "Psychiatric Problems of the Black Minority." In *American Handbook of Psychiatry*, ed. S. Arieti. New York: Basic Books, 1974.

Pitti, Gina Marie. "The Sociedades Guadalupanas in the San Francisco Archdiocese, 1942–1962." *U.S. Catholic Historian* 21 (Winter) 2003: 91–109.

Plascencia, Luis. *Disenchanting Citizenship: Mexican Migrants and the Boundaries of Belonging.* New Brunswick, N.J.: Rutgers University Press, 2012.

Portes, Alejandro. "Migration, Development, and Segmented Assimilation: A Conceptual Review of the Evidence." *Annals of the American Academy of Political and Social Sciences* 610 (2007): 270–72.

Portes, Alejandro, and Robert L. Bach. *Latin Journey: Cuban and Mexican Immigrants in the United States.* Berkeley: University of California Press, 1985.

Portes, Alejandro, and Min Zhou. "The New Second Generation: Segmented Assimilation and Its Variants." *The Annals of the American Academy of Political and Social Science* 530 (1993): 74–96.

Price, Marie, and Courtney Whitworth. "Soccer and Latino Cultural Space: Metropolitan Washington Futbol Leagues." In *Hispanic Spaces, Latino Places: Community and Cultural Diversity in Contemporize America*, ed. David Arreola, 167–86. Austin: University of Texas Press, 2004.

Puar, Jasbir K. *Terrorist Assemblages: Homonationalism in Queer Times.* Durham, N.C.: Duke University Press, 2007.

Raijman, Rebeca, and Marta Tienda. "Immigrant Pathways to Business Ownership: A Comparative Ethnic Perspective." *International Immigration Review* 34 (3) 2000: 682–706.

Ramirez, Daniel. "Public Lives in American Hispanic Churches: Expanding the Paradigm." In *Latino Religious and Civic Activism in the United States*, ed. Gastón Espinosa with Virgilio Elizondo and Jesse Miranda, 177–96. Oxford: Oxford University Press, 2005.

Ramos-Zayas, Ana Y. *National Performances: The Politics of Class, Race, and Space in Puerto Rican Chicago.* Chicago: University of Chicago Press, 2003.

———. "Delinquent Citizenship, National Performances: Racialization, Surveillance, and the Politics of 'Worthiness' in Puerto Rican Chicago." In *Latinos and Citizenship: The Dilemma of Belonging*, ed. Suzanne Oboler, 301–28. New York: Palgrave Macmillan, 2006.

Redfield, Robert. "The Antecedents of Mexican Immigration to the United States." *Mexican Journal of Sociology* 35 (1929): 433–38.

Reichmann, Eberhard, with LaVern J. Rippley and Jörg Nagler. *Emigration and Settlement Patterns of German Communities in North America.* Indianapolis: Max Kade German-American Center, 1995.

Relph, E. C. *Place and Placelessness*. London: Pion, 1976.

Rich, Brian, and Marta Miranda. "The Sociopolitical Dynamics of Mexican Immigration in Lexington, Kentucky, 1997–2002." In *New Destinations*, ed. Victor Zúñiga and Rubén Hernández-León, 187–219. New York: Russell Sage, 2005.

Rocco, Raymond. "Transforming Citizenship: Membership, Strategies of Containment, and the Public Sphere in Latino Communities." In *Latinos and Citizenship: The Dilemma of Belonging*, ed. Suzanne Oboler, 301–28. New York: Palgrave Macmillan, 2006.

Rodman, Margaret. "Empowering Place: Multilocality and Multivocality." *American Anthropologist* 94 (1992): 640–56.

Rodriguez, Marc Simon. *The Tejano Diaspora: Mexican Americanism and Ethnic Politics in Texas and Wisconsin*. Chapel Hill: University of North Carolina Press, 2011.

Rodriguez, Nestor. "The Battle for the Border: Notes on Autonomous Migration, Transnational Communities, and the State." *Social Justice* 23 (3) 1996: 21–37.

Rodriguez, Richard. *Hunger of Memory: The Education of Richard Rodriguez*. New York: Bantam Books, 1983.

Roediger, David R. *The Wages of Whiteness: Race and the Making of the American Working Class*. London: Verso, 1999.

Rojas, James. "The Latino Use of Urban Space in East Los Angeles." In *La Vida Latina en L.A.: Urban Latino Cultures*, ed. Gustavo Leclerc, Raul Villa, and Michael Dear. New York: Russell Sage, 1999.

Rosaldo, Renato. "From the Door of His Tent: The Fieldworker and the Inquisitor." In *Writing Culture: The Poetics and Politics of Ethnography*, ed. James Clifford and George E. Marcus, 77–97. Berkeley: University of California Press, 1986.

———. "Ideology, Place and People without Culture." *Cultural Anthropology* 3 (1988): 77–87.

———. *Culture and Truth: The Remaking of Social Analysis*. Boston: Beacon Press, 1993 [1989].

———. "Cultural Citizenship and Educational Democracy." *Cultural Anthropology* 9 (3) 1994: 402–11.

———. "Cultural Citizenship, Inequality, and Multiculturalism." In *Latino Cultural Citizenship: Claiming Identity, Space, and Rights*, ed. William V. Flores and Rina Benmayor, 27–38. Boston: Beacon Press, 1997.

Rosaldo, Renato, and William Flores. "Identity, Conflict, and Evolving Latino Communities: Cultural Citizenship in San Jose, California." In *Latino Cultural Citizenship: Claiming Identity, Space, and Rights*, ed. William V. Flores and Rina Benmayor, 57–96. Boston: Beacon Press, 1997.

Rosales, Francisco A. "Mexicanos in Indiana Harbor During the 1920s: Prosperity and Depression." *Revista Chicano-Requeña* 4 (4) 1976: 88–98.

Rosas, Gilberto. "The Thickening Borderlands: Diffused Exceptionality and 'Immigrant' Social Struggles during the 'War on Terror.'" *Cultural Dynamics* 18 (2006): 335–49.

Rouse, Roger. "Mexican Migration and the Social Space of Postmodernism." *Diaspora* 1 (1991): 8–23.

Russel y Rodriguez, Monica. "Confronting Anthropology's Silencing Praxis: Speaking of/from A Chicana Consciousness." *Qualitative Inquiry* 4 (1) 1998: 15–41.

Sadowski-Smith, Claudia. "Unskilled Labor Migration and the Illegality Spiral: Chinese, European, and Mexican Indocumentados in the United States, 1882–2007." *American Quarterly* 60 (3) 2008: 779–804.

Saenz, Benjamin A. "In the Borderland of Chicano Identity, There Are Only Fragments." In *Border Theory: The Limits of Cultural Politics*, ed. D. E. Johnson and S. Michaelsen, 68–96. Minneapolis: University of Minnesota Press, 1997.

Sagamore Institute. *Indiana Immigration and Workforce Patterns*. Policy Brief. Indianapolis, Indiana, 2007.

Saint Boniface—Roman Catholic Church. "100th Anniversary of the Consecration 1899–1999." 85-page history of the church. Archived at Sweezy Room of Indiana History, Tippecanoe County Public Library, 1999.

Sánchez, George J. *Becoming Mexican American: Ethnicity, Culture, and Identity in Chicano Los Angeles 1900–1945*. New York: Oxford University Press, 1993.

Sanchez, Thomas. "Negotiating Latino Immigrant Identity in Rural Nebraska." *The Journal of Latino-Latin American Studies* 3 (4) 2009: 115–57.

Santa Ana, Otto. *Brown Tide Rising: Metaphors of Latinos in Contemporary American Public Discourse*. Austin: University of Texas Press, 2002.

Sassen, Saskia. "Introduction: Whose City Is It? Globalization and the Formation of New Claims." In *Globalization and Its Discontents: Essays on The New Mobility of People and Money*. New York: The New Press, 1998.

———. "The Participation of States and Citizens in Global Governance." *Indiana Journal of Global Legal Studies* 10 (1) 2003: 5–28.

Schneider, Dorothee. "'I Know All about Emma Lazarus': Nationalism and Its Contradictions in Congressional Rhetoric of Immigration Restriction." *Cultural Anthropology* 13 (1) 1998: 82–99.

Segura, Denise A., and Patricia Zavella, eds. *Women and Migration: In the U.S.–Mexico Borderlands*. Durham, N.C.: Duke University Press, 2007.

Sellers, Robert M., and J. Nicole Shelton. "The Role of Racial Identity in Perceived Racial Discrimination." *Journal of Personality and Social Psychology* 84 (5) 2003: 1079–92.

Sepúlveda, Ciro. "Research Note: Una Colonia de Obreros: East Chicago, Indiana." *Aztlán* 7 (Summer 1976): 327–36.

Sidanius, Jim, and Rosemary C. Veniegas. "Gender and Race Discrimination: The Interactive Nature of Disadvantage." In *Reducing Prejudice and Discrimination: The Claremont Symposium on Applied Social Psychology*, ed. S. Oskamp. Hillsdale, N.J.: Lawrence Erlbaum Associates, 2000.

Smith, Andrea. "Heteropatriarchy and the Three Pillars of White Supremacy: Rethinking Women of Color Organizing." In *Color of Violence: The Incite! Anthology*, ed. Incite! Women of Color Against Violence. Cambridge, Mass.: South End Press, 2006.

Smith, Heather, and Owen J. Furuseth. *Latinos in the New South: Transformations of Place*. Burlington: Ashgate Publishing, 2006.

Smith, Michael Peter. "Power in Place/Places of Power: Contextualizing Transnational Research." *City & Society* 17 (2005): 5–34.

Smith, Michael Peter, and Luis Eduardo Guarnizo. *Transnationalism from Below: Comparative Urban & Community Research.* New Brunswick, N.J.: Transaction Publishers, 2006 [1998].

Smith-Nonini, Sandy. "Back to 'The Jungle': Processing Migrants in North Carolina's Meatpacking Plants." *Anthropology of Work Review* XXIV, 3–4 (Fall and Winter 2003).

Solorzano, Daniel, Miguel Ceja, and Tara Yosso. "Knocking at Freedom's Door: Race, Equity, and Affirmative Action in U.S. Higher Education." *The Journal of Negro Education* 69 (2000): 60–73.

Spiro, Melford E. "The Acculturation of American Ethnic Groups." *American Anthropologist* 57 (6) December 1955: 1240–52.

Stewart, Kathleen C. "An Occupied Place." In *Senses of Place,* ed. Steven Feld and Keith H. Basso. Santa Fe: School of American Research Press, 1996a.

———. *A Space on the Side of the Road: Cultural Poetics in an "Other" America.* Princeton, N.J.: Princeton University Press, 1996b.

———. *Ordinary Affects.* Durham, N.C.: Duke University Press, 2007.

Suarez-Orozco, Marcelo M. "California Dreaming: Proposition 187 and the Cultural Psychology of Racial and Ethnic Exclusion." *Anthropology and Education Quarterly* 27 (2) 1996: 151–67.

Sue, Derald Wing, et al. "Racial Microaggressions in Everyday Life: Implications for Clinical Practice." *American Psychologist* 62 (4) 2007: 271–86.

Terkenli, Theano. "Home as a Region," *Geographical Review* 85 (3) 1995: 324–34.

Thompson, Maurice. *Stories of Indiana.* New York: American Book Company, 1898.

Thrush, Coll. *Native Seattle: Histories from the Crossing-Over Place.* Seattle: University of Washington Press, 2007.

Torres-Saillant, Silvio. "Problematic Paradigms: Racial Diversity and Corporate Identity in the Latino Community." In *Latinos: Remaking America,* ed. Marcelo M. Suárez-Orozco and Mariela M. Páez, 435–55. Berkeley: University of California Press, 2002.

Treviño, Roberto R. *The Church in the Barrio: Mexican American Ethno-Catholicism in Houston.* Chapel Hill: University of North Carolina Press, 2006.

Trouillot, Michel-Rolph. *Silencing the Past: Power and the Production of History.* Boston: Beacon Press, 1995.

Tuan, Yi-Fu. *Space and Place.* Minneapolis: University of Minnesota Press, 1977.

Tucker, Richard K. *The Dragon and the Cross: The Rise and Fall of the Ku Klux Klan in Middle America.* Hamden, Conn.: Archon Books, 1991.

Turner, Victor. *The Forrest of Symbols.* Ithaca, N.Y.: Cornell University Press, 1967.

Urciuoli, Bonnie. "The Political Topography of Spanish and English: The View from a New York Puerto Rican Neighborhood." *American Ethnologist* 18 (2) 1991: 295–310.

———. "Acceptable Difference: The Cultural Evolution of the Model Ethnic American Citizen." *Political and Legal Anthropology Review* 17 (2) 1994: 19–36.

———. *Exposing Prejudice: Puerto Rican Experiences of Language, Race, and Class.* Boulder, Colo.: Westview Press, 1996.

———. "Boundaries, Language, and the Self: Issues Faced by Puerto Ricans and Other Latina/o College Students." *Journal of Latin American Anthropology* 8 (2) 2003: 152–72.

Valdes, Dionicio Nodin. *Barrios Norteños: St. Paul and Midwestern Mexican Communities in the Twentieth Century.* Austin: University of Texas Press, 2000.

Valle, Victor M., and Rodolfo D. Torres. *Latino Metropolis.* Minneapolis: University of Minnesota Press, 2000.

Vargas, Zaragosa. *Proletarians of the North: A History of Mexican Industrial Workers in Detroit and the Midwest, 1917–1933.* Berkeley: University of California Press, 1993.

Vélez-Ibañez, Carlos G. *Border Visions: Mexican Cultures of the Southwest.* Tucson: University of Arizona Press, 1996.

Vélez-Ibañez, Carlos G., and Anna Sampaio. *Transnational Latina/o Communities: Politics, Processes, and Cultures.* Lanham, Md.: Rowman & Littlefield, 2002.

Vila, Pablo. *Crossing Borders, Reinforcing Borders: Social Categories, Metaphors, and Narrative Identities on the U.S.–Mexico Frontier.* Austin: University of Texas Press, 2000.

Villanueva, Margaret A. "Ethnic Slurs or Free Speech? Politics of Representation in a Student Newspaper." *Anthropology and Education Quarterly* 27 (2) 1996: 168–85.

Villenas, Sofia A. "Latina Mothers and Small-Town Racism: Creating Narratives of Dignity and Moral Education in North Carolina." *Anthropology and Education Quarterly* 32 (1) 2001: 3–28.

———. "Diaspora and the Anthropology of Latino Education: Challenges, Affinities, and Intersections." *Anthropology & Education Quarterly* 38 (4) 2007: 419–25.

Walton, Sam. *Made in America: My Story.* New York: Bantam Books, 1993.

Weber, David Stafford. "Anglo Views of Mexican Immigrants: Popular Perceptions and Neighborhood Realities in Chicago, 1990–1940." Doctoral Dissertation: The Ohio State University, 1982.

Werbner, Pnina. "Stamping the Earth with the Name of Allah: Zikr and the Sacralizing of Space among British Muslims." *Cultural Anthropology* 11 (3) 1996: 309–38.

Williams, Brackette F. "A Class Act: Anthropology and the Race to Nation Across Ethnic Terrain." *Annual Review of Anthropology* 18 (1989): 401–44.

Williams, Patricia J. *The Alchemy of Race and Rights: Diary of a Law Professor.* Cambridge, Mass.: Harvard University Press, 1991.

Wilson, Tamara Diana. "Weak Ties, Strong Ties: Network Principles in Mexican Migration." *Human Organization* 57 (4) 1998: 394–403.

Woodrick, Anne C. "Preparing the Way: Hispanic Ministry and Community Transformation in Marshalltown, Iowa." *Urban Anthropology* 35 (2–3) 2006: 265–94.

Woods, Paula Alexander, and Fern Honeywell Martin. *Traveling Through Tippecanoe: Tippecanoe County, Indiana.* St. Louis: G. Bradley Publishing Inc., 1992.

Yoder, Michael S., and Renée LaPerrière de Gutiérrez. "Social Geography of Laredo Neighborhoods: Distinctiveness and Diversity in a Majority Hispanic Place." In

Hispanic Spaces, Latino Places: A Geography of Regional and Cultural Diversity, ed. Dan Arreola, 55–76. Austin: University of Texas Press, 2004.

Yuval-Davis, Nira. "Belonging and the Politics of Belonging." *Patterns of Prejudice* 40 (3) 2006: 197–214.

Zamudio, Margaret, Cecilia Aragón, Leticia Alvarez, and Francisco Rios. "Immigrant Rights Protest in the Rural West." Latino Studies 7 (1) 2009: 105–11.

Ziegler, James P. *The German-Language Press in Indiana: A Bibliography*. Indianapolis: Indiana German Heritage Society Publications, 1994.

Zúñiga, V., and Rubén Hernández-León, eds. *New Destinations: Mexican Immigration in the United States*. New York: Russell Sage, 2005.

INDEX

2006 immigration debate: H.R. 4437, xv–xvi, 1–4, 6–8, 103–104; influence on behavior, 141, 170–171; influence on local rhetoric, 22–23, 102–104, 112–117, 119–134, 136; Latino response to, 67, 72–73, 89, 176–179; manifested in schools, 209–213

Anzaldúa, Gloria, 6, 12, 74–75, 158, 214, 219
Anderson, Benedict, 23, 111, 119
Assimilation of immigrants, 16, 22–26, 51–55, 59, 67–69, 176, 202–203, 208

Borders/borderlands/border theory, 6–7, 74–75, 148–149; mental borders, 7, 111, 135, 149, 209–210

Celebrations/public festivals: 195; "Feast of the Hunter's Moon," 41; German Fest, 95; Tippecanoe Latino Festival, 195–196; Viacrucis performance, 113, 189–190, 203; Virgin of Guadalupe, 21–22, 61–65, 84–85, 89, 174–176
Chavez, Leo, 111, 127
Colt World Series, 203–207
Criminalization of immigrants: letters to the editor, 22–23, 106–107, 119–131; political fliers, 114–117; popular negative perceptions, 104–108, 117–118, 123–124, 136–137, 183–185
"Crossroads of America," 11–12, 30, 169, 214

DREAMERS, 99, 194, 221–224
"Driving while Mexican," 223–225

Economic revitalization: immigrant workforce, 9–10, 16, 147; Lafayette industries, 9–10, 122, 154, 156, 159; Latino entrepreneurship, xiii-xiv, 72
English: difficulties in learning, 36–37; early immigrant, 50–55; Latino willingness to speak 101–102, 156–158, 161–163
English as a New Language (ENL), 209–213
English-only debate: immigrants will not learn, 101–102, 126–132, 156–157, 162, 183–187, 191; in newspapers 53–54, 22–23, 126–128; in religion, 52–54, 91, 93–95; at school, 208–210, 221; at work, 162. *See also* National anthem
Ethnic belonging: definition of, 14–16, 179, 195–198, 214–215; in community organizations, 89, 171, 195, 198–200; for early German settlers, 50–55 in religion, xix, 38–39, 62, 67–69, 78–81, 90, 171; as resistance, 225–226; at school, x, 211–213; at sporting events, 203–208

Families: fictive kin, 79–80, 85–86, 88, 207; mixed status, 13, 150; recruitment, 9, 31–32
Fear of deportation, xvi, 13, 20, 149–150, 197
Fear toward globalization, 127–128, 145–147
Feminist analysis: intersectionality, xvi-xvii, 137, 157,160; performativity, 26, 73, 123, 138; "personal is political," 16, 197

ABOUT THE AUTHOR

Sujey Vega is Assistant Professor of Women and Gender Studies at Arizona State University. Her research centers on aggrieved communities and topics such as gender, intersectionality, immigration, and religion. Currently, her focus is on immigrant women and intimate partner violence in the Phoenix area. Additionally, she is working on the role of religious networks for immigrant women and Latino Mormons.